The Co Guide to Fo vation

Step-by-Step Instructions on How to Freeze, Dry, Can, and Preserve Food

by

Angela Williams Duea

THE COMPLETE GUIDE TO FOOD PRESERVATION: STEP-BY-STEP INSTRUCTIONS ON HOW TO FREEZE, DRY, CAN, AND PRESERVE FOOD

Library of Congress Cataloging-in-Publication Data

Williams Duea, Angela, 1966-
  The complete guide to food preservation : step-by-step instructions on how to freeze, dry, can, and preserve food / by Angela Williams Duea.
      p. cm.
  Includes bibliographical references and index.
  ISBN-13: 978-1-60138-342-6 (alk. paper)
  ISBN-10: 1-60138-342-8 (alk. paper)
  1. Food--Preservation. I. Title.
  TX601.W55 2010
  641.4--dc22
                        2010035164

Printed in the United States

PROJECT MANAGER: Melissa Peterson • mpeterson@atlantic-pub.com
INTERIOR LAYOUT: Antoinette D'Amore • addesign@videotron.ca
COVER DESIGN: Meg Buchner • meg@megbuchner.com
JACKET DESIGN: Jackie Miller • millerjackiej@gmail.com

Printed on Recycled Paper

We recently lost our beloved pet "Bear," who was not only our best and dearest friend but also the "Vice President of Sunshine" here at Atlantic Publishing. He did not receive a salary but worked tirelessly 24 hours a day to please his parents. Bear was a rescue dog that turned around and showered myself, my wife, Sherri, his grandparents Jean, Bob, and Nancy, and every person and animal he met (maybe not rabbits) with friendship and love. He made a lot of people smile every day.

We wanted you to know that a portion of the profits of this book will be donated to The Humane Society of the United States. *–Douglas & Sherri Brown*

The human-animal bond is as old as human history. We cherish our animal companions for their unconditional affection and acceptance. We feel a thrill when we glimpse wild creatures in their natural habitat or in our own backyard.

Unfortunately, the human-animal bond has at times been weakened. Humans have exploited some animal species to the point of extinction.

The Humane Society of the United States makes a difference in the lives of animals here at home and worldwide. The HSUS is dedicated to creating a world where our relationship with animals is guided by compassion. We seek a truly humane society in which animals are respected for their intrinsic value, and where the human-animal bond is strong.

Want to help animals? We have plenty of suggestions. Adopt a pet from a local shelter, join The Humane Society and be a part of our work to help companion animals and wildlife. You will be funding our educational, legislative, investigative and outreach projects in the U.S. and across the globe.

Or perhaps you'd like to make a memorial donation in honor of a pet, friend or relative? You can through our Kindred Spirits program. And if you'd like to contribute in a more structured way, our Planned Giving Office has suggestions about estate planning, annuities, and even gifts of stock that avoid capital gains taxes.

Maybe you have land that you would like to preserve as a lasting habitat for wildlife. Our Wildlife Land Trust can help you. Perhaps the land you want to share is a backyard—that's enough. Our Urban Wildlife Sanctuary Program will show you how to create a habitat for your wild neighbors.

So you see, it's easy to help animals. And The HSUS is here to help.

THE HUMANE SOCIETY
OF THE UNITED STATES.

2100 L Street NW • Washington, DC 20037 • 202-452-1100
www.hsus.org

Dedication and Trademark Disclaimer

This book is dedicated to my husband Joe,
who inspires me with his cooking and his love.

Table of Contents

Appendix C: Canning Vegetables
and Vegetable Products — Courtesy of the USDA 265

Appendix D: Canning Poultry, Red Meats,
and Seafood — Courtesy of the USDA.. 289

Appendix E: Canning Fermented Foods and
Pickled Vegetables — Courtesy of the USDA 305

Introduction

Before the canning and butchering industries became widespread, families had to preserve their own food by canning, drying, and salting produce and meat. Each year, a family's major efforts were focused on storing up enough food for the wintertime. Today, most people can run out to the grocery store to pick up a pound of bacon or a jar of applesauce, but some still enjoy the practice of preserving their own foods. Many people are more careful about the additives and quality of the food they eat, or prefer to select organic foods. Other people like to have several options for storing the produce from their own gardens — when the freezer is full, it is nice to be able to put away jarred fruits and vegetables in the pantry.

Storing food is a great option to increase the amount of available food for less money. By buying produce in season, you can get the best price. Then you can enjoy those foods in an off-season when the grocery store sells the same produce, picked and shipped from far away, for double or triple the cost of the in-season price. Canning can be a safe and economical way to preserve quality food at home. Disregarding the value of your labor, canning homegrown food may save you half the cost of buying commercially canned food. Preserving your own foods is economical. Once you make your investment in canning equipment, the only supplies you will need to buy in future years are the two-piece screw-top lids, a few freezer bags, plastic containers, or other equipment that can also be washed and re-used. Drying foods requires even less equipment to produce a large supply of healthful meals.

People are concerned about buying locally grown, in-season foods. Besides offering fresher produce, this reduces the amount of pollution and energy needed to get food from the farm to the consumer. Preserved foods are often more healthful than weeks-old "fresh" produce at the market. Think about buying tomatoes off-season — these fruits are harvested before they are ripe so that they will remain edible during handling and shipping. The unripe fruit is then often treated with a ripening agent and perhaps a preservative. The truck, train, plane, and/or ship that brings you the food spreads pollution across the country as the produce makes its way to your market. Then the fruit sits in a refrigerated bin until you buy it at an inflated price, and when you bring it home, you are eating a tasteless, over-processed tomato. Appetizing, right?

By contrast, you could harvest a tomato in season from your own — or a friend's — garden. Or, you could select produce at a farmers market or fruit stand from a farmer in your region who might have picked the tomatoes that morning. If you preserve the tomatoes while they are fresh, you will have a delicious source of soups, sauces, and other recipes all winter long. Granted, this does not mean that you will be able to enjoy a fresh tomato in January, but what you find in the grocery store is not so fresh, either.

Even when fruits and vegetables are refrigerated, their nutrition content has been declining since they were harvested. Within a week, up to 50 percent of the nutrients can be lost. Though the heat from canning destroys up to half of the Vitamin A, Vitamin C, riboflavin, and thiamin in foods, after the canning process is complete, the nutritional loss slows to 5 to 20 percent per year.

According to the National Frozen and Refrigerated Foods Association, freezing foods can add as much as 600 percent to the lifespan of many common refrigerated foods — and many people take advantage of that. Ball Corporation, one of the largest canning and packaging firms in the world, produces more than 50 billion containers per year. Clearly, even though our society is busier than ever, people still find the time and effort of preserving food to be worth it.

All of the methods of food preservation discussed in this book are techniques that can be learned easily. However, you will need to follow the directions exactly, and with some methods, you will need to buy certain supplies to preserve foods properly. If foods are not preserved properly, you run the risk of spoiling the foods or even making people ill from the foods.

This book will show you how to store food for future use and how to save money while doing it. You will learn to minimize the risk of damaging food or spreading food-borne illnesses. You will learn how to grow for harvest and how to handle that harvest with this book's crop-by-crop guide. You will learn how freezing works, how to organize your freezer, the various methods of freezing, and why failure occurs. In addition to freezing, you will learn about the canning and preserving processes, and the problems you may encounter. All of the equipment you might need is laid out in easy-to-read charts, and you will be shown the various final products you can expect.

Experts in food preservation and storage have been interviewed and their commentary has been included here to help you in storing foods. No matter your situation, this guide will help you learn how to store multiple forms of vegetables and fruits and to understand how they perform, why failure occurs, and what you need to be successful.

A History of Preserving Food

Before refrigerators and freezers were invented, people had few methods of storing food past the harvesting or butchering season. The oldest form of preserving food is salting and smoking meats and fish and drying fruits and vegetables. In fact, these were the only methods that early humans had to store food for later consumption, unless they lived in a frozen land where caches of food could be stored under ice. The first records of salting fish are about 5,500 years old.

These early preservers used either sea salt or mined rock salt for preserving meat. The sea salts contained minerals and substances, including nitrates, which people noticed gave a pinkish color to meat. It was not until the 20th Century that scientists discovered these nitrates could be harmful to humans, and the government regulated their use in commercially pre-pared foods.

Without refrigeration and before the invention of canning, a catch of cod or herring could not be transported far before it spoiled. Most of the haul from a fishery was smoked before being sent to markets throughout the country. This smoking removed the moisture that could cause bacteria and rot. Some fish were so heavily salted and smoked that homemakers had to soak the dried fish in water to remove excess salt and rehydrate the food for eating.

The canning method of storing food began in 1795, when the French government offered a reward of 12,000 francs to anyone who could invent a method of preserving food for the entire military. Chef Nicolas Appert was awarded this prize in 1810. He invented the "Appert method" of seal-ing food in bottles and jars covered with cork, wire, and sealing wax. These containers were then boiled for several hours to complete the preservation process. The popular Mason jars were invented in 1858 by New Yorker John L. Mason, who began his career as a tinsmith at a young age. The Ball Company soon followed by mass-producing canning jars and lids. By

1892, it operated three factories in New York and Indiana, run by more than 1,000 workers.

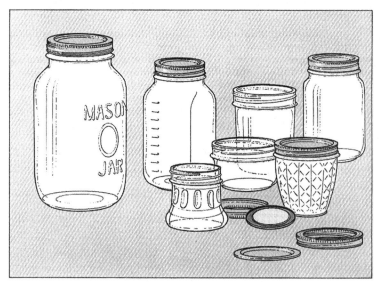

Illustration courtesy of the USDA

During World War II, Americans were encouraged to grow "Victory Gardens." Rather than using canned goods from the store, the government encouraged citizens to use their own canning jars and produce so that metal from the commercial canning supplies could be rerouted for the war effort. However, after the war, the popularity of canning waned. In the 1950s and 60s, Americans were more interested in TV dinners and fast food restaurants, and it was not until the recession of the 1970s that people once again became interested in fresh food from the land. Canning once again became popular.

The science of freezing foods was created much later than these other methods. In the early 20th century, some households had an icebox that consisted of a box with a container for ice at the top. An iceman would regularly bring new cakes of ice to replace the melted ice in this box. This arrangement kept foods cold for several days but was not considered a method of preserving foods. This changed when Clarence Birdseye, founder of the

Birdseye frozen foods empire, invented a double-belt freezer in 1928. Two years later, he introduced the first line of frozen foods, including several varieties of vegetables and fruits, 18 different cuts of meat, and seafood.

At first, frozen foods were not completely accepted. Merchants needed to buy expensive freezers to display these foods, and consumers were put off by the different textures and flavors of frozen foods. World War II provided a boost to the frozen food industry because tinned and canned foods were sent to feed the armed forces, and frozen foods were left for civilians. By the 1960s, most households had modern freezers and could easily store frozen foods. Since that time, freezing has become increasingly popular as frozen food companies develop meals for dieters and children, and offer more variety of foods. Refrigerator/freezer combos continue to grow larger, and people sometimes buy an additional chest freezer to store foods.

Safe preservation methods

Foods spoil for a number of reasons, but it mostly has to do with the growth of destructive microorganisms. All preservation techniques are designed to eliminate or neutralize these destructive microorganisms, so that food is safe to eat for long periods of time. One type of spoilage is caused by microorganisms called bacteria. Most bacteria are microscopic and are of no harm to people. Many forms of bacteria are actually beneficial, aiding in the production of such things as cheese, bread, butter, and alcoholic beverages. Only a small percentage of bacteria will cause food to spoil and can generate a form of food poisoning when consumed.

Most fresh foods contain a high percentage of water, which makes them perishable. Undesirable microorganisms, like bacteria, molds, and yeasts, can easily grow in unprocessed foods. Food enzymes can remain active, leading to over-ripening and spoilage. The oxygen in food tissues can dry out the foods and leave them tasteless and less nutritious. Microorganisms grow in bruised fruit, and are also present on food surfaces and inside the skin of fruits that have been damaged. These microorganisms multiply quickly and cause disease.

Another type of microorganism is mold. Usually mold affects the flavor of foods and often makes it inedible; however, some types of mold are actually beneficial, such as the mold that produces blue cheese, or the strain used to develop penicillin. Several strains of mold affect foods, and they appear as a gray, black, or white cottony growth on fruits and vegetables, and as blue or green spots on meats. Mold generally does not appear on foods that are kept frozen at the proper temperature, canned properly, or dried foods stored in the right environment. However, if you keep a root cellar, you will need to be vigilant about watching for mold and preventing it from spreading and wiping out your entire store. A layer of this mold on the surface of a jar of jelly does not necessarily mean the entire jar is spoiled, nor does it mean an entire loaf of bread is ruined because some mold appears on one slice. However, you will want to kill any mold spores on surfaces and utensils by thorough cleaning and by boiling utensils to 180 degrees Fahrenheit.

Yeasts are caused by the fermenting of sugars. Yeasts are helpful in raising bread and fermenting fruit and grains into alcoholic beverages. However, yeasts can also grow in a jar of fruit or vegetables and sour the produce so that it is inedible. In canning, this happens when the jars are sealed improperly and air containing yeast particles enter the jar. The first indication of yeast formation is a bubbly look to the product in the jar and a sour smell when it is opened. Yeasts have difficulty growing in a cold freezer or in dried foods, but they can be a problem in a root cellar.

Bacteria are a particular enemy of foods that contain low amounts of acid, like milk, meats, nuts, and legumes. As bacteria grow, it can create deadly growths of ptomaine and botulism, which may be difficult to detect and fatal to eat — even in tiny amounts. Unlike molds and yeasts, bacteria can survive temperatures greater than 212 degrees, which is the boiling point of water. These bacteria exist either as spores or as vegetative cells. The spores, which are comparable to plant seeds, can survive harmlessly in soil and water for many years. When ideal conditions exist for growth, the spores produce vegetative cells, which multiply rapidly and may produce a deadly toxin within 3 to 4 days of growth in an environment consisting of:

- a moist, low-acid food

- a temperature between 40 degrees and 120 degrees F

- less than 2 percent oxygen.

This makes it difficult to sterilize items that have come in contact with bacteria. Proper canning techniques such as adding lemon juice, lime juice, or vinegar prevent the growth of bacteria. Adding these liquids helps to raise the acid content high enough to destroy bacteria. Low-acid foods are canned only in a pressure canner that concentrates heat at a very high level for a long time to kill the microorganisms. In the drying process, proper handling of meat, the removal of moisture, and the addition of salt all work together to lessen the danger of bacterial poisoning. When freezing and thawing foods, it is crucial to handle food properly so that it does

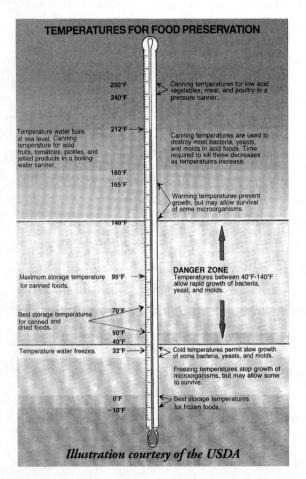

Illustration courtesy of the USDA

not come into contact with harmful bacteria, or that the food is not set in an environment where any bacteria already present have a chance to grow and multiply.

Foods also spoil because of the chemical and physical changes they can undergo. For example, fats such as oils or bacon grease will eventually turn rancid from a long reaction to oxygen; the oils in nuts can turn rancid for the same reason. Herbs and grains can become too dry and lose flavor and nutrition over long storage periods. Frozen foods have a specific storage period and if kept frozen too long or improperly sealed, the food becomes damaged and inedible. Often you will see ice crystals forming on foods that have been in the freezer too long; these ice crystals will damage the texture of the food and pull out enough moisture to spoil the flavor. You have probably seen frozen meats that have "freezer burn." Freezer burn happens when the moisture has been removed from exposed portions of meat, leaving a tough tasteless gray mass. Although these conditions are not life-threatening, they do not add to your enjoyment of a frozen meal.

There are many ways to prevent food poisoning and spoilage. The most obvious method is to keep all food preparation surfaces and utensils clean and to thoroughly wash your hands before handling food. A cleanser containing bleach is effective in killing microorganisms. However, if you are concerned about the effect of chlorine bleach on the environment, a strong vinegar solution in a spray bottle is an excellent alternative. If you are preparing meats for preservation, you should wash your hands and anything in contact with the meat before handling produce, herbs, or grains. Always wash your produce before preservation or cooking — and be sure to scrub the skins if you will be eating those.

It is best to preserve produce right after you pick and wash it, but if that is not possible, store your produce in the refrigerator to slow the growth of microorganisms. This will also slow the ripening process so your food is not past its prime by the time you are ready to preserve it. Make sure the produce is dry, whether you keep it in the refrigerator or on a counter. Moisture is a great enabler for the growth of yeasts, molds, and bacteria.

Commercially, our food is protected from spoiling in several ways. Have you ever seen a food label that contains the ingredients benzoic acid or sodium benzoate? These are chemical antiseptics added to foods as a preservative — and one benefit of home preservation is to eliminate those chemicals in our foods. Commercial food companies also protect foods like milk products by pasteurizing them. Pasteurized foods are heated past the boiling point to kill microorganisms, just as with home preservation.

At home, you can prevent preserved foods from spoiling through several methods. Hot water sterilization is the main method for canning. All your canning jars, lids, tongs, and other tools must be sterilized before adding the food; then the filled jars must be set in boiling water for a specified period of time, depending on the food. Fruits have a short boiling period — as short as ten minutes — and meats have the longest time period, at four hours or longer.

Drying and smoking foods prevents them from spoiling by removing moisture and making the food inhabitable for germs. Many meats and vegetables are dried with salt, which has an antiseptic action. Fruits are dried until the sugar concentrates to a level of 65 percent; the removal of much of the water slows spoilage. Smoking food helps preserve food through the removal of water, but also through the compound in the smoke.

Most bacteria, yeasts, and molds are difficult to remove from food surfaces. Washing fresh food reduces their numbers only slightly. Peeling root crops, underground stem crops, and tomatoes reduces their numbers greatly. Blanching also helps, but the vital controls are the method of canning and making sure the recommended research-based process times, found in these guides, are used.

The processing times in these guides ensure destruction of the largest expected number of heat-resistant microorganisms in home-canned foods. Properly sterilized canned food will be free of spoilage if lids seal and jars are stored below 95 degrees F. Storing jars at 50 degrees to 70 degrees F enhances retention of quality.

CASE STUDY: FOR SAFETY'S SAKE

Courtesy of the USDA

Pressure canning is the only recommended method for canning meat, poultry, seafood, and vegetables. The bacterium *Clostridium botulinum* is destroyed in low-acid foods when they are processed at the correct time and pressure in pressure canners. Using boiling water canners for these foods poses a real risk of botulism poisoning.

If *Clostridium botulinum* bacteria survive and grow inside a sealed jar of food, they can produce a poisonous toxin. Even a taste of food containing this toxin can be fatal. Boiling food 10 minutes at altitudes below 1,000 ft should destroy this poison when it is present. For altitudes at and above 1,000 ft, add 1 additional minute per 1,000 ft additional elevation. **Caution:** To prevent the risk of botulism, low-acid and tomato foods not canned according to the recommendations in this publication or according to other USDA-endorsed recommendations should be boiled as above in a saucepan before consuming, even if you detect no signs of spoilage. This is not intended to serve as a recommendation for consuming foods known to be significantly underprocessed according to current standards and recommended methods. It is not a guarantee that all possible defects and hazards with other methods can be overcome by this boiling process. All low-acid foods canned according to the approved recommendations may be eaten without boiling them when you are sure of all the following:

- Food was processed in a pressure canner.

- Gauge of the pressure canner was accurate.

- Up-to-date researched process times and pressures were used for the size of jar, style of pack, and kind of food being canned.

- The process time and pressure recommended for sterilizing the food at your altitude was followed.

- Jar lid is firmly sealed and concave.

- Nothing has leaked from jar.

- No liquid spurts out when jar is opened.

- No unnatural or "off" odors can be detected.

Do Your Canned Foods Pass This Test?

Overall appearance

- Good proportion of solid to liquid

- Full pack with proper headspace

- Liquid just covering solid

- Free of air bubbles

- Free of imperfections — stems, cores, seeds

- Good seals

- Practical pack that is done quickly and easily

Fruit and vegetables

- Pieces uniform in size and shape

- Characteristic, uniform color

- Shape retained — not broken or mushy

- Proper maturity

Liquid or syrup

- Clear and free from sediment

Acidic and alkaline foods — acid matters!

As mentioned before, heavily acidic foods are less conducive to the formation of bacteria than less-acidic (or alkaline) foods. Bacteria grow best in foods that are neutral or only slightly acidic. The quality known as "pH" indicates the level of acidity or alkalinity. The pH scale goes from 0.0 (very acidic) to 14.0 (very alkaline). Foods with a pH level of 7.0 are exactly neutral. Highly acidic foods such as fruits inhibit bacterial growth. For foods that are not highly acidic, you can add acidic ingredients to reduce the danger of bacterial growth, such as adding vinegar to pickles or lemon juice to sauces. However, meats and many other foods are in the optimal pH range for bacterial growth, so if the meat is not pickled (such as "corning" beef), extra effort must be expended to protect the food from bacteria.

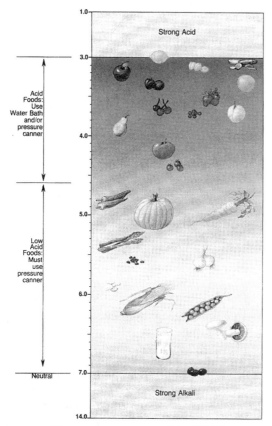

Illustration courtesy of the USDA

Botulinum spores are very hard to destroy at boiling-water temperatures; the higher the canner temperature, the more easily they are destroyed. Therefore, all low-acid foods should be sterilized at temperatures of 240 degrees to 250 degrees F, attainable with pressure canners operated at 10 to 15 PSIG. PSIG means pounds per square inch of pressure as measured by gauge. The more familiar "PSI" designation is used in this publication. At temperatures of 240 degrees to 250 degrees F, the time needed to destroy bacteria in low-acid canned food ranges from 20 to 100 minutes. The exact time depends on the kind of food being canned, the way it is packed into jars, and the size of jars. The time needed to safely process low-acid foods in a boiling-water canner ranges from 7 to 11 hours; the time needed to process acid foods in boiling water varies from 5 to 85 minutes.

Growing produce for preserving

Home gardening and food preservation go hand-in-hand. Watching plants grow and bud, and seeing produce ripen under the work of your own hands, is even more satisfying as you store it away in jars and bags. When you open that produce deep into a cold winter, you will be reminded of the fine sunny days when you stored them away.

By growing your own produce, you can choose to grow only the varieties of fruits and vegetables that you like. You can grow them with a minimum of harmful chemicals or waxes, pick them at the peak of freshness, and preserve them right away. Good produce at the peak of freshness is the best type of food to preserve. Storing mediocre fruits and vegetables will not improve their flavor. However, as your produce ripens in your backyard garden, you can preserve it in small batches, when it is ready.

Ensuring high-quality canned foods
Courtesy of the USDA

Begin with good-quality fresh foods suitable for canning. Quality varies among varieties of fruits and vegetables. Many county extension offices can recommend varieties best suited for canning. Examine food carefully for freshness and wholesomeness. Discard diseased and moldy food. Trim small diseased lesions or spots from food.

Can fruits and vegetables picked from your garden or purchased from nearby producers when the products are at their peak of quality — within 6 to

12 hours after harvest for most vegetables. For best quality, apricots, nectarines, peaches, pears, and plums should be ripened one or more days between harvest and canning. If you must delay the canning of other fresh produce, keep it in a shady, cool place.

Fresh home-slaughtered red meats and poultry should be chilled and canned without delay. Do not can meat from sickly or diseased animals. Ice fish and seafoods after harvest, eviscerate immediately, and can them within 2 days.

Most perennial fruits, like cherries and apples, will bear fruit at a certain time each year, allowing you to plan your food preservation schedule. With annual fruits and vegetables, you can plan by simultaneously planting early and late producing varieties that will bear at a certain number of weeks after planting. This is helpful in planting items like tomatoes — you can plant a small number of early bearing and another planting of late-bearing tomatoes to avoid being drowned in a flood of tomatoes all at once. Other vegetables with a short growing cycle, such as peas or salad greens, can be planted in a staggered schedule of two weeks apart, which will provide you with fresh produce throughout your region's entire growing season.

Succession planting is a way to use the same garden space continually through the growing year. With succession planting, one crop follows another through spring, summer, and fall, so your garden is continually producing. For example, you can harvest peas or carrots in the spring, broccoli in the summer, and Brussels sprouts in the fall. Another use for garden space is to intercrop plants. By planting two crops with different needs in a small area, you can get more use out of your garden space. For example, try planting rows of lettuce with shallow roots close to rows of onions or scallions, which need deep nutrients.

It is important to plan your garden ahead of time. In fact, it can be great fun to receive those seed catalogs in the heart of winter, and think ahead to your summer garden in bloom. Be sure to carefully plan your garden according to the amount of room, sun, and hours you will have available to tend the garden — you do not want to watch your garden go to seed because you cannot manage it all. Make sure you buy enough quantities of all seeds and plants in the spring, so that you are sure to have exactly the varieties you want. It can be disappointing to run out of lettuce seeds in July and find that all the nurseries and garden stores already put them away for the season.

Selecting fruits and vegetables for harvesting allows you to pick and preserve the best of your garden. The best time to store your produce is right when you pick it, before it loses any flavor or becomes overripe. Realistically, though, you do not always have the luxury of enough time or freedom to put up foods that day — or you may not have sufficient quantity to store. For most produce, it is important to chill your fruits and vegetables in the refrigerator so that the ripening process slows. However, tomatoes will lose their flavor in the refrigerator, so hold them on a counter or a sunny windowsill until ready to prepare. Herbs can also be harvested ahead of time and kept in a glass of water until ready for preparation.

Using ripe and healthy fruits like these strawberries will result in delicious preserves

The following table provides information on selecting and harvesting many popular fruits and vegetables for preserving.

Vegetable Harvesting Guide

Vegetable	Days to Harvest	Harvesting/Selecting	Preservation Method(s)
Beans: black, pinto, white, northern, fava, or lima	50-80	Harvest plump, unblemished pods as they ripen. If you plan to dry them, let them dry on the vine until hard. In damp weather, complete drying indoors.	Freezing, canning, and drying.
Beans: green or yellow	50-70	Harvest when pods are pencil size in thickness and seeds are barely visible.	Freezing, canning, pickling, and drying.
Beet	50-70	Up to 1/3 of the beet foliage can be harvested for greens without harming the root. Dig up roots when 1½" to 2" in diameter.	Canning, freezing, pickling, drying, juicing, or root cellaring.
Broccoli	50-65	Harvest before the green blossom buds open into yellow flowers. Side shoots can be harvested after main head is removed.	Canning, freezing, pickling, or drying.
Brussels Sprouts	100-150	Harvest when full size, green, and still firm. Harvesting after a frost will sweeten the flavor.	Freezing, root cellaring.
Cabbage	60-90	Cut off cabbage heads once they are large and solid. Chinese cabbage leaves can be harvested as needed.	Canning, freezing, pickling, drying, or root cellaring.
Carrot	60-80	Pull up when the orange shoulder pushes through the soil.	Canning, freezing, pickling, drying, juicing, or root cellaring.
Cauliflower	55-80	Cauliflower must be blanched in order to retain mild flavor. Blanch heads when 2" to 3" across by carefully tying leaves over heads.	Freezing, pickling, or drying.
Cucumber		All varieties should be harvested when they are slender and dark green. Pale-colored cucumbers will be seedy and watery.	Pickling, juicing, or fresh.

Vegetable	Days to Harvest	Harvesting/Selecting	Preservation Method(s)
Pickling	55-65	Harvest cucumbers at 1" to 4" long, depending on the pickling recipe. Leave small piece of stem attached to fruit.	
Slicing	55-65	Harvest cucumbers when they reach 1" to 2" in diameter.	
Corn: Sweet	60-100	Pick when silks and the tips of leaves are brown. Mature kernels exude milky sap when punctured.	Freezing, canning, pickling, or drying.
Corn: Popcorn/ Indian Corn		Pick when husks are brown and dry; in damp weather, continue drying indoors.	Drying.
Eggplant	75-90	Cultivate at maturity — before the produce grows too large and woody. It should have a shiny finish.	Freezing, pickling, or drying.
Garlic	90	Harvest when foliage topples over and dries or just before first frost.	Freezing, drying, or root cellaring.
Kohlrabi	55-70	Harvest when the stem is 2" to 3" wide. Store with leaves and roots removed.	Freezing or root cellaring.
Lettuce (leaf)	45-60	Cut off outer leaves with scissors as needed. Pull up baby greens as they reach the desired size. Hot weather causes bitterness and may slow the growth for some varieties.	Drying, freezing.
Melons: Honeydew, Cantaloupe, Watermelon	75-100	When mature, stem separates easily from melon.	Freezing, canning, pickling, or juicing.
Okra	50-65	Pick after flowers fall and pods are 1" to 3" long. Harvest frequently to maintain productivity and prevent old, woody pods.	Freezing, canning, pickling, and drying.

Vegetable	Days to Harvest	Harvesting/Selecting	Preservation Method(s)
Onion	100-120	Harvest when tops fall over and begin to dry.	Freezing, canning, root cellaring, pickling, or drying.
Parsnip	110-130	Dig up after heavy frost. Can be over wintered in the ground; mulch and dig before new growth starts in spring.	Freezing, canning, or root cellaring.
Pea: Snow (Sugar)	55-85	Harvest when pods are long and thin, just as the seeds begin to develop.	Freezing, canning, or drying
Pea: Snap	55-85	Pick when seeds are nearly full size.	Freezing, canning, or drying
Pea: Garden (Shell)	55-85	Harvest when peas are full size.	Freezing, canning, or drying
Peas: Black-eyed, cow, southern, or field	55-90	Harvest pods when young to eat like shelled peas; let them dry on the vine until peas are hard if you are planning to dry them.	Freezing, canning, or drying.
Peppers		Pick frequently to encourage new growth.	Freezing, canning, or drying.
Hot Peppers	60-90	Pick pods as they mature; use gloves when harvesting.	
Sweet Peppers	70-90	Usually harvested when green, but can be left on plant until red, orange, yellow, or purple.	
Potato	90-120	If new potatoes are desired, carefully dig them up after flowers die. Dig up mature potatoes when tops turn brown and die.	Freezing, canning, drying, root cellaring.
Pumpkin	85-120	Pick when uniformly orange, but leave 3" to 4" of stem attached. Rind should be hard and difficult to puncture with fingernail. Bring inside before a heavy frost.	Canning, freezing, root cellaring.
Radish		Pick when the color matures according to the cultivar.	Canning, freezing, root cellaring.

Vegetable	Days to Harvest	Harvesting/Selecting	Preservation Method(s)
Spring Radishes	25-40	Pull up radishes when they are about 1" to 1 1/2" in diameter.	
Winter Radishes	45-70	Can be left in the ground until frost.	
Spinach	45-60	Cut leaves with scissors; pull up the entire plant when plants begin to show signs of growing too large and tough.	Freezing, canning, pickling.
Summer squash		Harvest when squash is roughly 2" in diameter.	Freezing, canning, pickling.
Yellow squash	50-60	Harvest when skin is soft and the squash is 5" to 8" long. Dark yellow, warty squashes will be tougher and seedy.	
Zucchini	50-60	Skin should be soft and dark green. A tough outer skin will indicate a tough, seedy squash.	
Sweet Potato	100-125	Harvest just before or after a frost kills the vines.	Freezing, canning, drying, or root cellaring.
Tomato	70-90	Let tomatoes fully ripen on the vine, or ripen on a windowsill if streaks of green are present.	Freezing, canning, pickling, juicing, and drying.
Turnip	45-70	Foliage can be harvested for greens. Harvest turnips when 2" to 3" in diameter	Freezing, drying, or root cellaring.
Winter Squash	85-120	Pick when the rind has reached the proper color for the cultivar. Leave 3" to 4" of stem attached. Rind should be hard and difficult to puncture with fingernail. Bring inside before a heavy frost.	Canning, freezing, or root cellaring.

Fruit Harvesting Guide

Fruit	Harvest Time	Comments	Preservation Method(s)
Apples	Sept.– Nov.	Each type of apple has a characteristic flavor and aroma that will develop as the fruit ripens. Look for apples that have developed the mature color with a fragrance that is easily smelled. The under color of red apples will change from green to cream. In all varieties, the flesh will "give" slightly when squeezed. In some varieties, the apples will begin to fall off the tree when ripe. Other apples will release easily from the tree when ready to be picked.	Freezing, canning, pickling, juicing, drying, root cellaring.
Apricots	June-July	Harvest when the fruit begins to soften and develop characteristic flavor and aroma. Apricots will bruise easily and should be handled with great care.	Freezing, canning, juicing, and drying.
Blueberries	June-Aug.	Mature fruit is dark blue with a light blue overtone; it is slightly soft. Fruit falls readily when ready for picking.	Freezing, canning, juicing, and drying.
Blackberries	June-July	Fruit ripens to a dull black color and plump, juicy berries. Ripe berries will tumble from the white fruit cores by tugging lightly; unripe berries will not release easily. Harvest every 2 to 3 days.	Freezing, canning, juicing, and drying.
Cherries	July-Aug.	Mature fruit is juicy, soft, and full-flavored. Different varieties have varying colors as they ripen. Cherries will retain their flavor much better if picked with the stems on.	Freezing, canning, juicing, and drying.
Currants	July-Sept.	Mature fruit become softened and juicy with an intense color. If you will be making jelly with these fruits, harvest before completely ripe, when the pectin content is high.	Freezing, canning, juicing, and drying.

Fruit	Harvest Time	Comments	Preservation Method(s)
Elderberries	July–Sept.	Harvest when fruit is plump, color changes from shiny to dull purple, and it just beginning to soften.	Freezing, canning, juicing, and drying.
Gooseberries	July–Sept.	Harvest when the berries are still slightly firm and have turned light green in color. Some varieties may have pink blush.	Freezing, canning, juicing, and drying.
Grapes	Aug.–Nov.	Each type of grape will have a characteristic color and scent. Cut from the vines when the color has reached its peak and the stems have begun to turn brown. When removing the clusters, use scissors and be careful not to damage the vines.	Freezing, canning, juicing, and drying.
Peaches & Nectarines	July–Sept.	Each variety has a characteristic flavor and aroma; taste a sample to be sure it is ripe. Mature fruit is soft and juicy; skins may slide off easily. When ripe, the immature, green under-color changes to light green or cream. The fruit is very delicate; handle carefully to avoid bruising.	Freezing, canning, juicing, and drying.
Pears	July–Sept.	Pears should be picked before they are completely ripe, because they can become overripe quickly in storage. Pears that are picked too early will not develop full flavor and will become wrinkled in storage; pears that are picked when overripe will have poor flavor and hard, crunchy cells. Sample the fruit for flavor and ripeness, and look for fruit with small tan or brown spots on the surface. In all varieties, the flesh will "give" slightly when squeezed.	Freezing, canning, juicing, and drying.
Plums & Prunes	July–Sept.	Fruit softens and develops its characteristic flavor as it ripens. Handle the fruit carefully.	Freezing, canning, juicing, and drying.

Fruit	Harvest Time	Comments	Preservation Method(s)
Raspberries	June-Aug.	Harvest raspberries when they are deep red or bright magenta and can be easily pulled from the hull. Ripe raspberries should be very juicy and soft. Pick the berries every few days, as raspberries will ripen quickly.	Freezing, canning, juicing, and drying.
Rhubarb	June-Aug.	Harvest leaf stalks when they develop a reddish color and are 1/2 to 1" in diameter, and discard the leaves.	Freezing, canning, juicing, drying, and pickling.
Strawberries	May-June	Harvest strawberries when they develop a deep red color over most or the entire berry. Cream-colored sections indicate that part of the berry is fairly ripe but has not received enough sun to turn red. However, large sections of green on the berry mean that it is not yet ripe. The berries should be soft and slightly aromatic. Pick berries by pinching off from the stem, so that the green husk remains on top of the berry. The most flavorful berries are small, dark red ones.	Freezing, canning, juicing, and drying.

Herb Harvesting Guide

Herb	Comments	Preservation Method(s)
Basil	Pick healthy leaves all summer long. Plants will last until the first hard frost. Pinch off flower spikes to encourage leaf growth.	Freezing and drying.
Bee Balm	Harvest leaves or flowers throughout the summer. Plants will last until the first hard frost.	Freezing and drying.
Chamomile	Harvest flowers as they appear. Chamomile has a short growing season; you may want to stagger plantings to have flowers throughout the season.	Freezing and drying.

Herb	Comments	Preservation Method(s)
Chives	Cut flowers as they appear. Use scissors to cut chive spikes as needed. Periodically, cut the chive plant down to about 3" to encourage new, tender growth.	Freezing, drying, and pickling (flowers).
Cilantro/ Coriander	Snip leaves as needed; pinch off flower heads to encourage leaf growth. Cilantro has a short growing season; you may want to stagger plant-ings to have herbs throughout the season. If growing for coriander, allow flowers to develop. Carefully cut off seed heads when they have dried on the stem.	Freezing and drying.
Dill	Snip feathery leaves as needed; harvest young flower heads when they are light green. Leave some stem on the flower head. If harvesting for seeds, wait until the flowers have gone to seed, then cut the head off, leaving a 6" length of stem.	Freezing, drying, and pickling (flowers).
Fennel	Snip feathery leaves as needed; allow stems to flower and dry before harvesting the seeds. Dig up the bulb when the shoulders appear from the ground, before it becomes tough and stringy.	Freezing, drying, and root cellaring (bulbs).
Lavender	Clip flower heads once the entire stalk is in bloom.	Freezing and drying.
Lemon Balm	Snip off leaves as needed.	Freezing and drying.
Marjoram	Snip off leaves as needed.	Freezing and drying.
Mint	Snip off leaves as needed. **Note:** Mint is an extremely invasive plant. Cultivate it in an out-of-the-way spot in the garden or grow it in a pot.	Freezing and drying.
Oregano	Snip off leaves as needed.	Freezing and drying.
Parsley	Snip off leaves as needed.	Freezing and drying.
Rosemary	Snip off leaves as needed.	Freezing and drying.
Sage	Snip off leaves as needed.	Freezing and drying.

Herb	Comments	Preservation Method(s)
Tarragon	Snip off leaves as needed.	Freezing and drying.
Thyme	Snip off leaves as needed.	Freezing and drying.

Selecting food at a store

Without the space for a garden, or the desire to grow your own fruits and vegetables, you will need to be sure the foods you buy are at their best for preserving. One good source of fresh produce is a local farmers market or food exchange. These markets usually offer produce picked within a day or two of selling. Sometimes the markets sell these foods at a bargain price — but other farmers may charge a premium for locally grown, high-quality produce.

Whether you buy from one of these farmers or from your local grocery store, choose your produce wisely. It makes no sense to expend the effort to preserve sub-prime foods. Smell, squeeze, tap, or pinch your produce to make sure it is at the stage of freshness you need. Some foods are a particular concern. Ripe tomatoes should have an even, beautiful deep red color, and have some "give" when you squeeze them. However, if the skin starts to slip off the tomato, or it feels squishy, it is too ripe. Tomatoes that are somewhat hard or that have an orange-red color are under ripe, and may have been picked so early that they will never ripen completely.

Berries are another concern. Once they are picked, they have a short self-life and develop mold easily, even if refrigerated right away. Your best bet is to can berries the day you buy them. If any of your berries develop mold, discard the moldy berry as well as any berries touching it — they are already contaminated.

Wrinkly vegetables indicate old, dehydrated produce. Another sign of age is stem ends or leaves that are very brown and hard rather than a fresh, green color — these vegetables were harvested long ago. Herbs should always have fresh leaves with no dry edges, and should stand straight on their stems with no wilting. Many herbs will wilt completely once they have been mishandled; if you want to use them fresh, choose healthier plants.

Sometimes grocery stores will receive a new shipment of produce before the old shipment is sold. In that case, they will put the new produce at the bottom of the bin and the older food on top. It may be worth it to rummage a little to find the best food. You can also check with the store to see on which day they receive their produce, and make sure you shop that day to get the best pick of the new delivery.

When you select meats, choose items as far from the "sell by" date as possible. Red meats should have a rich, bright red color without discolored edges. The meats should always appear moist but any accumulated liquid should not appear cloudy. Meat, poultry, or seafood should not have a strong smell — especially seafood. If your grocery store has a butcher, be sure to ask when the meat was processed or packaged in the store. Again, it makes sense to determine the day they receive new shipments and plan your shopping for that day.

Chapter 1

How to Can Foods

Canning is one of the most popular preservation methods for food. However, it can be much more labor-intensive than freezing or drying foods, and you will need special equipment to process the food correctly. The benefits to canning, in spite of the extra trouble, are that many foods taste better when they are canned rather than frozen. Some produce, such as plums, apples, and carrots, develop a richer, complex taste in the canning process. In addition, your freezer usually has a small amount of room for storage, whereas canned foods can be piled up in a pantry, basement, or closet for years. Finally, there are some foods, such as pickles, that cannot complete the fermenting process in a freezer.

A Glossary of Canning Terms

Acid foods   Foods that contain enough acid to result in a pH of 4.6 or lower. This includes all fruits except figs; most tomatoes; fermented and pickled vegetables; relishes; and jams, jellies, and marmalades. Acid foods may be processed in boiling water.

Altitude   The vertical elevation of a location above sea level.

Ascorbic acid   The chemical name for vitamin C. Lemon juice con-
                        tains large quantities of ascorbic acid and is commonly
                        used to prevent browning of peeled, light-colored fruits
                        and vegetables.

Bacteria   A large group of one-celled microorganisms widely dis-
                        tributed in nature. See microorganism.

Blancher   A 6- to 8-quart lidded pot designed with a fitted perfo-
                        rated basket to hold food in boiling water, or with a fitted
                        rack to steam foods. Useful for loosening skins on fruits
                        to be peeled, or for heating foods to be hot packed.

**Boiling-water
canner**   A large standard-sized lidded kettle with jar rack, de-
                        signed for heat-processing 7 quarts or 8 to 9 pints in boil-
                        ing water.

Botulism   An illness caused by eating toxin produced by growth of
                        Clostridium botulinum bacteria in moist, low-acid food,
                        containing less than 2 percent oxygen, and stored be-
                        tween 40 degrees and 120 degrees F. Proper heat process-
                        ing destroys this bacterium in canned food. Freezer tem-
                        peratures inhibit its growth in frozen food. Low moisture
                        controls its growth in dried food. High oxygen controls
                        its growth in fresh foods.

Canning   A method of preserving food in air-tight vacuum-sealed
                        containers and heat processing sufficiently to enable stor-
                        ing the food at normal home temperatures.

Canning salt   Also called pickling salt. It is regular table salt without
                        the anticaking or iodine additives.

Citric acid   A form of acid that can be added to canned foods. It increases the acidity of low-acid foods and may improve the flavor and color.

Cold pack   Canning procedure in which jars are filled with raw food. "Raw pack" is the preferred term for describing this practice. "Cold pack" is often used incorrectly to refer to foods that are open-kettle canned or jars that are heat-processed in boiling water.

Enzymes   Proteins in food which accelerate many flavor, color, texture, and nutritional changes, especially when food is cut, sliced, crushed, bruised, and exposed to air. Proper blanching or hot-packing practices destroy enzymes and improve food quality.

Exhausting   Removal of air from within and around food and from jars and canners. Blanching exhausts air from live food tissues. Exhausting or venting of pressure canners is necessary to prevent a risk of botulism in low-acid canned foods.

Fermentation   Changes in food caused by intentional growth of bacteria, yeast, or mold. Native bacteria ferment natural sugars to lactic acid, a major flavoring and preservative in sauerkraut and in naturally fermented dills. Alcohol, vinegar, and some dairy products are also fermented foods.

Headspace   The unfilled space above food or liquid in jars. Allows for food expansion as jars are heated, and for forming vacuums as jars cool.

Heat processing   Treatment of jars with sufficient heat to enable storing food at normal home temperatures.

Hermetic seal   An absolutely airtight container seal that prevents reentry of air or microorganisms into packaged foods.

Hot pack   Heating of raw food in boiling water or steam and filling it hot into jars.

Low-acid foods   Foods that contain very little acid and have a pH above 4.6. The acidity in these foods is insufficient to prevent the growth of the bacterium *Clostridium botulinum*. Vegetables, some tomatoes, figs, all meats, fish, seafoods, and some dairy foods are low acid. To control all risks of botulism, jars of these foods must be (1) heat processed in a pressure canner, or (2) acidified to a pH of 4.6 or lower before processing in boiling water.

Micro-organisms   Independent organisms of microscopic size, including bacteria, yeast, and mold. When alive in a suitable environment, they grow rapidly and may divide or reproduce every 10 to 30 minutes. Therefore, they reach high populations very quickly. Undesirable microorganisms cause disease and food spoilage. Microorganisms are sometimes intentionally added to ferment foods, make antibiotics, and for other reasons.

Mold   A fungus-type microorganism whose growth on food is usually visible and colorful. Molds may grow on many foods, including acid foods like jams and jellies and canned fruits. Recommended heat processing and sealing practices prevent their growth on these foods.

Mycotoxins   Toxins produced by the growth of some molds on foods.

Open-kettle canning
A non-recommended canning method. Food is supposedly adequately heat processed in a covered kettle, and then filled hot and sealed in sterile jars. Foods canned this way have low vacuums or too much air, which permits rapid loss of quality in foods. Moreover, these foods often spoil because they become recontaminated while the jars are being filled.

Pasteurization
Heating of a specific food enough to destroy the most heat-resistant pathogenic or disease-causing microorganism known to be associated with that food.

pH
A measure of acidity or alkalinity. Values range from 0 to 14. A food is neutral when its pH is 7.0, lower values are increasingly more acidic, and higher values are increasingly more alkaline.

Pickling
The practice of adding enough vinegar or lemon juice to a low-acid food to lower its pH to 4.6 or lower. Properly pickled foods may be safely heat processed in boiling water.

Pressure Canner
A specifically designed metal kettle with a lockable lid used for heat processing low-acid food. These canners have jar racks, one or more safety devices, systems for exhausting air, and a way to measure or control pressure. Canners with 16- to 23- quart capacity are common. The minimum volume of canner that can be used is one that will contain 4 quart jars. Use of pressure saucepans with smaller capacities is not recommended.

Raw pack	The practice of filling jars with raw, unheated food. Acceptable for canning low-acid foods, but it allows more rapid quality losses in acid foods heat processed in boiling water.
Spice bag	A closeable fabric bag used to extract spice flavors in pickling solution.
Style of pack	Form of canned food, such as whole, sliced, piece, juice, or sauce. The term may also be used to reveal whether food is filled raw or hot into jars.
Vacuum	The state of negative pressure. Reflects how thoroughly air is removed from within a jar of processed food — the higher the vacuum, the less air left in the jar.
Yeasts	A group of microorganisms which reproduce by budding. They are used in fermenting some foods and in leavening breads.

The goal of proper canning is to remove oxygen, destroy enzymes, and kill harmful microorganisms like mold, bacteria, and yeast. Proper canning will also produce jars with a strong vacuum seal that will prevent liquid from leaking out or microorganisms from getting into the food. Properly canned foods can last for several years. Proper canning practices include:

- Selecting fresh, undamaged foods

- Carefully inspecting and washing fruits and vegetables

- Peeling fresh foods, if necessary

- Using the hot packing method where appropriate

- Adding acids (lemon juice or vinegar) to foods that need acid-packing

- Following recipes and directions precisely

- Using clean jars and lids that seal properly

- Using the right processing time when canning jars in a boiling-water or pressure canner

Collectively, these practices remove oxygen; destroy enzymes; prevent the growth of undesirable bacteria, yeasts, and molds; and help form a high vacuum in jars. Good vacuums form tight seals, which keep liquid in and air and microorganisms out. Most health-related problems arise when people do not follow the canning directions properly. Today, canning experts agree that old methods of canning and outdated cookbooks give unhealthy or inaccurate directions for food safety. However, the Center for Home Food Preservation, working with the University of Georgia, interviewed home canners and found that they often used unsafe directions or instructions from friends or relatives.

Different methods are now considered best for different types of foods. The USDA recommends water bath or pressure-canning methods when preserving high-acid products such as pickles, fruits, and tomatoes. In the past, people canned these products with open-kettle canning, but experts no longer considered this a safe canning method. Oven and microwave procedures are also considered unsafe.

Equipment and methods not recommended
Courtesy of the USDA

Open-kettle canning and the processing of freshly filled jars in conventional ovens, microwave ovens, and dishwashers are not recommended, because these practices do not prevent all risks of spoilage. Steam canners are not recommended because processing times for use with current models have not been adequately researched. Because steam canners do not heat foods in the same manner as boiling-water canners, their use with boiling-water process times may result in spoilage. It is not recommended that pressure processes in excess of 15 PSI be applied when using new pressure canning equipment. So-called canning powders are useless as preservatives and do not replace the need for proper heat processing. Jars with wire bails and glass caps make attractive antiques or storage containers for dry food ingredients, but they are not recommended for use in canning. One-piece zinc porcelain-lined caps are also no longer recommended. Both glass and zinc caps use flat rubber rings for sealing jars, but they too often fail to seal properly.

The canning process works to sterilize food and then seal the foods so that no contamination can enter the jar. Sterilization happens during the hot water processing, which also creates a vacuum seal in the jar. In the past, many homemakers poured a layer of wax over foods such as jams and preserves before processing the seal. Most experts now consider this unsafe and unnecessary. In fact, modern lids produce a good vacuum seal without this additional step.

The vacuum seal is crucial, and is affected by the quality of the lids as well as the proper level of food and liquid in the jar — known as "headspace." Each type of food has a different headspace depending on the food's shrinkage or swelling during the boiling process. Be sure to follow the directions closely and use a ruler if you have any doubts. More information on headspace can be found later in this chapter.

Each food has a different processing time to allow enough heat to kill microorganisms. In addition, these times increase with your altitude above sea level, because water boils at lower temperatures at higher altitudes. Foods with more acid, such as citrus fruits, tomatoes, and recipes with added vinegar or lemon juice have an additional antiseptic agent. The acid itself helps to sterilize the foods. Low-acid foods like meat and beans will need a much longer sterilization period.

Canning tools

You will need a few items to can your foods properly. The good news is that most of these items are probably already in your kitchen. Before you get started on a canning recipe, make sure you have the following accessories handy:

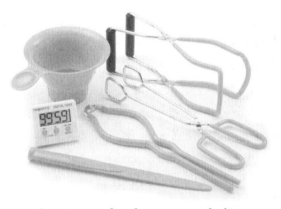

Canning supplies that are part of a kit

1. A jar lifter, which is a set of tongs specially made for canning jars with rubber-coated handles to lift hot jars out of the boiling water in the canner.

2. A small-bladed spatula — either plastic or rubber — to push out bubbles from jars before processing. Some instructions say to use a metal knife, but this may cause some fruits to change color.

3. An accurate kitchen timer, measuring cups, and spoons. Canning recipes are very exact, and proper timing and measuring are crucial to your success.

4. Saucepans to cook sauces and warm lids.

5. Colanders to drain.

6.   Knives and cutting boards to cut and process fruits and vegetables.

7.   Pot holders or mitts to protect hands from hot surfaces.

8.   A large spoon to use for stirring.

9.   Towels to use in the process of cooling your canning jars.

Canning jars

First, you will need to purchase or borrow canning jars. There are still many old-fashioned jars in circulation — perhaps you inherited some from a relative. These could be old, cracked jars or ones with a rubber gasket and clasp; these are likely to break during processing, and the clasp-type lids are not as safe for canning as modern jars and lids. Some recycled food containers are safe for use in a water-bath process, but cannot stand a pressure canner. Commercial mayonnaise jars are a particular concern due to their lack of heat-tempering and thin walls. They also have narrow rims that prevent a proper seal. Of course, many types of recycled food jars can be used for foods that you will refrigerate and use within a week or two. If you borrow or re-use canning jars, be sure to inspect them for nicks, cracks, or lid wear that could cause breakage — or even explosion in a pressure canner. Jars are safe to reuse if they can accommodate modern, flat canning lids and screw-on rings.

Your best choice is to purchase new jars made especially for canning from grocery stores, hardware stores, and the like. Quart jars are best for larger produce or meat pieces; pint and half-pint sizes are ideal for sauces, condiments, chutneys, jams, and jellies. Jars come in standard and wide-mouth varieties. Many prefer wide-mouth jars that are easier to fill and wash. Regular and wide-mouth Mason-type, threaded, home-canning jars with self-sealing lids are the best choice. They are available in ½ pint, 1 pint, 1 ½ pint, quart, and ½ gallon sizes. The standard jar mouth opening is about 2 3/8 inches. Wide-mouth jars have openings of about 3 inches, making them more easily filled and emptied. Half-gallon jars may be used for canning very acidic juices. Regular-mouth decorator jelly jars are available in 8 and 12 ounce sizes. With careful use and handling, Mason jars may be reused many times, requiring only new lids each time. When jars and lids are used properly, jar seals and vacuums are excellent and jar breakage is rare.

Today, safe canning requires the self-sealing, two-piece vacuum lid that can be found anywhere canning jars are purchased. These flat metal lids have a rubber gasket strip molded to a crimped underside. A metal band screws onto the jar to hold the lid in place. When you process the jars in a hot water bath, the compound softens and begins to seal while still allowing air to escape from the jar. When you allow the jars to cool after processing, the lid seals itself and creates a vacuum within the jar. For this reason, lids should never be re-used, but the metal bands can be removed after canning and used repeatedly. Be sure to check the metal bands for any signs of rust before using, because the rust can prevent a proper seal. Buy only the quantity of lids you will use in a year. To ensure a good seal, carefully follow the manufacturer's directions in preparing lids for use. Examine all metal lids carefully. Do not use old, dented, or deformed lids, or lids with gaps or other defects in the sealing gasket.

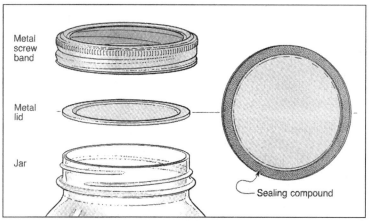

Courtesy of the USDA

Jar cleaning and preparation

Before every use, wash empty jars in hot water with detergent and rinse well by hand, or wash in a dishwasher. Unrinsed detergent residues may cause unnatural flavors and colors. Jars should be kept hot until ready to fill with food. Submerge the clean empty jars in enough water to cover them in a large stockpot or boiling water canner. Bring the water to a simmer (180 degrees F) and keep the jars in the simmering water until it is time to fill them with food. A dishwasher may be used for preheating jars if they are washed and dried on a complete, regular cycle. Keep the jars in the closed dishwasher until needed for filling.

These washing and preheating methods do not sterilize jars. Some used jars may have a white film on the exterior surface caused by mineral deposits. This scale or hard-water film on jars is easily removed by soaking jars several hours in a solution containing 1 cup of vinegar (5 percent acidity) per gallon of water prior to washing and preheating the jars.

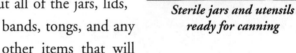

Sterile jars and utensils ready for canning

These peppers were hot packed, preserving their bright colors

Another method is to put all of the jars, lids, bands, tongs, and any other items that will contact the food into a large pot and boil the items for ten minutes. Keep the sterile items in the pot until you are ready to use them. Do not touch sterilized supplies with your hands or any unsterilized tools — this will contaminate your sterile supplies. If you boil the equipment at the time you are preparing your foods for packing, the hot-pack foods will go straight into hot jars and minimize stress on the glass.

Canning Guidelines

Hot pack vs. raw pack

When packing food (and any juices or spices) into canning jars, there are two ways you can do it: hot pack or raw pack. To hot pack food, you will boil some kind of liquid, juice, or broth, and cook the food slightly before putting it into hot jars. The raw pack method requires you to tightly pack raw food into jars, and then cover with boiling water, syrup, juice, or broth to the proper headspace. Each canning recipe will indicate which method is best, though some items can be packed either raw or hot.

The hot pack method works best for firm produce or meats that either need a cooked sauce or will taste best with a processed syrup or broth. In addition, hot-packed foods will contain less air, will inactivate enzymes, and preserve the bright color of the produce. To hot pack foods, fold them into a boiling syrup, juice, or water. Then pack the produce into hot, sterile jars to prevent the glass from cracking, and to eliminate food-borne illnesses. Ladle the juice or broth into the jars until it reaches the required headspace. You may need to tap the jar on a counter or slide a spatula down between the jar and produce to remove any bubbles. Seal the jars, and then

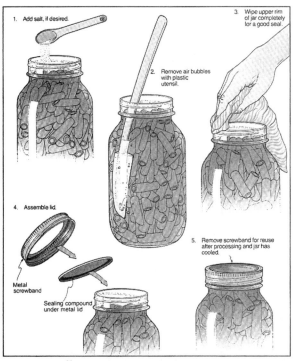

Illustration courtesy of the USDA

process them in a water-bath canner. Because these foods are partially cooked, hot packed produce requires less processing time. Recipes should indicate the proper processing time and the hot pack process.

Raw pack (or cold pack) works best for delicate foods like berries or some types of pickles. Cold packing is quicker and easier, but the processing time is longer. Make sure to pack the produce as tightly as possible into hot, sterile jars. Then pour in the hot syrup, juice, or water to fill spaces and submerge the contents. Again, you may need to tap the jar on a counter or slide a spatula down the insides of the jars to remove any bubbles. Seal the jars, and then follow the recipe's directions to process them in a hot water canner.

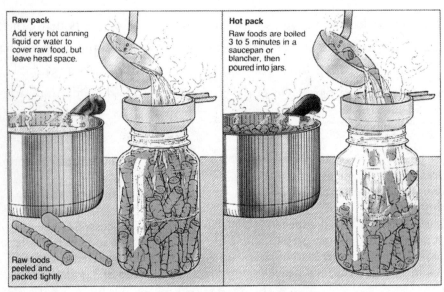

Illustration courtesy of the USDA

Headspace

The space between the food and liquid and the top rim of the jar is called the headspace. Proper headspace is crucial to a good seal. This space will allow the food and air to expand and move while it is heated. The air will expand much more than the food does, and the higher the temperature, the more the air will expand. If you fill the jar too full, the food will swell and spurt out of the jar, ruining the seal. This causes a mess in your canner, too. Even if you wipe off the jar, food may be trapped under the seal and will cause the food to rot. The best remedy is to sterilize the jar and lid, and re-process that jar with the correct headspace.

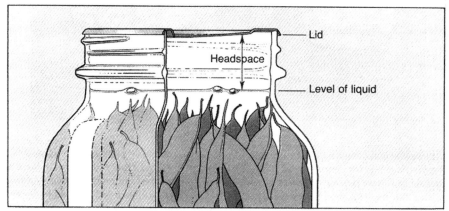

Illustration courtesy of the USDA

As the jars cool, the food, liquid, and air begins to contract; this pulls down the lid to create a vacuum seal that protects your food. You have probably noticed the characteristic hiss as you open a jar of food and the vacuum releases. However, if there is too much headspace for the specific food, the product has too much room to set a strong vacuum as the jars cool. Always make sure the lid is concave when fully cooled, as this indicates a good seal.

Canning recipes should always indicate the right amount of headspace. Make sure you follow the instructions carefully. As a general guideline, vegetables and fruits usually need ½ inch of headspace if processed in a boiling water canner. Produce, meat, and other recipes processed in a pressure canner should generally have 1 inch of headspace. Jams and jellies need ¼ inch of headspace.

Altitude adjustments

The canning recipes in this book call for a specific processing time and, with pressure canners, a specific amount of pressure. These instructions are intended for people who are processing food at altitudes ranging from sea level to 1,000 feet above sea level. However, those same processing times used at higher altitudes may not be sufficient and can cause the food to spoil. The reason for this is that water boils at a lower temperature at higher altitudes; the lower temperature may not be sufficient to destroy all the bacteria and mold.

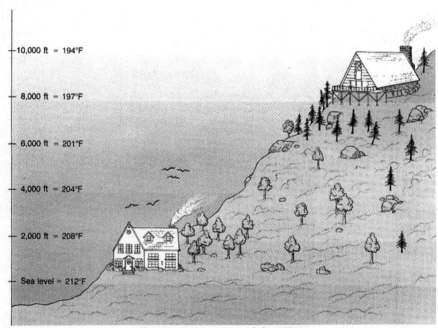

10,000 ft = 194°F

8,000 ft = 197°F

6,000 ft = 201°F

4,000 ft = 204°F

2,000 ft = 208°F

Sea level = 212°F

Illustration courtesy of the USDA

If you live at a high altitude, you are probably familiar with adjusting many types of recipes to work with your area. When using a pressure canner at altitudes above 1,000 feet, add ½ pound more pressure for each 1,000 in altitude. If your pressure canner does not have a dial gauge that allows you to make small adjustments, increase the weighted gauge to the next mark. For example, if your recipe calls for 10 pounds of pressure at 1,000 feet, process it at 15 pounds of pressure at high altitudes. When processing high-acid foods in a water-bath canner at altitudes above 1,000 feet, add 5 minutes of processing time. For low-acid foods, add 10 minutes for each 1,000 in altitude. These are only general guidelines; your particular area may vary. If you have questions about your altitude, proper pressures, or canning times, check with your county extension office.

Determining Your Altitude Above Sea Level
Courtesy of the USDA

It is important to know your approximate elevation or altitude above sea level in order to determine a safe processing time for canned foods. Because the boiling temperature of liquid is lower at higher elevations, it is critical that additional time be given for the safe processing of foods at altitudes above sea level.

It is not practical to include a list of altitudes in this guide, because there is wide variation within a state and even a county. For example, the state of Kansas has areas with altitudes varying between 75 ft to 4,039 ft above sea level. Kansas is not generally thought to have high altitudes, but there are many areas of the state where adjustments for altitude must be considered. Colorado, on the other hand, has people living in areas between 3,000 and 10,000 ft above sea level. They tend to be more conscious of the need to make altitude adjustments in the various processing schedules. To list altitudes for specific counties may actually be misleading, due to the differences in geographic terrain within a county.

If you are unsure about the altitude where you will be canning foods, consult your county extension agent. An alternative source of information would be your local district conservationist with the Soil Conservation Service.

Boiling water bath canners

These types of canners are large metal or porcelain-lined pots that have a removable canning rack and a lid. These are inexpensive and easily found in department or hardware stores. Buy a size that will be no more than 4 inches wider than your stove burners, so that the water will process food evenly.

During water-bath processing, jars are placed on top of the canning rack, and then the pot is filled with water. Make sure you fill the canner so at least an inch of water covers the tops of the jars. The water is heated to boiling, and once a full rolling boil is attained, you begin timing the processing according to the recipe's directions. Some boiling-water canners do not have flat bottoms. A flat bottom must be used on an electric range. Either a flat or ridged bottom can be used on a gas burner. To ensure uniform processing of all jars with an electric range, the canner should be no more than 4 inches wider in diameter than the element on which it is heated.

Boiling water bath canning is suitable only for foods containing high acid, like many fruits and pickles; the acid content helps to destroy toxins and harmful microorganisms. Lower-acid foods need a longer processing time and the heat concentration of a pressure canner to raise the temperature high enough to kill the same microorganisms.

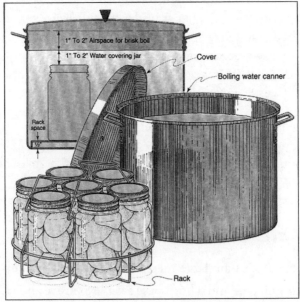

Illustration courtesy of the USDA

How to use a water bath canner
Instructions courtesy of the USDA

1. Before you start preparing your food, fill the canner halfway with clean water. This is approximately the level needed for a canner load of pint jars. For other sizes and numbers of jars, the amount of water in the canner will need to be adjusted so it will be 1 to 2 inches over the top of the filled jars.

2. Preheat water to 140 degrees F for raw-packed foods and to 180 degrees F for hot-packed foods. Food preparation can begin while this water is preheating.

3. Load filled jars, fitted with lids, into the canner rack and use the handles to lower the rack into the water; or fill the canner with the rack in the bottom, one jar at a time, using a jar lifter. When using a jar lifter, make sure it is securely positioned below the neck of the jar (below the screw band of the lid). Keep the jar upright at all times. Tilting the jar could cause food to spill into the sealing area of the lid.

4. Add more boiling water, if needed, so the water level is at least 1 inch above jar tops. For process times longer than 30 minutes, the water level should be at least 2 inches above the tops of the jars.

5. Turn heat to its highest position, cover the canner with its lid, and heat until the water in the canner boils vigorously.

6. Set a timer for the total minutes required for processing the food.

7. Keep the canner covered and maintain a boil throughout the process schedule. The heat setting may be lowered a little as long as a complete boil is maintained for the entire process time. If the water stops boiling at any time during the process, bring the water

back to a vigorous boil and begin the timing of the process over, from the beginning.

8. Add more boiling water, if needed, to keep the water level above the jars.

9. When jars have been boiled for the recommended time, turn off the heat and remove the canner lid. Wait 5 minutes before removing jars.

10. Using a jar lifter, remove the jars and place them on a towel, leaving at least 1 inch spaces between the jars during cooling. Let jars sit undisturbed to cool at room temperature for 12 to 24 hours.

Pressure canners

Pressure canners for use in the home have been extensively redesigned in recent years. Models made before the 1970s were heavy-walled kettles with clamp-on or turn-on lids. They were fitted with a dial gauge, a vent port in the form of a petcock or counterweight, and a safety fuse. All low-acid foods must be processed in a pressure canner. This is a different kitchen appliance than a pressure cooker — it is designed to accommodate large canning jars and produces the proper temperature for canned food processing. An average canner can hold about seven quart jars or up to nine pint jars. Smaller canners can hold four quart jars.

Pressure does not destroy microorganisms, but high temperatures applied for an adequate period of time do kill microorganisms. The success of destroying all microorganisms capable of growing in canned food is based on the temperature obtained in pure steam, free of air, at sea

A 16-quart pressure canner

level. At sea level, a canner operated at a gauge pressure of 10.5 lbs provides an internal temperature of 240 degrees F.

A pressure canner has a locking lid that holds in the steam and allows the pressure to build up, along with the heat. Either a pressure canner has a pressure gauge that shows the settings — 5,10, or 15 pounds — or a dial gauge that monitors rises in pressure from 5 to 15 pounds. If you live at a higher altitude, the dial gauge will be easier for you to use, because you must increase the pressure by a ½ pound for each 1,000 feet above sea level. If you use a dial gauge, be sure to have it checked every year at your county extension office.

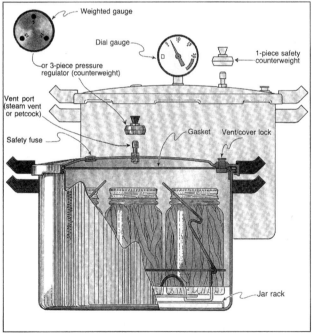

Illustration courtesy of the USDA

Two serious *errors* in temperatures obtained in pressure canners occur because:

1. **Internal canner temperatures are lower at higher altitudes.** To correct this error, canners must be operated at the increased pressures.

2. **Air trapped in a canner lowers the temperature obtained at 5, 10, or 15 pounds of pressure and results in under processing.** The highest volume of air trapped in a canner occurs in processing raw-packed foods in dial-gauge canners. These canners do not vent air during processing. To be safe, all types of pressure canners must be vented 10 minutes before they are pressurized.

To vent a canner, leave the vent port uncovered on newer models or manually open petcocks on some older models. Heating the filled canner with its lid locked into place boils water and generates steam that escapes through the petcock or vent port. When steam first escapes, set a timer for 10 minutes. After venting 10 minutes, close the petcock or place the counterweight or weighted gauge over the vent port to pressurize the canner.

Weighted-gauge models exhaust tiny amounts of air and steam each time their gauge rocks or jiggles during processing. They control pressure precisely and need neither watching during processing nor checking for accuracy. The sound of the weight rocking or jiggling indicates that the canner is maintaining the recommended pressure. The single disadvantage of weighted-gauge canners is that they cannot correct precisely for higher altitudes. At altitudes above 1,000 feet, they must be operated at canner pressures of 10 instead of 5, or 15 instead of 10, PSI.

Check dial gauges for accuracy before use each year. Gauges that read high cause under-processing and may result in unsafe food. Low readings cause over-processing. Pressure adjustments can be made if the gauge reads up to 2 pounds high or low. Replace gauges that differ by more than 2 pounds. Every pound of pressure is very important to the temperature needed inside the canner for producing safe food, so accurate gauges and adjustments are essential when a gauge reads higher than it should. If a gauge is reading lower than it should, adjustments may be made to avoid over processing, but are not essential to safety. Gauges may be checked at many county cooperative extension offices, or consumers can contact the pressure canner manufacturer for other options.

Handle canner lid gaskets carefully and clean them according to the manufacturer's directions. Nicked or dried gaskets will allow steam leaks during pressurization of canners. Keep gaskets clean between uses. Gaskets on older model canners may require a light coat of vegetable oil once per year. Gaskets on newer model canners are prelubricated and do not benefit from oiling. Check your canner's instructions if there is doubt that the particular gasket you use has been prelubricated.

Lid safety fuses are thin metal inserts or rubber plugs designed to relieve excessive pressure from the canner. Do not pick at or scratch fuses while cleaning lids. Use only canners that have the Underwriters Laboratory (UL) approval to ensure their safety.

Replacement gauges and other parts for canners are often available at stores offering canning equipment or from canner manufacturers. When ordering parts, give your canner model number and describe the parts needed.

Using pressure canners

Instructions courtesy of the USDA

Follow these steps for successful pressure canning:

1. Put 2 to 3 inches of hot water in the canner. Some specific products in this guide require that you start with even more water in the canner. Always follow the directions for specific foods if they require more water added to the canner. Place filled jars on the rack, using a jar lifter. When using a jar lifter, make sure it is securely positioned below the neck of the jar (below the screw band of the lid). Keep the jar upright at all times. Tilting the jar could cause food to spill into the sealing area of the lid. Fasten canner lid securely.

2. Leave weight off vent port or open petcock. Heat at the highest setting until steam flows freely from the open petcock or vent port.

3. While maintaining the high heat setting, let the steam flow (exhaust) continuously for 10 minutes, and then place the weight on the vent port or close the petcock. The canner will pressurize during the next 3 to 5 minutes.

4. Start timing the process when the pressure reading on the dial gauge indicates that the recommended pressure has been reached, or when the weighted gauge begins to jiggle or rock as the canner manufacturer describes.

Illustration courtesy of the USDA

5. Regulate heat under the canner to maintain a steady pressure at, or slightly above, the correct gauge pressure. Quick and large pressure variations during processing may cause unnecessary liquid losses from jars. Follow the canner manufacturer's directions for how a weighted gauge should indicate it is maintaining the desired pressure.

    IMPORTANT: If at any time pressure goes below the recommended amount, bring the canner back to pressure and begin the timing of the process over, from the beginning (using the total original process time). This is important for the safety of the food.

6. When the timed process is completed, turn off the heat, remove the canner from heat if possible, and let the canner depressurize. **Do not force-cool the canner.** Forced cooling may result in unsafe food or food spoilage. Cooling the canner with cold running water or opening the vent port before the canner is fully depressurized will cause loss of liquid from jars and seal failures. Force-cooling may also warp the canner lid of older model canners, causing steam leaks. Depressurization of older models without dial gauges should be timed. Standard-size heavy-walled canners require about 30 minutes when loaded with pints and 45 minutes with quarts. Newer thin-walled canners cool more rapidly and are equipped with vent locks. These canners are depressurized when their vent lock piston drops to a normal position.

7. After the canner is depressurized, remove the weight from the vent port or open the petcock. Wait 10 minutes, unfasten the lid, and remove it carefully. Lift the lid away from you so that the steam does not burn your face.

8. Remove jars with a jar lifter, and place them on a towel, leaving at least 1-inch spaces between the jars during cooling. Let jars sit undisturbed to cool at room temperature for 12 to 24 hours.

Cooling jars

When you remove hot jars from a canner, do not retighten their jar lids. Retightening of hot lids may cut through the gasket and cause seal failures. Cool the jars at room temperature for 12 to 24 hours. Jars can be cooled on racks or towels to minimize heat damage to counters. The food level and liquid volume of raw-packed jars will be noticeably lower after cooling. Air is exhausted during processing and food shrinks. If a jar loses excessive liquid during processing, do not open it to add more liquid.

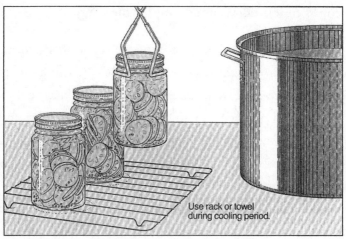

Use rack or towel
during cooling period.

Illustration courtesy of the USDA

Testing jar seals

After cooling jars for 12 to 24 hours, remove the screw bands and test seals with one of the following options:

- Press the middle of the lid with a finger or thumb. If the lid springs up when you release your finger, the lid is unsealed.

- Tap the lid with the bottom of a teaspoon. If it makes a dull sound, the lid is not sealed. If food is in contact with the underside of the lid, it will also cause a dull sound. If the jar is sealed correctly, it will make a ringing, high-pitched sound.

- Hold the jar at eye level and look across the lid. The lid should be concave (curved down slightly in the center). If center of the lid is either flat or bulging, it might not be sealed.

Illustration courtesy of the USDA

Reprocessing unsealed jars

If a lid fails to seal on a jar, remove the lid and check the jar-sealing surface for tiny nicks. If necessary, change the jar, add a new, properly prepared lid, and reprocess within 24 hours using the same processing time. Headspace in unsealed jars may be adjusted to 1 ½ inches and jars could be frozen instead of reprocessed. Foods in single unsealed jars could be stored in the refrigerator and consumed within several days.

Storing jars

Store your jars in a dark, dry, cool place away from heat sources, and protect them from freezing. You can remove the screw bands from the lids if you wish, but some prefer to use those bands to secure the

Stored jars of canned drinks and food

lids after the first time you open the jar. Label and date the jars and store them in a clean, cool, dark, dry place. Do not store jars above 95 degrees F or near hot pipes, a range, a furnace, under a sink, in a non-insulated attic, or in direct sunlight. Under these conditions, food will lose quality in a few weeks or months and may spoil. Dampness may corrode metal lids, break seals, and allow recontamination and spoilage.

What to Can?

Canned pickles and mushrooms — just two of many vegetables you may can

There are many different foods you are able to can. The following section discusses popular foods to can and how these foods should be prepared. Also discussed are variations you can use in your canning for special diets.

Preparing pickled and fermented foods

The many varieties of pickled and fermented foods are classified by ingredients and method of preparation.

Regular dill pickles and sauerkraut are fermented and cured for about 3 weeks. Refrigerator dills are fermented for about 1 week. During curing, colors and flavors change and acidity increases. Fresh-pack or quick-process pickles are not fermented; some are brined several hours or overnight, then drained and covered with vinegar and seasonings. Fruit pickles usually are prepared by heating fruit in a seasoned syrup acidified with either lemon juice or vinegar. Relishes are made from chopped fruits and vegetables that are cooked with seasonings and vinegar.

Be sure to remove and discard a 1/16-inch slice from the blossom end of fresh cucumbers. Blossoms may contain an enzyme which causes excessive softening of pickles.

Caution: The level of acidity in a pickled product is as important to its safety as it is to taste and texture.

- **Do not alter vinegar, food, or water proportions in a recipe or use a vinegar with unknown acidity.**

- **Use only recipes with tested proportions of ingredients.**

- **There must be a minimum, uniform level of acid throughout the mixed product to prevent the growth of botulinum bacteria.**

Pickling ingredients

Select fresh, firm fruits or vegetables free of spoilage. Measure or weigh amounts carefully, because the proportion of fresh food to other ingredients will affect flavor and, in many instances, safety.

Use canning or pickling salt. Noncaking material added to other salts may make the brine cloudy. Because flake salt varies in density, it is not recommended for making pickled and fermented foods. White granulated and brown sugars are most often used. Corn syrup and honey, unless called for in reliable recipes, may produce undesirable flavors. White distilled and cider vinegars of 5 percent acidity (50 grain) are recommended. White vinegar is usually preferred when light color is desirable, as is the case with fruits and cauliflower.

You can pickle many different fruits and vegetables
— photo courtesy of Blue Ridge Farms

Pickles with reduced salt content

In the making of fresh-pack pickles, cucumbers are acidified quickly with vinegar. Use only tested recipes formulated to produce the proper acidity. Although these pickles may be prepared safely with reduced or no salt, their quality may be noticeably lower. Both texture and flavor might be slightly, but noticeably, different than expected. You may wish to make small quantities first to determine if you like them.

However, the salt used in making fermented sauerkraut and brined pickles not only provides characteristic flavor but also is vital to safety and texture. In fermented foods, salt favors the growth of desirable bacteria while inhibiting the growth of others. **Caution: Do not attempt to make sauerkraut or fermented pickles by cutting back on the salt required.**

Firming agents

Alum may be safely used to firm fermented pickles. However, it is unnecessary and is not included in the recipes in this publication. Alum does not improve the firmness of quick-process pickles. The calcium in lime definitely improves pickle firmness. Food-grade lime may be used as a lime-water solution for soaking fresh cucumbers 12 to 24 hours before pickling them. Excess lime absorbed by the cucumbers must be removed to make safe pickles. To remove excess lime, drain the lime-water solution, rinse, and then resoak the cucumbers in fresh water for 1 hour. Repeat the rinsing and soaking steps two more times.

To further improve pickle firmness, you may process cucumber pickles for 30 minutes in water at 180 degrees Fahrenheit. This process also prevents spoilage, **but the water temperature should not fall below 180 degrees F.** Use a candy or jelly thermometer to check the water temperature.

Preventing spoilage

Pickle products are subject to spoilage from microorganisms, particularly yeasts and molds, as well as enzymes that may affect flavor, color, and texture. Processing the pickles in a boiling-water canner will prevent both of these problems. Standard canning jars and self-sealing lids are recommended. Processing times and procedures will vary according to food acidity and the size of food pieces.

Preparing butters, jams, jellies, and marmalades

Sweet spreads are a class of foods with many textures, flavors, and colors. They all consist of fruits preserved mostly by means of sugar and they are thickened or jellied to some extent. Fruit jelly is a semi-solid mixture of fruit juice and sugar that is clear and firm enough to hold its shape. Other spreads are made from crushed or ground fruit.

Jam also will hold its shape, but it is less firm than jelly. Jam is made from crushed or chopped fruits and sugar. Jams made from a mixture of fruits are usually called conserves, especially when they include citrus fruits, nuts, raisins, or coconut. Preserves are made of small, whole fruits or uniform-size pieces of fruits in a clear, thick, slightly jellied syrup. Marmalades are soft fruit jellies with small pieces of fruit or citrus peel evenly suspended in a transparent jelly. Fruit butters are made from fruit pulp cooked with sugar until thickened to a spreadable consistency.

Use strawberry jam on toast, bagels, or English muffins

Ingredients

For proper texture, jellied fruit products require the correct combination of fruit, pectin, acid, and sugar. The fruit gives each spread its unique flavor and color. It also supplies the water to dissolve the rest of the necessary ingredients and furnishes some or all of the pectin and acid. Good-quality, flavorful fruits make the best jellied products.

Pectins are substances in fruits that form a gel if they are in the right combination with acid and sugar. All fruits contain some pectin. Apples, crab apples, gooseberries, and some plums and grapes usually contain enough natural pectin to form a gel. Other fruits, such as strawberries, cherries, and blueberries, contain little pectin and must be combined with other fruits high in pectin or with commercial pectin products to obtain gels. Because fully ripened fruit has less pectin, one-fourth of the fruit used in making jellies without added pectin should be under-ripe.

Caution: Commercially frozen and canned juices may be low in natural pectins and make soft-textured spreads.

The proper level of acidity is critical to gel formation. If there is too little acid, the gel will never set; if there is too much acid, the gel will lose liquid (weep). For fruits low in acid, add lemon juice or other acid ingredients as directed. Commercial pectin products contain acids, which help to ensure gelling.

Sugar serves as a preserving agent, contributes flavor, and aids in gelling. Cane and beet sugar are the usual sources of sugar for jelly or jam. Corn syrup and honey may be used to replace part of the sugar in recipes, but too much will mask the fruit flavor and alter the gel structure. Use tested recipes for replacing sugar with honey and corn syrup. Do not try to reduce the amount of sugar in traditional recipes. Too little sugar prevents gelling and may allow yeasts and molds to grow.

Jams and jellies with reduced sugar

Jellies and jams that contain modified pectin, gelatin, or gums may be made with noncaloric sweeteners. Jams with less sugar than usual also can be made with concentrated fruit pulp, which contains less liquid and less sugar.

Two types of modified pectin are available for home use. One gels with one-third less sugar. The other is a low-methoxyl pectin, which requires a source of calcium for gelling. To prevent spoilage, jars of these products might need to be processed longer in a boiling-water canner. Recipes and processing times provided with each modified pectin product must be followed carefully. The proportions of acids and fruits should not be altered, because spoilage may result. Acceptably gelled refrigerator fruit spreads also may be made with gelatin and sugar substitutes. Such products spoil at room temperature, must be refrigerated, and should be eaten within 1 month.

Preventing spoilage

Even though sugar helps preserve jellies and jams, molds can grow on the surface of these products. Research now indicates that the mold, which people usually scrape off the surface of jellies, may not be as harmless as it seems. Mycotoxins have been found in some jars of jelly having surface mold growth. Mycotoxins are known to cause cancer in animals; their effects on humans are still being researched. Because of possible mold contamination, paraffin or wax seals are no longer recommended for any sweet spread, including jellies. To prevent growth of molds and loss of good flavor or color, fill products hot into sterile Mason jars, leaving ¼-inch headspace, seal with self-sealing lids, and process 5 minutes in a boiling-water canner. Correct process time at higher elevations by adding 1 additional minute per 1,000 ft above sea level. If unsterile jars are used, the filled jars should be processed for 10 minutes. Use of sterile jars is preferred, especially when fruits are low in pectin, because the added 5-minute process time may cause weak gels.

Methods of making jams and jellies

There are two methods to make jams and jellies. The standard method, which does not require added pectin, works best with fruits naturally high in pectin. The other method, which requires the use of commercial liquid or powdered pectin, is much quicker. The gelling ability of various pectins differs. To make uniformly gelled products, be sure to add the quantities of commercial pectins to specific fruits as instructed on each package. Overcooking can break down pectin and prevent proper gelling. When using either method, make one batch at a time, according to the recipe. Increasing the quantities often results in soft gels. Stir constantly while cooking to prevent burning. Recipes are developed for specific jar sizes. If jellies are filled into larger jars, excessively soft products may result.

You can dress up small jars of jam with
decorative paper and ribbon to give as gifts

Canned foods for special diets

The cost of commercially canned special-diet food often prompts interest in preparing these products at home. Some low-sugar and low-salt foods may be easily and safely canned at home. However, the color, flavor, and texture of these foods may be different than expected and be less acceptable.

Canning without sugar

In canning regular fruits without sugar, it is very important to select fully ripe but firm fruits of the best quality. Prepare these as described for hot-packs, but use water or regular unsweetened fruit juices instead of sugar syrup. Juice made from the fruit being canned is best. Blends of unsweetened apple, pineapple, and white grape juice are also good for filling over solid fruit pieces. Adjust headspaces and lids and use the processing recommendations given for regular fruits. Splenda® is the only sugar substitute currently in the marketplace that can be added to covering liquids before canning fruits. Other sugar substitutes, if desired, should be added when serving.

Canning without salt (reduced sodium)

To can tomatoes, vegetables, meats, poultry, and seafood with reduced sodium, simply omit the salt. In these products, salt seasons the food but is not necessary to ensure its safety. Add salt substitutes, if desired, when serving.

Canning fruit-based baby foods

You may prepare any chunk-style or pureed fruit with or without sugar. Pack in half-pint, preferably, or pint jars and use the following processing times.

Recommended process time for fruit-based baby foods in a boiling-water canner

Style of Pack	Jar Size	Process Time at Altitudes of		
		0-1,000 ft	1,001-6,000 ft	Above 6,000 ft
Hot	Pints	20 min	25 min	30 min

Caution: Do not attempt to can pureed vegetables, red meats, or poultry meats, because proper processing times for pureed foods have not been determined for home use. Instead, can and store these foods using the standard processing procedures; puree or blend them at serving time. Heat the blended foods to boiling, simmer for 10 minutes, cool, and serve. Store unused portions in the refrigerator and use within 2 days for best quality.

How much should you can?

The amount of food to preserve for your family, either by canning or freezing, should be based on individual choices. The following table can serve as a worksheet to plan how much food you should can for use within a year.

Suggested Preservation Plan for Canned and Frozen Foods									
		Servings/week[a]			My family needs				
	Serv-ing Size	Per Person		My Fami-ly[b]	Cups/ Week[0]	Qts/ Week[d]	Weeks served/ yr[3]	Quarts/year	
Kind of Food		Sug-gest	Ac-tual					To-tal[e]	Can-ned[3]	Fro-zen[3]
Example: Family of 4										
Fruits	1/2 cup	12	12	48	24	6	36	216	72	144
My Plan:										
Fruits – apples, berries, peaches, plums, pears, tomatoes	1/2 cup	12								
Juices – apple, berry, grape, tomato	1 cup	7								
Vegetables – beets, beans, carrots, corn, peas, pumpkin, squash	1/2 cup	16								
Meat & Seafood – red meat, poultry, shellfish, fish	1/2 cup	14								
Soups	1 cup	2								
Pickles & Relishes – ketchup, fruit pickles, vegetable pickles, rel-ish, etc.		1/2 cup								

Suggested Preservation Plan for Canned and Frozen Foods									
		Servings/week[a]			My family needs				
	Serving Size	Per Person		My Family[b]	Cups/Week[0]	Qts/Week[d]	Weeks served/yr[3]	Quarts/year	
Kind of Food		Suggest	Actual					Total[e]	Canned[3]	Frozen[3]
Fruit Spreads- honey, jellies, jam, syrups, preserves, etc.	-	1/2 cup								
Sauces-to-mato, etc.	1/2 cup	2								

Your family should make these decisions.

Servings/week for my family = actual weekly servings/person multiplied by number of family members who eat that food.

Cups/week = servings/week multiplied by recommended serving size.

Quarts/week = cups/week divided by 4.

Total quarts/year = quarts/week multiplied by weeks served/year.

Chapter 2

Troubleshooting Canning Problems

anning requires strict adherence to directions, and many problems can result from not following recipes precisely. If you are new to canning, you may be tempted to come up with your own canning recipe or add extra thickeners, vegetables, or liquids to your food — resist the temptation. Canning recipes have been developed and tested to ensure a delicious, quality product that will withstand the stress of canning, and will provide healthy food even after long storage.

There are common mistakes that people make during canning. This chapter focuses on how to examine your finished products for problems, and what to do when you see a problem. Not every funny-looking jar

Homemade preserves like these will be delicious and last a long time if you follow instructions

must be discarded; sometimes, the problem is minor or just a symptom of produce subjected to high temperatures. However, the rule is: if in doubt, throw it out.

Here are some other mistakes people often make while canning:

- Failing to adjust the recipe for their altitudes.

- Forgetting to vent the pressure cooker.

- Neglecting to have their pressure cooker gauges checked and adjusted before each canning season.

- When processing "hot pack" foods, allowing the food to cool before placing it in jars.

Check Your Food!

When you open up a jar of food, there are several things to check for to ensure your food has not spoiled. Look for the following indications:

1. The outside of the jar is soiled or moldy. This means that food has seeped out of the jar through a bad seal — and therefore mold and bacteria have seeped in. Toss it out.

2. Bubbly liquid or a spurt of liquid when you open the jar. This means that food has developed gases through improper processing.

3. Change in texture or color — this indicates the food has spoiled since canning.

4. Mold on the lid or in the food. An improper seal or processing has allowed mold spores to grow.

Common Canning Problems

Because the canning process requires several steps and careful attention to details, many things can go wrong with your food. In addition, before you eat food from any jar, check it again for problems. Once you complete a batch of canning and allow it to cool for 24 hours, check each jar for problems. Do not diagnose problems by tasting the food.

This guide will describe some common problems, how they occurred, and how to avoid these problems next time. Some of the problems are merely appearance issues, but other problems will affect the taste or texture of the food and hamper your enjoyment of your products.

However, some of the problems are health issues. These are the most important problems for you to monitor. Once you complete a batch of canning, always check your food against these health signs to be sure you do not harm anyone with the food. If you see signs that food has become contaminated, take care with your disposal method. Some bacteria are deadly even in small amounts; you could spill a tiny splash on your hand and then wipe your mouth. Then, the bacterium has entered your system. It is best to dump bad products down the drain, where the water treatment plants will neutralize contaminants, then scrub your sink and sterilize the jars. Make sure you *always* discard the self-seal lids after using them. The screw ring can be re-used once it is sterilized. Alternatively, you can boil the jars in a water bath canner for 30 minutes to neutralize the contents, and then place the unopened jars in the trash.

Spoiled food

Spoiled food usually has several indicators; just one sign might not be a problem. For example, some foods, such as juices, may be cloudy after processing because of the pulp present in the juice. However, if you open the jar and the food smells off, rather than the food's ordinary smell, or if you see feathery mold growing on the rim or in the jar, it is clearly a spoiled product. For this reason, if you notice something odd with the food, check for anything else that may indicate a problem: the color, smell, increase in bubbles, seepage from the jar, obvious growth of bacteria or contaminants, etc. Remember; **do not** test food by tasting it.

If you notice the following problems with your jars, carefully discard the food and lid, and sterilize the jar immediately. It is better to lose a little food than make yourself sick. To prevent these problems in the future, take these precautions to process the food properly in the future:

- Make sure the jars are not overstuffed and that they are filled to the proper headspace. Remove air bubbles before putting the lids on the jars.

- Follow the processing method and time exactly.

- Check to be sure you have a good seal: concave, good vacuum, and no bulging at the lid.

- Make sure the pressure gauge on your pressure canner is checked and calibrated for accuracy at the beginning of each canning season.

- Check jars and lids for cracks, chips, rust, or damage. Always use new lids and sterilized equipment.

- Choose the freshest foods that have no rotten or moldy parts. Prepare the product properly.

- Carefully wipe the rim of each jar after it is filled. Make sure no food remains on the rim to hamper the seal or cause spoilage later.

Illustration courtesy of the USDA

Problem	Possible Causes
Product at the top of the jar is dark and/or thicker than normal.	This may not be a sign of spoiled food; check the table on appearance changes to rule out other problems. If other signs of spoilage exist, this is probably the result of improper processing.
The liquid in the jar is cloudy.	This may not be a sign of spoiled food; check the table on appearance changes to rule out other problems. If other signs of spoilage exist, this is probably the result of improper processing.
The liquid in the jar contains sediment.	This may not be a sign of spoiled food; check the table on appearance changes to rule out other problems. If other signs of spoilage exist, this is probably the result of improper processing.
Non-pickled or fermented food has a sour, strange, or foul smell.	The food or jar has been contaminated — especially if bubbles also appear within the jar.

Problem	Possible Causes
Non-pickled or fermented food is bubbly.	The food or jar has been contaminated and fermentation has occurred, especially if the food has a strange or foul smell.
Food has an unusual color.	This may not be a sign of spoiled food; check the table on appearance changes to rule out other problems. If other signs of spoilage exist, this is probably the result of improper processing.
Jar lid, rim, or the surface of the food contains mold.	Although some molds are harmless and can be removed so the rest of the food can be eaten, it is best to be safe and discard the entire contents. This is the result of improper processing.

Cleaning up the area
Courtesy of the USDA

Contact with botulinum toxin can be fatal whether it is ingested or enters through the skin. Take care to avoid contact with suspect foods or liquids. Wear rubber or heavy plastic gloves when handling suspect foods or cleaning up contaminated work surfaces and equipment. A fresh solution of 1 part unscented liquid household chlorine bleach (5 to 6 percent sodium hypochlorite) to 5 parts clean water should be used to treat work surfaces, equipment, or other items, including can openers and clothing, that might have come in contact with suspect foods or liquids. Spray or wet contaminated surfaces with the bleach solution and let stand for 30 minutes. Wearing gloves, wipe up treated spills with paper towels being careful to minimize the spread of contamination. Dispose of these paper towels by placing them in a plastic bag before putting them in the trash. Next, apply the bleach solution to all surfaces and equipment again, and let stand for 30 minutes and rinse. As a last step, thoroughly wash all detoxified counters, containers, equipment, clothing, etc. Discard gloves when cleaning process is complete. (Note: Bleach is an irritant itself and should not be inhaled or allowed to come in contact with the skin.)

Problem	Possible Causes	How To Avoid
Product at the top of the jar is dark and/or thicker than normal.	Too much air in the jar has caused the top layer of food to become oxidized.	Do not overstuff jars, but be careful that the food and liquid reach the recipe's proper headspace. Remove bubbles from the jar before processing.
	The food in the jar is not completely covered with liquid.	Do not overstuff jars, but be careful that the liquid completely covers the food and reaches the recipe's proper headspace.
	Food is spoiled, because it was not processed correctly.	Follow preparation and processing instructions exactly.
Food has an unusual color.	Some substances in foods react to the canning process by changing color. For example, peaches, pears, cauliflower, or apples may turn slightly pink or blue.	Freezing, drying, and pickling (flowers).
	Food that is white, blue, black, or green (unless it is naturally that color) is spoiled. If other signs of spoilage exist, the food has been contaminated.	Follow preparation and processing instructions exactly.
Food has pale color.	The jars have been stored improperly.	Store the jars in a cool, dark place, free from drafts or excess humidity.
The liquid in the jar is cloudy.	Minerals or additives in the water or salt may have clouded the liquid.	Choose pure salt with no additives, and use soft or distilled water for canning.
	The starchy foods have released some starch, which has clouded the liquid. Meat products often produce cloudy liquid during processing; this is normal.	Choose fresh, ripe products that are not overripe. If cutting up starchy foods like potatoes, rinse them in cold water before processing; then when you add liquid to the jars, use fresh water instead of the cooking water.

Problem	Possible Causes	How To Avoid
	If the product is juice, it is possible that extra pulp has drained into the juice.	This is not a problem — the pulp will add extra flavor and nutrients to the finished product. However, if you prefer a clear juice, strain the juice several times before processing, and do not squeeze or press the pulp while straining.
	If other signs of spoilage exist, the food has been contaminated.	Follow preparation and processing instructions exactly.
The liquid in the jar contains sediment.	Minerals or additives in the water or salt may have clouded the liquid.	Choose pure salt with no additives, and use soft or distilled water for canning.
	If other signs of spoilage exist, the food has been contaminated.	Follow preparation and processing instructions exactly.
Food is floating in the jar.	The syrup used in canning is heavier than the product.	Prepare ripe, firm fruit properly, and use the hot pack method. Use thinner syrup that contains less sugar.
	The produce or jar contains too much air.	Use the hot pack method to remove more air from the product. Make sure all bubbles are removed from the jar before processing. Pack the produce firmly in the jar.
Tomato juice has separated into yellow liquid on top and thick red juice at the bottom.	This is a natural enzymatic action that occurs when tomatoes are cut up for processing.	If you prefer not to shake up the jar before pouring some juice, make sure that during the hot pack process, you bring the tomatoes to a boil immediately after chopping them.

Jar is not sealed properly

If you discover any of the following problems, you can refrigerate the food and eat it within a few days. Alternatively, if you discover a bad seal within the first 12 to 24 hours, and the band and lid are undamaged, you can re-process the jar using the original method and timing.

Problem	Possible Causes	How To Avoid
Not enough liquid in jars.	Uneven pressure in the pressure canner.	Make sure pressure remains constant during processing. Allow pressure canner to release the pressure and heat naturally. Wait at least 10 minutes before opening the canner.
	Bubbles were left in the jar while packing food.	Slide a knife or spatula inside the jar to remove air bubbles; adjust headspace if necessary.
	Liquid escaped through a bad seal.	Use new, undamaged lids and ring bands that screw on properly. Make sure the jars do not have any chips or cracks. Make sure no food is on the rim of the jar by wiping the rims before putting on the lids. Wipe sealing surface of jar clean after filling, before applying lid.
	The water bath canner did not have sufficient water.	Make sure the water is at least 2 inches over the tops of the jars throughout the entire processing time.
	The food absorbed too much liquid.	Starchy foods will need a larger ratio of liquid to product. Make sure you hot pack these items.
	The food was packed too tightly.	Allow enough headspace so that the food does not boil out of the jars.

Problem	Possible Causes	How To Avoid
The jar did not seal; the lid is not concave and does not have a vacuum seal.	There was food between the rim and seal, or the rim was damaged.	Check jars before using. Wipe the rims of jars after filling them.
	Ring bands were damaged or not screwed on properly.	Check ring bands before using. Always screw bands on finger-tight.

Special problems with jams and jellies

Problem	Possible Causes	How To Avoid
The product contains crystals.	Too much sugar might have been added, or the sugar was not completely dissolved during processing.	Reduce the amount of sugar; follow tested recipes exactly and remove from heat once the product reaches the jellying point.
	If appearing in products made from grape juice, naturally occurring tartrate crystals may have formed.	Settle the crystals in the juice by refrigerating overnight and then straining the juice before making the product.
Bubbles.	Jelly set while air bubbles were still in the jar.	Skim foam from the liquid before filling jars, and quickly slide a spatula through the product to remove air bubbles.
	If other signs of spoilage exist, the food has been contaminated.	Follow preparation and processing instructions exactly.
Jam or jelly is too soft.	There may be several causes: The juice was overcooked. Too much water was used to make the juice. The sugar and juice proportions were not correct. The product was undercooked, so that the sugar was not concentrated enough.	Follow tested recipes exactly.

Problem	Possible Causes	How To Avoid
	The product did not contain enough acid.	Add a small amount of lemon juice to the juice before making the jam or jelly.
	Making too much jelly/jam at once.	Process jams and jellies in small batches, such as 4-6 pint jars at a time. You will need approximately 8-12 cups of fruit juice to produce 4-6 pint jars; follow recipes for specific amounts.
	Not allowing enough time before moving jars.	Wait at least 12 hours after processing before you move the jars.
	Using the product before it has had time to properly gel.	Most jams or jellies will take about two weeks to completely gel; jellies take a little longer than jams. Some fruits, such as plums, will take longer than two weeks; fruit butters will not completely gel. Shaking the jar might help you determine if the product is ready.
The product is darker than normal.	The juice may have cooked too long, or the sugar may have scorched.	Follow the instructions precisely; smaller batches of product will be easier to manage.
	The jam or jelly may be too old, or may have been stored in a very warm environment.	Once the product has set, store it in a cool, dark place and use within the next year. Refrigerate the jar after it has been opened.
The product is cloudy.	The juice used to make the jam/jelly has too much pulp drained into the juice.	This is not a problem — the pulp will add extra flavor and nutrients to the finished product. However, if you prefer a clear juice, strain the juice several times before processing, and do not squeeze or press the pulp while straining.

Problem	Possible Causes	How To Avoid
	The completed jelly/jam sat before it was poured into the jars, or was poured too slowly.	The product will begin to gel immediately upon removal from the heat. Pour into the jars quickly and carefully.
The jam or jelly is stiff or too thick	The product has been overcooked so that too much of the liquid has boiled away.	Follow cooking instructions precisely and stop cooking once the product forms a sheet on the cooking spoon.
	Inaccurate proportion of pectin to fruit.	Use less pectin; tested recipes should not present this problem.

Chapter 3

Freezing Foods

As mentioned in the introduction, preserving foods through freezing only became available in much of the world since the invention of refrigerators and freezers, about 75 years ago. However, many cultures have been freezing foods for millennia. People who lived in extremely cold climates, such as the Arctic Circle, dug storage places for the meat from hunting, or built a cache out of rocks. The meat was protected from predators, and when the people needed some food, they would chop a hunk off the frozen meat and cook it.

Other early cultures invented clever ways to keep food frozen during the summer months. The Chinese used ice cellars more than three thousand years ago. The ancient Incas, living in the Andes, learned how to freeze-dry food by removing the water content during the freezing process. In warmer climates, the Egyptians and Indians discovered that they could produce ice crystals by causing clay jars to evaporate water quickly. In addition, many cultures, including the Greeks and Romans, collected snow and ice from mountains during the winter months to line cellars that would keep food frozen during the summer.

Today, freezing is the safest, quickest, and easiest method to store food until you are ready to eat it. Freezing is also an economical method, because you can buy meat and produce when it is on sale or in season, and pack it away for later. Whether you have a large chest freezer, or a refrigerator/freezer combination, this chapter will explain how to pack and freeze foods properly. This chapter discusses how to keep frozen foods tasting as delicious as possible, and how long you should keep items in your freezer. It will also show you what to do when something goes wrong — such as handling a power outage or an unexpected thaw.

Freezing occurs when food is kept in a freezer at 0 degrees Fahrenheit (-18 degrees Celsius) for 24 hours or longer. Of course, the amount and texture of the food determines how quickly it will reach the optimal freezing state. Once the food is completely frozen, bacteria, yeasts, and molds that could cause food to spoil are rendered completely inactive. This means that though the bacteria is still present, it does not reproduce and cannot spoil the food. Some bacteria are destroyed by freezing, but many can begin to multiply once the food is thawed and begin to cause illness again. It is possible that sub-zero freezing can destroy trichina and other parasites, but it is still a good idea to rely on proper cooking to kill any parasites. Freezing also changes the enzymes present in food. This can be especially important in fruits and vegetables that may continue to ripen slightly while they are frozen. In these cases, a few extra steps, described in this chapter, are needed to stop the enzymatic process.

A well-stocked freezer means less trips to the grocery store

Although freezing meat produces food that tastes closest to fresh meat, all methods of preservation will change the flavor and texture of the food. Freezing can toughen some produce and soften other foods. In addition, food can take on a stale "freezer taste" or absorb odors from newly-frozen foods. To prevent this, defrost the refrigerator occasionally and wipe it down with cleaner and a wet rag. Frost-free freezers, which are standard appliances today, should not require ice removal but will still benefit from a periodic cleaning. Between cleanings, keep an open box of baking soda in the freezer to absorb odors and ensure foods have the best taste possible. Change the box every three to four months — you can pour it down your kitchen sink to get rid of odors there, as well.

Problems with freezing

You may notice two problems in your freezer — foods that take on a tough, dried-out texture and foods entirely covered with ice crystals. Neither of these conditions is dangerous to your health, but they will not add to your enjoyment of the food. Freezer burn happens when food is inadequately wrapped against the cold, and frozen air dries out the surface and damages the fibers of the food.

Ice crystals generally form when food is not packed properly or freezes too slowly. Later in this chapter, you will find tips on how to package food to protect it against freezer burn. Large ice crystals will form on food as it slowly releases moisture directly from the produce or meat. When you defrost these products, you end up with a great deal of water and a tough, dry portion of food. Ice crystals also form when a freezer has fluctuations in temperature that may cause slight thawing — again, releasing moisture from your food. An older or malfunctioning freezer will most likely cause temperature fluctuations, so it is smart to check your freezer now and then for a stable, cold environment. Food that has been frozen long past its lifetime will also be susceptible to ice crystals, but it is not harmful.

You will be most successful at freezing foods, and produce food with the best possible quality, if you use containers, bags, and wraps designed for the freezer. These are designed to be thick enough to keep moisture in and freezer odors out. Plastic wrap and sandwich bags are not thick enough, and often leave gaps that will cause freezer burn on your food. Foil is a good freezer wrap, but the disadvantage is that it is hard to tell what food is under the layer of foil. Plastic containers and casserole dishes designed to go from freezer to oven (or vice versa) are good choices as well, but some plastic containers can give your food a plastic taste — especially when new. Some people also use vacuum-seal machines that remove the air from a thick plastic bag, and then seal the open edge with heat.

Regardless of the storage container you use, always write the date and the contents of the package on the outside. Nothing is more frustrating than riffling through anonymous packages looking for that bag of eggplant from last month.

Freeze smarter

There are ways to freeze smarter so your food will taste better and your freezer will be more energy-efficient. Cold foods need much less energy to freeze than hot ones, so wait for hot foods to cool before freezing. If you live in a cold climate, you can save energy by placing the warm container outside and letting the weather cool it for you. Then place it in the freezer at a spot where there is plenty of space around the container so cold air can circulate around it. Once it is frozen solid, you can place it with the rest of the foods.

Remember to freeze food in small portions. The food will freeze faster and will taste fresher when it is thawed, and your freezer will have to produce less cold air to keep the food frozen. Freezing food in serving portions is also a smart idea; it can be hard to chip one chicken breast out of a package of six, or remove a few slices of bread from a frozen loaf. However, if you individually wrap meats, you can take out just what you need and save the rest.

When sealing the bags, make sure you remove as much air from the bag as you can. Any air remaining in the bag can cause freezer burn or allow condensing moisture to create ice crystals. If you use a container rather than a

These frozen shrimp will make a great addition to any meal

bag, make sure that the food fills the entire container. On the other hand, if freezing soups, sauces, or stews, leave some headspace at the top of the container to prevent the liquid, which expands as it freezes, from freezing to the lid — or popping the lid right off the container.

The following charts will help you remember the foods that freeze worst and best, how long to keep various foods in the freezer, and the best way to prepare them to be frozen.

Foods that do not freeze well:

- Buttermilk

- Eggs in the shell, whether cooked or raw

- Raw egg yolks

- Any products made of eggs, such as pudding, custard sauces, or pastries and cakes containing custard

- Sour cream

- Dips made with sour cream

- Whipped topping, including those in a frozen carton, an aerosol can, or prepared from a mix

- Whipped cream and half-and-half

- Yogurt

- Prepared salads: egg, chicken, ham, tuna, and macaroni salads

- Opened bottles of salad dressing

- Lettuce and other salad greens

- Radishes

- Green onions

- Cucumbers

- Opened cans of meat, poultry, fish, or seafood

Freezer storage times

The following chart shows various foods that freeze well, and the foods' recommended storage times. These times are for quality purposes, rather than safety, because frozen food can stay safe forever.

Raspberries kept fresh in the freezer can be thawed for recipes, or even eaten frozen for a refreshing treat

If you take a food out of the freezer and are unsure about its quality after you defrost it, smell it to determine if it still good. If it smells odd, off, or rancid, discard it. If a food smells fine, but looks odd, it is still probably good enough to serve cooked in a stew or soup. You can cook suspect foods first and if they taste good after cooking, use them as ingredients.

Item	Months
Bacon and sausage	1 to 2
Casseroles	2 to 3
Egg whites or egg substitutes	12
Frozen dinners and entrees	3 to 4
Gravy, meat, or poultry	2 to 3
Ham, hotdogs, and lunchmeats	1 to 2
Meat, uncooked roasts	4 to 12
Meat, uncooked steaks or chops	4 to 12
Meat, uncooked ground	3 to 4
Meat, cooked	2 to 3
Poultry, uncooked whole	12
Poultry, uncooked parts	9
Poultry, uncooked giblets	3 to 4
Poultry, cooked	4
Soups and stews	2 to 3
Wild game, uncooked	8 to 12

Information courtesy of the USDA Food Safety and Inspection Service, public domain fact sheet at www.fsis.usda.gov/Fact_Sheets/Focus_On_Freezing.

Defrosting food

When you are ready to eat something that you froze, how you defrost it will have an impact on the food's flavor, texture, and it could even have an impact on your health. The best way to thaw meat or a dairy product, for example, is to remove it from the freezer several days before it is to be cooked, place it in the refrigerator, and let it thaw slowly. A quick application of heat will start the multiplication process of any dangerous organisms. *Never* leave meat out at room temperature to thaw.

A quicker method is to keep the meat in a plastic bag and submerge it in cool water until it is thawed. This could take several hours depending on the size of the meat portion, but again, it will slow the growth of bacteria and parasites. Using the microwave to defrost your meat is also a good option, but watch the process so that the meat is not browned or overheated in some areas and still frozen in others. Any quick acceleration of heat will have an effect on the inactive microorganisms in the food.

Vegetables can be cooked from their frozen state — there is no need to thaw them. Any fruits or vegetables that will be used raw can be thawed in the refrigerator, where they will keep some firmness while defrosting. Fruits and vegetables do not pose as many health threats as defrosting meats. Many fruits and vegetables may lose liquid during the defrosting process, so you might want to drain them before using.

What to do when your freezer stops working

It could happen at any time — your freezer could fail, and then all of your investment in food and time could be lost. Your freezer may have mechanical problems, or someone could accidentally change the temperature, or a power failure could occur. A terrible thunderstorm could knock your power out for a week.

It is wise to know ahead of time what you should do to minimize your losses, and prevent illness due to spoiled food. At the moment of an emergency, you may have other things to worry about. So ahead of time, find local commercial or institutional freezers that may accept your food. Locate a dry ice supplier. If your area is subject to frequent power failures or you know there is a scheduled outage, set your freezer temperature between -10 degrees Fahrenheit and -20 degrees Fahrenheit, so that the food will be colder during the outage and less likely to thaw.

Once your freezer stops working, keep the door closed at all times. A freezer packed with foods that are frozen solid will continue to keep those foods frozen for about two days if the doors are kept shut. Putting blankets or other types of insulating objects around the freezer will also help keep foods cold, but be sure not to close off air vents, in case the freezer starts up again. Separate the meat from other foods, so that if the meat thaws, it will not drip juices onto other food.

Next, determine the cause of the failure. It could be as simple as an accidental disconnection, a tripped circuit breaker, a blown fuse, or an electrical shortage. In these cases, fix the problem as quickly as possible, and then check for any food that might be thawing. If the problem is the result of a power failure, contact the utility company to find out how long it will be before power is restored.

If the problem is not a simple one, or the result of a power failure, check the operating instructions for your freezer to see if there are any additional solutions before you call a technician. You might save yourself a service call.

Protect your food from thawing

Though a sealed freezer that is not operational may keep food frozen for a day or two, it is wise to plan ahead to protect your food from thawing. If you are in the middle of winter and temperatures will be well below zero for several days, you could pack your food in coolers and store them in a garage or shed, but do not store the cooler in sunlight. You might want to ask a friend or neighbor if you can store your food in his or her freezer — or perhaps distribute the food among several freezers. You could also check with a school, church, or social organization to see if they have freezer space for you to use temporarily. If there is a local freezing plant in your area, you may ask to store your food there.

When you move your food, be sure to protect it from thawing, as well. Place the packages into insulated coolers, or boxes that are lined with Styrofoam, thick layers of newspaper, or blankets. Once you take the food out of your freezer, get it to an operating freezer as soon as possible.

If you cannot find another freezer to store your food, you might be able to purchase dry ice and place it in your freezer to keep things cold. Check your phone book or the Internet for a local place that sells dry ice or carbonic gas. A full 20-cubic foot freezer will use a 50-pound cake of dry ice to keep the packages frozen for three to four days; a 10-cubic foot freezer will use a 25-pound cake. Note that if your freezer is half full, it will need more dry ice to keep it cold. When you buy dry ice, ask the company to cut it to the right size for you, and have them wrap each piece in plastic or other protective material. Dry ice is dangerous; you can lose layers of skin or give yourself frostbite by touching it with bare skin. Handle it quickly and always wear protective gloves to prevent the ice from burning your hands.

Place heavy cardboard or newspapers on top of your frozen food packages, put the dry ice on top of the cardboard, and close the freezer. Make sure the freezer is not opened again unless you must replace the dry ice, or the freezer is working again. The dry ice will gradually form a vapor that you can dispel by opening the door. The vapor is harmless and will dissipate quickly.

If you had to move your food to another freezer, this is the perfect time to unplug it, defrost, and clean it out. Use mild cleaners and wipe it down one last time with plain water so the freezer will not impart the taste to the foods that will be put back. While your freezer is not in use, leave the door open slightly to air it out. As a safety precaution for young children, be sure the door is propped so it cannot be closed.

What to do with thawed foods

Some thawed foods can be refrozen; others should be kept refrigerated and eaten quickly. Some foods must be discarded after a thaw. Note that refreezing a food will break down its texture and taste. If you find you have too much edible thawed food to eat in the next few days, contact a church, shelter, or charitable organization to share your food before it spoils.

Here are some guidelines for food that is thawed:

Food	How to Handle
Baked goods	If the product is still solidly frozen, it can be returned to the freezer. Baked goods that are partially or completely thawed will have a poor texture and flavor if re-frozen. Instead, refrigerate the product and eat within the next few days.
Cheese	If the product is still solidly frozen, it can be returned to the freezer. If the cheese started to thaw, do not refreeze, because the flavor and texture will degrade. Refrigerate the cheese and use as soon as possible.
Fish	If the package is solidly frozen, it can be returned to the freezer. If the meat thawed but is still cold, check for bad smell or discoloration. If it looks and smells normal, cook and eat immediately. If the fish reached room temperature, it should be thrown away.
Frozen fruit juices	Juices that are still frozen can be returned to the freezer. Thawed juices should be refrigerated and used in the same timeframe as fresh juice.
Frozen prepared foods	If the package still has a layer of ice crystals, it can be re-frozen. Completely thawed foods should be cooked and eaten immediately. If the product reached room temperature, it should be thrown away.
Fruits	Check the package. If the food is mostly thawed but does not smell "off" or look spoiled or discolored, it can be refrozen; however, it may lose some taste and texture. Thawed fruits may be used in cooking or making jams, jellies, and preserves.
Ice cream	Discard thawed or partially thawed ice cream or frozen desserts.
Meat	Check the package. If the food is mostly thawed but does not smell "off" or look spoiled or discolored, it can be used within the next day or two. If the package is still very cold or mostly frozen, or has a layer of ice crystals, it can be re-frozen after packaging in new wrap. If the meat reached room temperature, it should be thrown away.

Food	How to Handle
Poultry	If the package is still very cold or mostly frozen, or has a layer of ice crystals, it can be re-frozen after packaging in new wrap. If the meat thawed but is still cold, check for bad smell or discoloration. If it looks and smells normal, cook and eat immediately. Make sure any poultry juices from thawed meat do not touch any other food.
Smoked or cured meat	If the package is still frozen or very cold, it can be placed back in the freezer. Check for bad smell or discoloration of thawed meat; if it looks and smells normal, refrigerate and use within a day or two.
Vegetables	If the package is still very cold or mostly frozen, or has a layer of ice crystals, it can be re-frozen after packaging in new wrap. Thawed vegetables will lose most of the flavor and texture if you attempt to refreeze them; instead, refrigerate and cook within the next few days.

Chapter 4

Smoking and Preserving Meat

When most of the world lived in the agricultural age, farmers raised their own stock, and hunted and fished to provide food. All of this meat had to be preserved for lean times, and one of the most popular methods was to smoke or preserve it through salting, curing, or brining. Today, these methods are somewhat less popular, because it is so much easier to buy high-quality meat at a store. However, many people are still passionate about making their own sausages, hams, bacon, and smoked meats. People who want to return to pastoral living, homesteading, or organic lifestyles may choose to preserve their own foods, and have more control over the content of the things they eat.

Meat spoils in several ways, just like other foods. Moisture in the meat will hasten the breakdown of the meat,

Hanging smoked fish

and the fat attached to the meat will become rancid far quicker than the meat fibers. And just like other foods, meat is susceptible to decay through the growth of mold, bacteria, and other organisms. Meat also contains a greater risk for sickness than any other food. Bacteria are present in all meats, but some of the most dangerous pathogens are Salmonella, Botulism, Campylobacter, and *Escherichia coli* (E. coli). Unless meat is well prepared, the preservation method will not kill these microorganisms, and people can become gravely ill by eating the food.

Some meat also contains parasites; this is most common in wild game, fish, and home-raised pork. Trichinella is a worm-like parasite that can infest the human body. Some saltwater fish and shellfish can contain various parasites, viruses, and worms. All of these organisms can be destroyed if proper processing techniques are followed. In addition, take special care when field-dressing wild game, especially because the preparation will occur in a fairly unclean environment. If a wound opens the animal's intestines, the meat can become contaminated with other pathogens.

Because meat can transfer more parasites and bacteria than most other foods, be very careful when processing meat. Keep the cooking area clean, and wash hands, knives, and tools between tasks. Make sure that utensils used to process meat are separated from other foods and utensils. Wipe up spills and meat juices right away.

Curing Meat

Meat is preserved through several ways. Curing refers to all the ways that meat can be preserved — whether it is through soaking in a brine mixture, dry preserved with a rub of salt, sugar, and preserving substances like nitrites, smoking the meat, or pickling or marinating. Most of these methods work through removing moisture from the meat and replacing it with salt and preserving agents that inhibit the growth of bacteria and decay. Smoking also involves the use of salt, sugar, and marinades, but the heat and by-products of the smoke also help the meat to remain edible for longer periods of time. Meat may be cured and then smoked, for additional flavor and shelf life. Adding spices to sausages, and sealing them in casing, also adds to the preservation of those meats. A cook's job is to remove as much fat and water from the meat as possible, and then to use other ingredients to prolong freshness before packaging the meat for storage.

Salting meat

Although today's nutritionists tell us that consuming large amounts of nitrites can be harmful to our health, small amounts used in meat preservation are used to prevent food poisoning, improve the color of the meat, and retain the texture of the food. In fact, it is possible to cure meat without using any chemicals at all, if you follow extra precautions when processing the food, and do not store the finished product outside refrigeration or freezing for longer than a few weeks.

When curing meat through salting, there are a few factors that will determine the length of the processing time and the quality of the completed product. Thicker meat will need longer processing times so that the brine or dry rub will fully penetrate the meat. If dry curing the meat, more moisture in the meat will require longer drying times as well. Larger amounts of salt and nitrite in the brine or rub will reduce the curing time, while larger amounts of fat in the meat will take longer to process. However, rather than adjusting recipes designed by experts, it is better for beginners to take the time to follow instructions exactly, even if the meat takes a long time to process. Part of the fun of preserving your own food is an appreciation of the process.

Brining

To brine meat, cut the meat into uniform pieces and immerse them in a solution of salt and water, and perhaps other ingredients such as spices. This will make the meat more tender and flavorful, and will produce a moister cooked meat. Brined meat is usually cooked or smoked before it is eaten.

Any kind of meat can be brined. The process can range from soaking the meat for less than an hour, to being submerged in brine for several weeks in order to begin a fermentation process. In some recipes, such as those for salt pork and fish, the meat can remain in the brine solution until ready to be eaten, preserving it for 9 months to a year.

Dry rub preserving

Another curing method is to use a rub of salt, sugar, nitrites, spices, and herbs to flavor the meat, remove moisture, and begin the preservation process. Salt and sugar are both preservatives that slow the growth of bacteria and replace moisture in the cells of meat with preserving agents. Although any kind of meat can theoretically be dry cured, the process works best on cuts of meat with few bones, skin, fat, or gristle on them — these animal parts will not cure quite so well, and can cause spoilage. The best choices are roasts, pork bellies, briskets, whole breast meat, and the like. However, people have been salting fish, large and small, including the skin and bones, for thousands of years with absolutely no problems. Obviously, the important thing is to pay attention to the details.

To dry cure meat, you start by trimming fat and gristle from the meat. Mix the dry ingredients together to create the dry cure mixture. Then, rub part of the dry cure mixture into the prepared meat, covering all surfaces. The meat can be hung or set in an uncovered container in a dark, cool place to rest for several days. The meat is rubbed again with more of the dry cure mixture, and rests in intervals between rubbings. Depending on the size, type, and cut of the meat, the dry cure process could go on for a couple of weeks to a few months. Very strong dry-cured sausages, such as an artisanal pepperoni, can be cured for up to 6 months in controlled conditions before it is used.

Smoking meat

Smoking is done through the principle of low, slow heating. The smoker surrounds the meat with wood smoke, which permeates the meat and dries it without cooking. The smoke also deposits creosote on the meat, which also helps to preserve it. The simplest and cheapest way to smoke meat is to fire up your gas or charcoal grill at a low heat, add wood chips directly to the coals or flames, and allow the meat to cure slowly with the cover closed while being surrounded by smoke. Check the meat temperature occasionally and remove when the meat reaches the safe minimum internal temperature (see the chart later in this chapter). Any kind of meat can be smoked, and often meat is smoked after it is preserved another way, such as dry-cured ham that is then smoked for added flavor. In addition, some people enjoy smoking other foods, such as nuts (almonds are a favorite), figs, dried apple slices, and eggplant.

This homemade smoker was designed to preserve fish and meat

If you are going to smoke larger quantities of meat, or try specialized recipes, you will need some specific equipment. Smokers can range in shape and size from small, inexpensive models to deluxe smokers with many features. A basic beginner's model can cost $50 to $100. Smoking aficionados even build their own smokehouses, in which they can process large amounts of meat at once — and then store them right in the smokehouse.

You will need to buy a good meat thermometer, because accurate testing of the temperature is crucial to proper preservation and will prevent food-borne sickness. Expert smokers have several favorite wood chips that they prefer, and many varieties are easy to find in grocery stores or on the Internet. Generally, hard woods are preferable because they will burn longer and produce more smoke; some common woods are hickory, apple, cherry, alder, mesquite, or maple. Each of these woods will give a characteristic flavor to the meat. Smoking equipment burns wood through one of three fuels — electric, propane, or a simple wood fire. To increase the amount of smoke produced by the low heat, experts usually soak the wood chips for a period of time before adding it to the coals or heater.

Before smoking, meat is commonly rubbed with salt, sugar, and/or spices. Try a mixture of salt, paprika, oregano, and cayenne pepper for poultry and

Smoked meat hanging outside

game. For beef brisket or ribs, combine brown sugar, chili powder, dry mustard, salt, and garlic powder. The meat can also be soaked in a brine solution or marinade for several hours or overnight before beginning the smoking process. A good pork marinade can combine honey, pineapple juice, sage, chili powder, and vinegar. More recently, cooks use tools to inject flavorings into the meat. This gives the advantage of a seasoning permeating all the meat, not just the surface.

Smoking safety information

To ensure meat and poultry are smoked safely, you will need two types of thermometers: one for the food and one for the smoker. A thermometer is needed to monitor the air temperature in the smoker or grill to be sure the heat stays between 225 and 300 degrees Fahrenheit throughout the cooking process. Many smokers have built-in thermometers.

Use a food thermometer to determine the temperature of the meat or poultry. Oven-safe thermometers can be inserted in the meat and remain there during smoking. Use an instant-read thermometer after the meat is taken out of the smoker.

Cooking time depends on many factors: the type of meat, its size and shape, the distance of food from the heat, the temperature of the coals, and the weather. It can take anywhere from 4 to 8 hours to smoke meat or poultry, so it is imperative to use thermometers to monitor temperatures.

Smoke food to a safe minimum internal temperature:

- Beef, veal, and lamb steaks, roasts, and chops may be cooked to 145 degrees Fahrenheit.

- All cuts of pork to 160 degrees Fahrenheit.

- Ground beef, veal, and lamb to 160 degrees Fahrenheit.

- All poultry should reach a safe minimum internal temperature of 165 degrees Fahrenheit.

If using a sauce, apply it during the last 15 to 30 minutes of smoking to prevent excess browning or burning.

Smoking Safety Information courtesy of the USDA Food Safety and Inspection Service, public domain fact sheet at www.fsis.usda.gov/fact_sheets/Smoking_Meat_and_Poultry/ index.asp

Curing Instructions by Type of Meat

Pork

There are several common foods made by preserving pork: ham, bacon, and salt pork. This can be a particularly satisfying meat to preserve, because there are a variety of seasonings and methods to try. Think for a moment of the kinds of bacon you find in the grocery store: hickory smoked, salt cured, maple flavored, thick-sliced, among others. When you make your own, you can make the meat specifically to your taste. In addition, there are many ethnic and regional types of cured pork, from the Italian pancetta to the thick-cut Canadian bacon; because some ethnic foods can be difficult to find, it is worthwhile to make your own.

Ham

Ham is made from the front and rear legs of the hog; each cut has a specific name. A regular ham is made from the hind legs, and is more tender and juicy; meat from the front legs (and shoulders) of the hog are called a picnic shoulder or picnic ham, and this cut is tougher and less flavorful. To prepare the meat, remove the bones unless you prefer a bone-in ham, but remember that the meat will preserve better without any bones. Make sure to remove the skin and as much fat and gristle as possible. Once prepared this way, the meat is a low fat and lean cut of meat.

There are several ways to cure a ham. Dry-cured hams are made by rubbing salt, sugar, nitrites, and spices into the meat and allowing the rub to remove moisture and fat. Nitrites and other preservatives can be found in specialty stores or on the Internet. The rub is applied several times during the curing process. This method takes a few months and will shrink the meat considerably. However, the benefit is that the end product is extremely flavorful; it is also an easy method for beginners, because it does not require special equipment or a great deal of effort. After the meat has cured for about a month, it can be smoked or eaten as-is.

Pork can also be cured in brine, in a process somewhat similar to pickling. Brine curing will produce a ham that is more tender than dry-cured meat. In this method, sugar, salt, and nitrites are combined with water, and the ham is submerged in the brine for 1 to 2 weeks. After the cure is completed, the ham can be boiled, smoked, or eaten as-is.

Bacon

The meat used to make bacon comes from the hog's belly. This meat tends to be fatty, with veins of meat and fat striped throughout. Canadian bacon is meat from the same area, but cut from a section of the belly with more muscle and less fat. Because pork belly is not commonly sold at a regular grocery store, you may have to seek out a specialty butcher for fresh pork belly. It is generally not an expensive cut of meat. Because of the high fat content, there is a greater risk of the meat turning rancid, so follow curing instructions precisely.

Like ham, bacon can be either dry-cured or brined. Bacon is usually smoked after curing; if you use the brine-curing method on the bacon, it must dry completely before smoking, or the smoke will not penetrate the meat. One benefit to making bacon at home is that it will not contain the preservatives and phosphates added to speed up the curing process. You can also adjust recipes to your own taste.

To make the bacon, cut the pork belly into squares or rectangles about 8" x 11" in size — about the size of a page of notebook or printer paper. After curing the meat, use special bacon hangers with multiple hooks that pierce the meat and allow it to hang within the smoker. Bacon is usually smoked thoroughly within eight hours in a 100 degree Fahrenheit smoker. When the meat is finished smoking, cut the hard rind side off the bacon and slice the bacon into strips of the width you prefer.

Salt pork

Salt pork is salted pork belly fat. It is not usually smoked, but it is preserved in containers without other seasonings. To make salt pork, cut fresh pork belly into 6-inch squares. Rub all surfaces with fine salt and pack tightly into a ceramic, stoneware, or plastic container. Allow to stand overnight. The next day, mix 6 cups of salt with 4 cups of water, and pour over the meat. Make sure the meat is packed down below the liquid, and allow it to cure for at least 3 weeks. Change the brine if it becomes slimy or ropy. The meat can be stored in the container for up to 4 months, in a cool, dark place.

Beef

Beef can be smoked, salted, dry-cured, or brined. Some common products made from smoked or salted beef included corned beef, pastrami, chipped beef, and smoked ribs. Preserved beef is usually made from cheaper, fattier cuts of meat such as the rump roast, brisket, or ribs. If the meat will be dry-cured or smoked, cut off fat and gristle to reduce the risk of the fat turning rancid and spoiling the meat. Fattier cuts of meat are more desirable for salted preservation methods.

To make salted beef or corned beef, cut the meat into six-inch squares. Rub all surfaces with fine salt. Sprinkle a ceramic, stoneware, or plastic container with salt, and then pack a layer of beef into the container. Rub several tablespoons of coarse salt into the meat, and continue layering salt and meat. Allow to stand overnight. The next day, mix 6 cups of water with 1 teaspoon of nitrite and 1/3 cup sugar. Pour over the meat until it is submerged. Make sure the meat is packed down below the liquid, and allow it to cure for at least 6 weeks. Change the brine if it becomes slimy or ropy. The meat can be stored in the container for up to 4 months, in a cool, dark place.

Poultry

Chicken, turkey, goose, duck, or any game bird can be smoked. The white meat is particularly tasty when smoked, and the meat develops a slight pink color in a smoker. The instructions for smoking poultry are the same as for other meats; all poultry should be skinned and

A raw, crude-cut chicken waiting to be smoked

cut into pieces, and fatty poultry like duck and goose should be carefully trimmed of excess fat. Poultry is more often rubbed with spices and herbs, or marinated overnight and then smoked immediately. Depending on the size of the poultry pieces, the meat will take 3 to 8 hours to smoke in a 120 degrees smoker. Aspen, hickory, and mesquite woods lend poultry a special flavor. Experiment with the woods to see which you prefer. Try rubbing the meat with a mixture of salt, sage, thyme, and paprika. Another blend is rosemary, salt, sugar, onion powder, and tarragon. You will soon find your own favorite blends for smoking poultry. Smoked poultry can be wrapped and hung in a cool, dark storage area for up to 3 months.

Fish

Any fish can be salted and smoked. To process large fish, like tuna, salmon, and shad, cut off the head, and tail; scale the fish, cut it in half lengthwise, and remove the bones and viscera. Rinse well in cold water before curing. Slash across skin in several places to allow the salt or rub to penetrate the flesh. Alternatively, you can skin the fish and/or cut it into large pieces.

Smaller fish can be processed whole. Cut off the head and tail, scale, and remove the viscera. Very small fish, like sardines, herring, or alewives, can

be processed without boning if you prefer. If you pickle these fish, the bones will soften and sometimes dissolve, releasing their nutrients into the fish. You should bone larger fish.

Fresh fish and seafood will give you the best finished product

Immerse the fish in a solution of 3 parts salt to 1 part water for two days, layering a weight on top of the fish to keep them under the brine. Drain off the brine. If you plan to smoke the fish, rub them with any mixture of salt, herbs, and spices that you prefer. Hang them on hooks or place in racks in the smoker. Alder wood is a nice choice for smoking most fish, though heavier, oilier fish like salmon or trout may taste better with a heavier smoke, like hickory, cherry, or oak. Depending on the size of the fish pieces, they will take 8 to 12 hours to smoke in a 120 degrees Fahrenheit smoker. Then the fish should be hung to dry for 24 hours before packaging.

To preserve fish by salting, drain off the brine. Rub a layer of coarse salt into the fish, and pack into a ceramic, stoneware, or plastic container. Sprinkle with a small amount of salt, and then continue layering fish and salt. Place a heavy lid or plate onto the fish, and store in a dark, cool place.

Check the fish once a week to be sure the product has not become too slimy or developed an off color or odor. After one month, drain off the oily liquid and replace it with a brine of 2 parts salt to 1 part water. Place the weight on it again, and let it continue to process for 4 to 5 months, checking weekly to be sure the brine is not fermenting. If it does, replace the liquid. Fish will stay preserved in this method for up to 9 months.

Game

In rural areas, wild game is still an essential part of many diets. Some of the most common meats are venison (deer), bear, elk, wild boar, wild turkey, rabbit, squirrel, pheasant, and quail, among others. In fact, most wild animals are good for eating, especially if processed by salting or smoking. Some people who are unused to wild game might find the taste a little strange, but most people come to enjoy the unique flavor.

Care must be taken when obtaining wild game. As mentioned before, the location of a wound could spill intestinal contamination into the flesh. Experienced hunters will recognize the signs of disease in animals and discard that meat; they should also be familiar with field dressing the meat so that the viscera and blood do not cause contamination. If you are given wild game, make sure the meat is fresh and has been processed correctly. Unlike domestic animals, there is no inspection or processing requirements for wild meat.

Wild game can be salted or smoked according to the same directions for similar domestic animals (for example, venison and elk can be processed as beef; pheasant and rabbit can be processed like poultry). Bear meat requires a little extra attention, because it is one of the only wild game animals that has a heavy layer of fat to be trimmed, and because its omnivorous diet may introduce more bacteria and parasites into the food. Process as you would handle fatty pork.

Sausage

Generally, sausage is made from meat ground to different consistencies and heavily flavored with herbs and spices. The mixture may be formed into patties or links, or stuffed into skins. Sausage may be smoked or preserved in other ways.

According to the U.S. Department of Agriculture (USDA), there are several categories of sausages:

1. Fresh sausages are a coarse or finely "comminuted" (reduced to minute particles) meat food product prepared from one or more kinds of meat, or meat and meat "byproducts" (heart, kidney, or liver, for example). They may contain water not exceeding 3 percent of the total ingredients in the product. They are usually seasoned, frequently cured, and may contain binders and extenders (for example, wheat flour, and non-fat dry milk). They must be kept refrigerated and thoroughly cooked before eating.

2. Cooked and/or smoked sausages are made of one or more different kinds of chopped or ground meats, which have been seasoned, cooked and/or smoked. Meat byproducts may be used. Included in this category are:

- liverwurst

- hot dogs

- bologna

- knockwurst

- cooked bratwurst

- braunschweiger

- cooked Thuringer

- cooked salami*

*Cooked salami (not dry) is made from fresh meats, which are cured, stuffed into casings and cooked in a smokehouse at high temperature. It may be air dried for a short time. It has a softer texture than dry and semi-dry sausages and must be refrigerated.

3. Meat specialties are ready-to-eat sausage-like products. These are made from comminuted meats that are seasoned and usually cooked or baked rather than smoked. They are usually sliced and served cold. Included in this category are:

   - chopped ham loaf

   - peppered loaf

   - head cheese

   - jellied corned beef

   - ham and cheese loaf

   - honey loaf

- old fashioned loaf

- olive loaf

- pickle and pimento loaf

- scrapple

- souse

- veal loaf

4. Dry and semi-dry sausages are possibly the largest category of dried meats, particularly in the United States. These products can be fermented by bacterial growth for preservation and to produce the typical tangy flavor. Alternatively, they may be cultured with lactic acid — much as cheese, pickle, and yogurt makers do — to eliminate the fermentation phase and shorten the process. They are, with a few exceptions, cooked.

   Fermentation is one of the oldest methods of preserving meats. Dry sausages — such as pepperoni, and semi-dry sausages such as Lebanon bologna and summer sausage, have had a good safety record for hundreds of years.

   In this procedure, a mixture of curing ingredients, such as salt and sodium nitrite, and a "starter" culture of lactic acid-bacteria, is mixed with chopped and ground meat. The meat is placed in casings, fermented, and then dried by a carefully controlled, long, and continuous air-drying process. The amount of acid produced during fermentation and the lack of moisture in the finished product after drying typically have been shown to cause pathogenic bacteria to die.

Dry sausages require more time to make than other types of sausages and are a more concentrated form of meat. Dried sausages range from 60 percent to 80 percent of their original weight before drying.

Semi-dry sausages are usually heated in the smokehouse to fully cook the meat and partially dry it. Semi-dry sausages are semi-soft with good keeping qualities due to their lactic acid fermentation and heavy application of smoke. Some are mildly seasoned and some are quite spicy and strongly flavored.

Dry sausages include:

- Sopressata (a name of a salami)

- Pepperoni (not cooked, air dried)

- Genoa salami, which is an Italian meat made of pork and may contain a small amount of beef. The meat is seasoned with garlic and moistened with grape juice or wine.

Semi-dry sausages include:

- Summer sausage

- Lebanon bologna

- Cervelat

- Thuringer

Some dry sausages are shelf stable (in other words, they do not need to be refrigerated or frozen to be stored safely). Dry sausages require more production time than other types of sausage and result in a concentrated form of meat.

Information courtesy of the USDA Food Safety and Inspection Service, public domain fact sheet at www.fsis.usda.gov/PDF/Sausage_and_Food_Safety.pdf

To make fresh sausage at home, you will need some specific equipment. Unless you are making large batches of sausage, this equipment will not be too expensive. At a minimum, making sausage links requires a funnel, a manual pump stuffer, and sausage casings. This will cost you less than $100 and you will only need to replenish the casings before making a new batch. More advanced techniques require a meat grinder and high-output sausage stuffer, but the results will be the same.

First, you will need to buy or grind pork, beef, lamb, venison, or other meat. If you are grinding your own meat, choose a cheaper cut like a pork shoulder, because the flavorings and processing will improve the flavor and the best cuts of meat are not wasted on sausages. Next, place the meat in a large bowl or mixing container, and add spices and herbs. Sage, fennel seed, garlic, black pepper, and dried red pepper are all traditional seasoning for sausage, but you can experiment with your favorite flavors. Thoroughly mix the meat and flavorings; add some water to make the mix more pliable. If you choose to make sausage patties, you can form patties with your hands, wrap them individually in plastic wrap, and place in a freezer-safe bag. The patties will keep fresh for up to one year.

If making sausage links, put the meat into the funnel or stuffing cylinder, pressing out air pockets as you pack it. Put a sausage casing on the spout end (hog casing for large sausages; sheep casings for thin sausages), and brush the casing with vegetable oil or food-grade lubricating oil so that the casing will not burst. Tie a knot at the end of the casing. Next, begin to crank or press the meat through the funnel and into the casing. This is a two-person job; one person must press the meat through the machine, while another person eases off the filled casing as it is stuffed. Gently squeeze out air bubbles while the casing fills.

Once the casing is filled, it is time to twist the sausage into links. Pinch the casing at the length of the first link, and very gently twist it once in a clockwise direction. At the next link, twist it in the opposite direction. Continue until you have twisted the entire sausage into links. If you will be cutting the links, twist several times and then cut the link.

Fresh sausage can be stored in a refrigerator for a few days, but for longer periods, it must be wrapped and stored in the freezer.

Chapter 5

Preserving Food by Drying

lthough canning is a relatively new invention, and people used freezing sporadically for thousands of years, all ancient cultures were skilled in drying foods to preserve them for lean times. In fact, for much of history, drying was virtually the only preservation method available. It was a relatively easy process; the elements of wind, sun, and fire did almost all the work, and the end result was food that was easily stored and very portable. Today, these dried foods are popular with campers and backpackers, because these foods are easy to carry and need only fresh water to make a nutritious meal. And trail mixes, seeds, dried fruits, and nuts are even more popular as snack items, and provide more nutrition than snacks like potato chips.

A delicious, healthy snack of dried fruit

Drying foods today is just as easy as in the past, and requires no special equipment — though if you wish, you can purchase special dehydrators, drying racks, and other tools. Besides being economical, dried foods are more nutritious than many other types of preserved foods. Fewer vitamins are destroyed during drying than in methods such as canning or freezing. The protein in meat and the sugars in fruit become more concentrated — so your snack or your lunch is easier to carry but still satisfies that sweet tooth. Because dehydrated foods reduce in size, and have a stable shelf-life if kept in the right environment, drying is a great way to stock up your pantry.

It is likely that your first taste of dried foods were raisins — one of California's biggest yearly crops. Other dried staples of our diets are rice, beans, pasta, prepared cereals, and whole grains. These foods have been prepared for you with the same techniques shown in this book for your own use. As you select your own produce and meat, and carefully dry it, you will have the satisfaction of knowing that your food is prepared exactly as you want it.

The drying process, which is also called dehydration, is merely removing the water from the food to the point that the food becomes storable. This prevents bacteria, yeasts, and molds from growing and causing spoilage. The drying process also interferes with the enzyme activity in food, which can cause color, texture, and flavor changes. Some dried foods are eaten dry, but others are rehydrated, or given moisture, before used.

Foods that do not dry well

Although most produce and meat can be preserved through drying, there are some foods that will give unsatisfactory results. It is recommended that you do not try drying these items:

- Any dairy products

- Cucumbers

- Lettuce, cabbage, and other greens

- Asparagus

- Melons

- Avocados

Some unusual foods to try

Looking for new flavors? Try drying some of these items:

- Rosehips

- Nasturtium or sweet violet flowers

- Edible seaweed (know your species first!)

- Edible mushrooms (know your species first!)

- Juniper berries

- Chive blossoms

Drying Methods

Foods can be dried several ways. The oldest method is sun drying. Other methods include a food dehydrator, room drying, or drying in an oven. Microwave drying is not recommended because of the uneven heating and the trapped moisture inside the microwave. For best results a combination of warm temperature, low humidity, and air circulation helps to dry foods properly. As air moves over the food, it absorbs moisture, but the warmer the air, the more moisture it can absorb. Each 27 degree F increase in heat will double the amount of moisture the air can carry. However, controlled heat and humidity are the keys to successful dehydrating. Too little heat and too much moisture will mean that organisms grow faster than the food is being preserved. This food is either spoiled immediately, or the microorganisms remain inactive until the food is rehydrated — and then make you sick. Too much heat and your food will be too tough or burnt.

When you dry foods, they are actually preserved by removing the moisture that can accelerate decay. If the food is not dried adequately, it will encourage the growth of mold, which is the primary reason that dried foods become spoiled when they are stored. Bacteria and other organisms can also grow in food that has sufficient moisture content. For that reason, it is better to over-dry your foods than to not dry them enough.

Sun-dried foods

The best candidates for sun-drying foods are fresh fruits and vegetables. The thin leaves of herbs contain volatile oils that will actually help burn the plants — and then dissipate, leaving little flavor. And though it is still possible to dry meats outdoors, it is healthier to use indoor methods to prepare meat to better control the heat and timing that is necessary.

Climate is a big factor in successful solar drying. If you live in a climate without much humidity and many long days of sunlight, you will have the best luck drying foods outdoors. Sun-drying requires about 3 to 5 days of temperatures above 90 degrees F and low humidity — a rarity in the Midwest U.S. If you live in a place that has high humidity or gets plenty of rain, your best choice may be to dry foods with a dehydrator or in the oven. If you live in a place that has bad air pollution or heavy traffic nearby, your food may be contaminated from airborne emissions.

Solar drying is done on a drying tray, which might also be used for home or oven drying. Drying trays are easy to make. Cover a wooden frame with cheesecloth or plastic screen. Metal screens should not be used unless you cover them with cheese cloth, because the metal may contaminate food that is placed on the metal. Old windows, doors, or discarded screens all make good frames for drying trays. Stretch the screens as tightly as possible and tack or staple the screens to the back of the frame. Then crisscross the back with sting to provide extra support across the middle of the screen.

The tray must be able to receive air circulation on all sides so that evaporation happens as quickly as possible. To solar dry your food, first prepare it for drying according to the chart at the end of this chapter. The prepared foods should always be arranged in a single layer on your drying trays without allowing the food pieces to touch each other. Make sure that strong-flavored or strong-smelling foods are dried by themselves so that their flavors do not overpower other foods. Drying trays should be set at least a foot or so above the ground in a spot that will be sunny all day and provide good air circulation (but away from wind gusts that could blow your food away). You can set the drying trays on blocks, bricks, or pieces of wood to keep them off the ground. Loosely drape cheesecloth or a light layer of fabric over the food to prevent insects from eating their share. Do not allow the fabric to touch the food, because it may stick.

Turn food at least daily. To intensify the heat from the sun, set another layer of bricks or wood above the frame, and place a piece of glass or hard plastic on the second layer of bricks. The space between the bricks and glass should provide several inches of space for air circulation. Placing the frame in a hot area, like a hot driveway or rooftop, can intensify the heat, as well. You want the drying temperature to be between 95 degrees and 130 degrees F. Check the temperature occasionally to make sure it is not burning your food or keeping it too cool for evaporation. If rain is in the forecast, or you might have heavy dew overnight, be sure to bring your trays inside. Finish drying in the oven or on your stove if necessary.

Oven-dried foods

If you choose to oven-dry your food, you do not need any special equipment, and your drying can continue day and night without much intervention from you — if you do not need the oven for something else. Oven-drying is also more satisfactory than sun-drying, because you do not have to worry about insects, wildlife, or pollution during the drying process.

To properly dry food in an oven, your appliance must be able to be set at the low temperature of 140 degrees F. Because an oven does not provide much air circulation, you will need to keep the door cracked open a few inches, and keep checking that the temperature remains stable throughout drying time. A fan in front of the stove or an overhead fan will also keep the air circulating as moisture-filled air seeps from the oven.

Your produce or meat should be prepared according to this section's directions. Note that variations in food slices, maturity of produce, or size of the portions will all affect drying time. If you want to err on the side of caution, it is better to slightly over-dry your food rather than under-dry it, because remaining moisture will encourage mold and rot.

To oven dry, place your food on cookie trays or drying trays (as described above). Make sure the pieces do not touch each other. Dry strong-tasting or strong–smelling produce, such as onions or garlic, at a different time so the smell does not transfer to other foods. It is also wise not to dry produce and meat at the same time.

Place your oven racks at least 2 to 3 inches apart. Make sure that your trays or pans are a few inches shorter than the oven from front to back, to maximize circulation. Do not overcrowd the oven, because this will slow the drying process enormously, and the pieces at the edges will dry much more quickly than the ones in the center.

Drying times will vary greatly according to the type of food and size of the pieces; at least 12 hours are usually needed. Check the oven after four hours, and several times a day after that until the product is completely dry.

Using dehydrator appliances

A dehydrator is a small appliance that can be used to quickly dry batches of produce and meat. In fact, dehydrators work in half the time that sun-drying

or oven-drying takes, so the method can be very energy efficient. If you plan to dry food regularly, the $100 to $300 price tag can be well worth it. The best places to find dehydrators are in health-food stores, garden and cooking catalogs, and department stores.

Apple slices dried with a dehydrator

Dehydrators contain rows of non-reactive drying screens above a heating element and a fan that continually circulates air. Good-quality dehydrators will also have a thermostat so that you can monitor an even temperature.

These appliances come in different sizes, so you should consider the amount of food you will dry each year. Each square foot of shelf space will hold about 1 or 2 pounds of fresh food. Some dehydrators run at louder volumes than others, so if you are running it frequently, you may want to choose a quiet model.

A dehydrator makes drying foods quick and easy

Like all other methods of drying, the amount of time needed to dry the food will vary. However, there is no harm in leaving the food in the dehydrator for longer than a day, because the goal is to get the food as dry as possible.

Air-drying

Herbs are commonly air-dried without the application of heat or sun, and many other foods you eat daily are also dried solely by the circulation of air. For example, many beans, rice, and grains can be dried by simply leaving them on racks or pans, and shaking them from time to time. The best candidates for air-drying are foods that are small and have less moisture content.

Onions are popular vegetables to air dry

Some vegetables and legumes can be dried right on the vine or stem. If you grow peas, white beans, fava beans, lima beans, kidney beans, soybeans, or other legumes, you can let them field-dry in a spell of warm weather. The crop should be kept off the ground and free of mildew or insect pests. When they are thoroughly dry, but not damaged by frost, pick the pods. Make sure to collect them before they over-dry and the pods break open, or you will have lost the seeds to the ground or to hungry animals. If your dry season is interrupted by wet weather, harvest the pods before rot or mildew sets in, and dry them in an oven or dehydrator.

Once you pick your bean pods, you will notice that the pods are hard and brittle. To remove the shells, place them in a strong plastic bag or old pillowcase, and beat them with a mallet or crush them with your feet. Alternatively, you can put the pods in a pillowcase, tie the end shut, and toss it in the dryer on low heat for about 30 minutes. If any pods remain unopened, shell them by hand.

Corn and popcorn can be partially field-dried, until the kernels are past maturity and begin to harden. Check the corn often to be sure the leaves are not developing mildew — this might affect the taste of the corn. Once you notice the kernels firming up, pick the ears and shuck all the leaves and tassels from them. Put them in paper bags in a cool, dry place with good circulation, like a basement or garage, for about one month. Check occasionally for rot. When you can rub your finger over the ear with a little pressure and the kernels fall off, it is time to remove the kernels from the cob. If you have many ears to shell, you can buy an inexpensive gadget called a corn sheller at a farming-supply store or an internet gardening source. It is best to try popping an ear or two of popcorn to see if it is ready. If you do not get much popcorn but plenty of kernels, let it dry longer before shelling any other cobs.

Peel back the husks of field-dried corn and tie with baling twine to make festive fall decorations

Dried corn can be ground for flour, polenta, corn meal, or grits, depending on the variety. Check your blender or food processor to see if it can handle the hard, tough kernels. If not, you can purchase tools to grind up the corn to the desired consistency.

Garlic, peppers, and onions are other popular foods for air-drying. In old pioneer movies, you may remember seeing strings of these vegetables hanging in kitchens. As warm air dries the produce, a piece can be snipped off to use whenever needed. The best onions for air-drying are young, small ones — slightly larger than a bulb of garlic. Dig up the onions and garlic with the tops intact, because this is what you will use to string the vegetables. Rinse any dirt from the bulbs and clip off any diseased leaves. Small peppers, such as jalapenos, scotch bonnets, cayennes, anchos, and others should be harvested as they mature. *Always* wear gloves when handling hot peppers.

Use a length of string or twine and a thick needle to string the stems of the bulbs together. String the peppers by piercing the stem of the pepper. The

Strings of chile peppers at a Santa Fe market

string can be placed like a clothesline in a cool, dry place with good air circulation, such as a shed, garage, or basement. Alternatively, you can braid together the stems of garlic and onions and let them hang from a string in your drying area for approximately two weeks. Check occasionally for signs of rot. Once the produce starts to dry, these strings can be coiled around themselves to produce long, bountiful columns of produce. Garlic and onions are completely dried when they are tough and have no "give" when you squeeze them; dried peppers will be wrinkly, crispy, and tough (note: the volatile oils in peppers become concentrated during drying — do not squeeze a pepper without your gloves).

Dried chili peppers ready to add spice to a Mexican dish

Food Dehydration Guide

Drying herbs

One of the easiest and cheapest ways to dry fresh herbs is simply to allow them to dry in the air. One benefit is that the slow drying process retains all the essential oils in the herbs, adding more flavor and health to the dried produce. As a last resort, you can use an oven to dry the herbs, but this process will also cook the plants slightly, and will reduce the herbs' oil content and flavor.

Harvest before the herbs begin flowering. Alternatively, harvest throughout the season, making sure you cut off tops so that your plants will continue to grow in a bushy pattern, rather than a tall spike or one long vine. If you harvested herbs throughout the gardening season, your plants probably

have not set flowers. However, herbs that are sensitive to cool weather will start to decline in early fall, so late summer is the best time to start cutting and drying herbs. Some herbs have a short growing season.

A spoon of aromatic and flavorful dried rosemary

Whether you are harvesting seeds, roots, or leaves, you must take care with the finished item. Once your herbs are completely dry, they should be stored in labeled paper or plastic bags, or in glass jars. Keep them out of sunlight and extreme temperatures, and check them for signs of mold. It is best to toss out last year's harvest once a new harvest is ready, but well-dried herbs will keep their flavor in a jar for several years.

Drying whole herbs

Cut healthy branches, full of undamaged leaves. The longer the branches, the easier it will be to dry them. If you wait until mid-morning to harvest, the morning dew will dry off the leaves, and you will avoid clipping plants that suffer wilting in hot afternoon sun. Cut off any dry or diseased leaves, and then rinse the foliage. Pat dry with towels or napkins; leaves that remain wet will be susceptible to mold or mildew.

Cut off the leaves growing on the bottom inch or two of the branch. Take 4 to 8 branches at a time, and tie them together at the bare end of the stems with twine, string, or rubber bands. Make sure the knot is tight; as the bundles dry, they will begin to shrink, and the stems could slip apart. **Note:** if you are drying herbs with high water content, such as basil, tarragon, or mint, use smaller bundles.

Hang the herbs upside down by the string in a warm, airy room. If you are drying the herbs in the summertime, anywhere outside that is not in direct sunlight is ideal, including a garage or a shed. However, many people love

the mingled scent of many herbs drying together, so they hang the herbs with twine in a hallway, where they can catch a good whiff every time they walk by.

Dried herbs and gourds hanging in an ancient ranch house kitchen storeroom

Within two weeks, most herbs are dry enough for permanent storage. They should be as crispy as old autumn leaves, and leave no feel of moisture when you crumple one between your fingers. You may want to strip the leaves from the stems and put them in labeled jars, or you may want to save the bundles until needed.

If you store whole leaves from the plants, and then crush the leaves as you use them in recipes, they will have the freshest, strongest flavor. Note that dried herb leaves are much more potent than fresh herbs. The rule of thumb is to use about one teaspoon of crushed dried herbs in place of a tablespoon of fresh leaves.

Drying herb seeds, flowers, and roots

Sometimes the leaves of an herb are not the part you want — you may be after the seeds of cilantro, called coriander, or the roots of angelica or ginger. The process is similar to drying herbal leaves and stems. Bundle roots together and tie them tightly, then place in a paper bag with holes punched in for air circulation. Label the bag with the name of the root you are drying. For seeds or flowers, bundle the stems upside down and place them in a paper bag.

Check on the bag every few weeks to see how the plants are drying. After the bundle is thoroughly dry, you can shake the seeds off the stems or pick the flowers. These can be stored either in paper or plastic bags, or in glass jars. Be sure to label the containers, because many herb seeds look alike.

Drying meat

For most of history, humans preserved their meat by drying or smoking it over a fire. Early dried meats were mostly wild game, domesticated birds, and fish. Later in history, people began to dry and smoke domesticated large animals, creating beef jerky, ham, bacon, and pemmican. Today, most of us who have tried beef jerky (or jerky made from any other sort of meat) are familiar with the spicy taste

Pork drying in a smokehouse

and leathery texture. The spiciness of jerky dates back to earlier generations, who liberally sprinkled their meat with pepper to chase away insects as the meat dried in the sun.

Like any other food, meat and seafood can certainly be dried in the sun, but you must be cautious about contamination from insects or the growth of harmful microorganisms. Raw animal products may be contaminated with dangerous microorganisms such as *Campylobacter, Clostridium perfringens, E. coli, Listeria, Salmonella, Shigella,* and others. Marinating or salting the meat will help kill some of these organisms, while tenderizing the meat. Meat can also be dried in an oven or dehydrator.

You also want your meat, especially fish, to be as fresh as possible. Depending on the type of animal or fish, the meat must be cut into specific uniform pieces. The right shape and thickness of the piece is key to even, successful drying; the outer surface of the meat should not dry so soon that moisture in the inside cannot escape through the "crust." Meat will complete drying outdoors in 3 to 7 days during ideal conditions; during this time, it will lose 60 to 70 percent of its weight. Plan ahead when buying or preparing your meat so that you have the desired yield.

Fish

Fish is generally salted before drying; some fish are traditionally heavily salted and then soaked to release the salt and rehydrate the meat before eating. Different types of fish will require different preparation, but the drying process remains the same.

- If you are drying larger fish, from trout to large deep-water fish, skin the fish and bone it, then slice along the grain in ½ to 1-inch thick fillets. Try to keep each slice about the same size and thickness.

- If you are drying small fish, such as sardines or perch, remove the head, tail, entrails, and bones, but leave the skin intact. Split the fish in half length-wise. Rinse the fish in cold water.

In a large bowl or pan, add 1 cup of salt to 1 gallon of cold water. Soak the fish or fillets in this solution for 30 minutes. Drain the fish and rinse the flesh again. Next, cover the fish with coarse pickling or sea salt. Press the salt into the flesh of the fish to help firm up the flesh of the fish. If you wish, you can add marinades, dry rubs, herbs, or flavorings to the fish.

If you will be drying your fish outside, place the fish on wooden drying racks in a sunny place. Do not use metal racks, because they can corrode and harm the taste and appearance of the fish. Cover the meat with light cheesecloth to discourage bugs, and move the racks indoors at night to prevent wildlife from stealing your fish. Each day, turn the meat and check it for dryness. Press on the flesh of the fish to squeeze out excess salt water, as this hastens drying.

If you will be drying your fish in an oven, turn the oven to 170 degrees Fahrenheit, and prop it open 1 to 2 inches. Spray the tray or pan with a bit of non-stick spray, and then place the fish on the trays without any pieces touching. Make such the oven racks are several inches apart and there is ample circulation room. Dry for 2 hours. Take the trays out and squeeze any water from the fish and drain it off the pans. Flip over the fish and dry for another 4 to 6 hours. Check again for dryness and if it is not ready, squeeze it, flip it again, and return it to the oven. When the fish is done, the flesh will yield to your touch, but it will not spring back.

This same process can be followed by using a food dehydrator, but depending on the size, you may have to cut your fish into smaller pieces.

Store the dried fish in a plastic bag in the refrigerator or pantry, away from light and extremes of temperature. Make sure you squeeze as much air as possible out of the bag. If you pack your fish in small portions, such as enough for one meal, you will lose less of the product if the contents go bad. The fish should keep for 1 month in the pantry when completely dried, 3 to 6 months if refrigerated, or up to a year if stored in a freezer. Check the package occasionally for signs of rot, foul smell, or mold; discard the entire package if it is spoiled.

Meat

Dried meat is generally called jerky, and can consist of practically any meat, such as beef, lamb, pork, goat, deer, caribou, moose, elk, bear, or small game. Poultry, wild or domestic, does not produce a texture and flavor as good as other meats, but it can be dried, as well. Jerky was a food staple of explorers, trappers, hunters, American Indian tribes, and settlers in early years of the U.S. In earlier times, meat was soaked in salty water and then dried in small pieces over a fire. The wood smoke helped keep insects away and flavored the meat. Jerky is still popular with everyone from city dwellers to mountain climbers. Meat can be dried into jerky in three ways: By drying in a dehydrator, in the sun, or in on oven. Again, oven drying is the easiest method.

If you kill and dress your own meat, make sure the carcass is completely cooled before cutting meat for drying. Take particular care with wild game; the wound can affect the safety of the meat. For example, if the wound pierced the entrails, the contents may contaminate all the meat and make

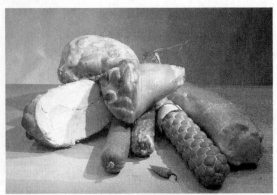

it unsafe for jerky. This meat should be thoroughly cooked instead. Decrease the risk of causing illness with home-dried jerky by constantly using a meat thermometer

Most meats can be preserved

to check that the meat's temperature is a constant 160 degrees Fahrenheit during drying.

When selecting your meat, you do not necessarily need an expensive cut; in fact, cheaper cuts of meat can be a very cost-effective method for adding protein to your diet. Lean meat is best, because the fat content will oxidize and could cause an unpleasant taste; trim off as much fat as you can. About 4 pounds of fresh meat will produce 1 pound of jerky. Begin by partially freezing the meat to make slicing easier. Slice meat no thicker than ¼ inch. You can slice with the grain if you like chewy jerky, or slice across the grain if you prefer a tougher, brittle jerky. Your pieces should be shaped like ribbons or tongues, 2 to 3 inches wide and as long as you have room for in your oven or drying racks.

If desired, you can also sprinkle the meat with a prepared tenderizer. Marinating the meat will make it more tender and flavorful. Marinade recipes can include all kinds of ingredients such as sauces, vinegar, and herbs; many recipes are included in the index for you to try. Once you begin making jerky, you will probably want to experiment with different flavorings and marinades.

If you will be drying your meat outside, place the slices on wooden drying racks in a sunny place. Do not use metal racks, because they can corrode and harm the taste and appearance of the meat. Cover the meat with light cheesecloth to discourage bugs, and move the racks indoors at night to prevent wildlife from stealing your food. Each day, turn the meat and check it for dryness. The meat should be completely dry all the way through and flexible, but as brittle as a dry twig. Your marinade might change the color of the meat, but it should have a pleasant odor and no signs of rot or insect damage.

If you will be drying your meat in an oven, heat your oven to 160 degrees Fahrenheit. Make sure the oven racks are several inches apart and there is ample circulation room. Spray nonstick spray directly on the oven racks and spread the meat evenly on the racks in the oven. Try not to have the meat pieces touch each other. Place a cookie sheet under the drying racks, to catch any drippings. Leave the door propped open 1 to 2 inches to permit moisture to escape.

After about 2 hours, check on the meat and turn it over. Meat will dry into jerky in 4 to 10 hours, depending on the size of the pieces, the cut of meat, and the amount of meat you are drying at once. Meat will dry more quickly if the pieces are spread far apart. Your meat is ready when you can bend it slightly; once the jerky cools, it will become more brittle, so make sure you do not dry it too much. It should look dehydrated and dark in color. Jerky is usually eaten dry, but you can rehydrate it with water and use it in casseroles, stews, and other recipes.

If you will make jerky in a dehydrator, spray the drying racks with nonstick spray and then arrange the meat pieces in a single layer without any piece touching another. Rotate trays periodically to ensure an even consistency. A dehydrator will dry the meat in approximately 3 to 5 hours.

Jerky can be stored in a labeled bag or screw-top jar. Squeeze as much air as possible out of the container. If you pack the meat in small portions, enough for one meal, you will lose less food if the contents go bad. Keep jerky in an airtight container in a cool, dark place, or store it in the refrigerator or freezer. Well-dried jerky will last about a month in a pantry, 3 to 6 months if refrigerated, or up to a year if frozen. Check the package occasionally for signs of rot, foul smell, or mold, and discard the entire package if it is spoiled.

Drying fruits and vegetables

Dried fruits are especially delicious because of the concentrated sugar content, the intense fruit flavor, and chewy texture. Dried legumes and grains are the staple of many diets. Dried vegetables are convenience foods, and make it easy to store a large amount of produce. Depending on the amount of juice in the produce, the dried product can be up to 75 percent less weight and volume than the fresh item.

Fruits and vegetables can be dried by the sun, oven, or dehydrator. Always use the freshest produce you can find. There are many ways to prepare produce, because of the vast variety of fruits and vegetables that can be dried. The moisture content and chemical makeup will affect how each kind of produce should be prepared. For instance, before you dry some

kinds of fruit, they should be dipped in ascorbic acid or shaken with lemon juice to prevent browning from exposure to air. Make sure fruits and vegetables are prepared according to the chart shown below.

A bowl of dried fruit — a perfect snack

Some vegetables should be partially cooked (blanched in hot water) before being dehydrated, to stop the enzymatic ripening process that will reduce the flavor and texture of the food. Blanch vegetables with a ratio of 1 gallon of water for each pound of vegetables. After the vegetables are boiled for the specified time, they will be chilled for an equal time in ice water. Place the prepared vegetables in the boiling water for the recipe's stated time. When finished, remove the vegetables and immediately pour them into the bowl of cold water. After an equal time cooling in the water, pat the slices dry and begin the drying process.

If you will be drying your produce outside, place the fruits or vegetables on wooden drying racks in a sunny place. Do not use metal screens, because they can corrode and harm the taste and appearance of the food. Cover the vegetables with light cheesecloth to ward away bugs and birds; move the racks indoors at night to prevent wildlife from stealing your food. Each day, turn the pieces and check for dryness. Produce generally dries completely in 4 to 7 days; very tough or large items, such as popcorn ears, will take 2 weeks or longer.

If you will be drying your produce in an oven, turn the oven to 160 degrees Fahrenheit and prop it open 1 to 2 inches. Place produce on the trays without any pieces touching. Make such the oven racks are several inches apart and there is ample circulation room. Dry for 4 hours. Take the trays out and flip the pieces. Dry for another 2 to 4 hours and check again for dryness. Depending on the moisture content and size, produce can take 4 to 12 hours to dry in the oven.

If using a dehydrator, spread the pieces evenly on the racks without touching each other. Try to place produce of a similar size in the dehydrator together, so it will finish at approximately the same time (check your owners' manual for instructions). Rotate trays periodically to ensure an even consistency. Depending on the produce, a dehydrator can dry the food in approximately 2 to 8 hours.

Fruits and vegetables should be stored in labeled plastic bags or air-proof containers. Squeeze as much air as possible out of the container. If you pack the food in small portions, such as enough for one meal, you will lose less food if the contents go bad. These foods will keep for up to 1 year; check occasionally for spoilage or mold. If you want to rehydrate the food before using it, soak it in hot water for 30 minutes and then drain before using.

Vegetable drying guide

Once vegetables are completely dry, they should have a leathery to brittle consistency. Follow proper storage techniques to maximize the storage time; remember that

Dried tomatoes — a perfect pizza topper

dried food will store for longer periods at temperatures less than 55 degrees Fahrenheit.

Vegetable	Preparation	Storage Months At 70 Degrees
Beans, green or yellow	Cut off ends and slice into 1 inch pieces. Steam 3 minutes.	4
Broccoli	Cut off stem and cut head into small florets. Steam 3 minutes.	1
Carrots and parsnips	Slice ¼ to 1/8 inch thick.	6
Corn	Steam whole ears for 3 minutes, then cut the kernels from the cob.	4
Eggplant	Cut into ¼ inch thick slices or small chunks. Steam for 3 minutes.	2
Onions	Cut off ends and cut into 1/8 inch slices.	2
Peas and shell beans	Shell and steam for 3 minutes.	8
Peppers	Slice ¼ to ½ inch thick.	6
Potatoes	Peel potatoes if desired. Cut into ¼ inch slices. Steam for 3 minutes.	4
Summer Squash and Zucchini	Cut off ends and slice ¼ inch thick.	1
Tomatoes	Cut off stem end and slice ½ inch thick.	3
Winter Squash	Cut flesh from rind and cut into small chunks or slices. Steam 3 minutes.	8

Fruit drying guide

Pretreat any fruit that will start to turn brown after slicing, such as apples, bananas, or pears. This will prevent them from turning an unappetizing color while they dry. To make a pretreatment solution, mix a proportion of 1 cup of water to 1 teaspoon of ascorbic acid (found in the canning section of local stores) or 2 teaspoons lemon juice. After preparing the fruit for drying, dip them in this solution and then arrange them on drying trays or pans.

Most fruits are completely dry when they are leathery and no longer moist; berries should be slightly harder, and bananas should be slightly crisp or brittle when done.

Fruit	Preparation	Storage Months At 70 Degrees
Apples	Wash ripe, firm fruit. Peel off skin and core. Cut into ¼ inch slices or thin sections.	6
Apricots	Wash ripe, firm fruit. Cut in half and cut out the pit.	8
Bananas	Peel firm, ripe fruit. Cut out any bruised sections. Slice ⅛ inch thick.	6
Berries	Wash ripe, firm fruit and drain well. Dry whole berries or cut in half, depending on size.	6
Cherries	Wash ripe, firm fruit. Remove stems and pits.	12
Coconut	Break open shell. Cut out flesh and slice into ⅛ inch sections.	
Dates and figs	Wash ripe, firm fruit and drain well. Remove skin if desired. Slice ¼ inch thick.	6
Grapes	Wash seedless grapes and drain well. Remove stems.	6
Nectarines and peaches	Wash ripe, firm fruit. Remove stems. Cut in half and remove pit. Slice into ⅛ inch pieces or sections.	6
Papayas and mangoes	Wash ripe, firm fruit. Remove stems and peel fruit. Cut in half and remove pit. Slice into ⅛ inch pieces or sections.	6
Pears	Wash ripe, firm fruit. Peel off skin. Cut in half and remove core. Cut into ⅛ to ¼ inch slices.	6
Plums	Wash ripe, firm fruit. Remove stems. Cut in half and remove pit.	8
Rhubarb	Wash tender stalks. Cut off tough ends and slice into 1 inch sections.	4

Drying nuts and seeds

The word 'nut' is a general term for the large, oily seeds or fruit from certain plants and trees. On the other hand, seeds come from fruit, and can be removed from the fruit. Nuts are both the seed and the fruit, and cannot be separated. So all nuts are seeds, but not all seeds are nuts.

Some people have (serious) allergic reactions to peanuts, tree nuts, ground nuts, seeds, or wheat. If you are able to eat them, they are a great addition to your diet. Note that if someone close to you has a serious nut allergy, you could endanger his or her health even by processing these foods in your kitchen. Be cautious, and ask questions of your allergic friends.

Nuts and seeds are powerhouse foods, providing concentrated protein and vitamins in small packages. Their nutrients include heart-healthy Omega 6 and Omega 3 fats, monounsaturated fats, and the antioxidant vitamin E. Almost all nuts and seeds contain high amounts of fat, but the fat is unsaturated and can actually aid weight loss and reduce the saturated fat and calories in your overall diet, if eaten in moderation. Eating portion-controlled amounts of the good kind of fat can placate your cravings and keep you from gorging on something far less healthy.

Some commonly dried nuts include:

- Almonds

- Walnuts

- Brazil nuts

- Cashews

- Chestnuts

- Peanuts

- Pine nut

- Pistachios

Commonly-dried seeds include:

- Sesame seeds

- Sunflower seeds

- Pumpkin and squash seeds

- Poppy seeds

- Flax seeds

- Wheat kernels

Drying nuts and seeds will preserve them for about 4 months. They can be dried raw, toasted, or baked after drying to bring out more flavors. Many seeds and nuts should be soaked before drying. Nuts and seeds that are not soaked and are raw have enzyme inhibitors, which prevent human bodies from absorbing healthy enzymes. In addition, raw nuts and seeds that are not soaked contain phytic acid, which is indigestible, and bonds with minerals in the digestive tract, instead of allowing the minerals to be absorbed by bodies. It is sufficient to submerge nuts and seeds in warm water for 30 minutes before draining thoroughly.

Most nuts must be shelled before drying, but pistachios and peanuts can also be dried in the shell, if you prefer. When shelling walnuts, be careful not to punch through the hard shell and crush the nut inside. Special picks can be purchased to pull all the nutmeats out of the shell. When shelling chestnuts and Brazil nuts, remove all the papery brown skin on the nut; it will leave a bitter taste if it remains. Pine nuts are particularly hard to remove from the cones, but the taste is certainly worth it.

Pumpkin seeds should be carefully washed, while rubbing the seeds with your hands, to remove all the fibers and pumpkin flesh that clings to the seeds. Make sure the seeds are not slippery — this means that all the pumpkin meat has been removed. Wrap the flower of the sunflower in cheesecloth as it starts to ripen during the harvest. You will notice that during this ripening process, birds and squirrels will be checking the sunflowers daily to see when they will ripen —make sure you get to the seeds before they do. Sunflower seeds may be dried in the sun right on the stalk, in the oven, or in a dehydrator at 100 degrees Fahrenheit.

All seeds and nuts can be dried without adding any further seasoning, but many people enjoy salted nuts and seeds. This is achieved by soaking them in salt water for 3 to 6 hours, and then draining well before drying them. To salt the nuts, try the following proportions, and then adjust for your personal taste:

1 cup raw nuts or seeds

2 cups water

2 teaspoons salt

When your seeds or nuts are prepared, spread them on a baking sheet in a single layer and put in a 200 degree Fahrenheit oven for 4 hours. Alternatively, you can dry them in a dehydrator at 100 degrees Fahrenheit for 2 to 4 hours.

Peanuts, pistachios, and sunflower seeds are dry when the shells are hard and easy to crack. Inside, the meat should be tender, but not wrinkled up. Shelled nuts are dry when the surface is slightly leathery, but upon breaking one open the inside is tender not moist. Wheat kernels and other seeds will be hard and dry.

Dry nuts to add to a trail mix

Store these seeds and nuts in labeled plastic bags or air-tight containers. If you prefer to toast seeds or nuts before use, spray a little non-stick spray on a frying pan, and warm to medium heat. Pour in the food and allow it to toast, stirring or shaking constantly. The seeds, especially small ones, can burn easily. If you will be storing them after toasting, allow them to cool on paper towels before packaging them.

If you would like to roast nuts before storing, turn the oven to 400 degrees Fahrenheit. Spray non-stick cooking spray on a baking pan. Spread the nuts in a single layer on the sheet. You may want to add seasonings such as salt, pepper, chili powder, garlic salt, or brown sugar before roasting. Cook for several minutes and then stir the nuts, making sure they are browning on all sides. When the seeds are golden brown, remove them from the oven. Allow them to cool on paper towels before packaging them.

Chapter 6

Juicing

Fruit and vegetable juicing is becoming a popular way to consume your daily allowance of produce — you can find juice bars in almost every town and mall, and the juice aisle of your grocery store probably has more blends than you could imagine. However, commercially prepared juices must contain preservatives to keep them shelf-stable, and they also can contain dyes, fillers, and other ingredients you might prefer to live without. Commercial juices are also much more expensive than the ones you can make at home, and you can create blends that suit you, not a manufacturer.

People juice citrus fruits by hand with a small tool that twists the liquid from lemons, limes, and oranges, but this is a time-consuming, difficult process. Another juicing device is the grape press, which uses a hand crank to press a board down over grapes or apples to produce grape juice, apple juice, or cider. Some people also use kitchen blenders or juicing appliances to make juices. Whichever method you choose, you are sure to enjoy the rich tastes of homemade juices.

Juicing for Health

Juicing vegetables allows you to obtain all the benefits of fresh vegetables, without indigestible portions of the produce that your intestines might find difficult to handle. Additionally, fresh, uncooked fruits and vegetables have the maximum amount of nutrients. Though cooking destroys some to all of the nutrients your body might absorb from the food, you will absorb nearly all the nutrients by drinking them in a raw produce beverage. Many people have less-than-ideal digestion from eating less healthful food throughout their lives; this limits the body's ability to take up the vitamins and minerals from fruits and vegetables you eat. Juicing these foods begins the breakdown process of digestion, so the body will absorb more of the nutrition. Many people swear by the weight loss and detoxifying effects of drinking fresh vegetable and fruit juices. In addition, when you remove the pulp and fiber from fruits and vegetables, the remaining juice will stay preserved longer in a refrigerator, freezer, or can. The USDA food pyramid states that each day, adults should eat five servings of fruits and vegetables. That is plenty to consume — and most people do not consume nearly that amount of produce. However, getting that amount of produce is easier if you drink it in vegetable juice form. When you juice your produce, you will consume the maximum amount of vegetable nutrients most efficiently. In addition, fresh juices can be used in place of broth or water in many recipes, stirred into yogurts, or frozen in cubes for ice teas and drinks. In addition, juicing gives you more options for processing your produce. Juices take up much less room than whole fruits and vegetables, and if you can not consume all the produce at once, the juice can be frozen or canned.

When making your own juices, you can add more types of fruits and vegetables to your diet. Oftentimes, people tend to eat the same vegetables, fruits, or salads every day. Rotating your foods and adding new produce to your menu will keep you interested in produce, as well as exposing your body to new and healthful alternatives. Even if you do not care for a particular fruit or vegetable, you may find you like it better in juice form.

Juicing Methods

The following methods are the best ways to juice your fruits and vegetables. You may find that you already have all the equipment you need to start making your own juice.

Pressing juices

Apple cider straight from the press is a staple of fall. Nothing brings back memories of autumn more than a taste of homemade juices and cider. This is one of the reasons that people love to produce their own juice.

Fruits that are best for this type of juicing are slightly tart. Fruit with bruises can be used for juice when they cannot be canned or dried — a reason to combine juicing and preserving of produce. However, fruit with any mold or decay will ruin an entire batch of juice. Sort and wash your fruit carefully. You can use larger fruits such as apples, pears, peaches, quinces, persimmons, pineapples, any kind of melon, citrus fruits, apricots, tomatoes, or pomegranates as long as you cut them into smaller pieces. Grapes, cherry and grape tomatoes, blueberries, blackberries, currants, raspberries, strawberries, gooseberries, loganberries, and cherries are excellent choices for juicing whole. However, very sweet fruits like strawberries and cherries will be improved by the addition of some lemon juice, or by blending the juice with another type of fruit that adds some tartness. Make sure you remove the stems of fruit before juicing them, because the stems will make the juice bitter. Depending on the water content of the fruit, a pound of raw fruit will yield about a cup of juice.

The type of fruit you choose will determine the best method for juicing. Here are some of the most commonly juiced fruits and the best methods juice them:

- **Stovetop juicing:** grapes, peaches, berries, cherries, and tomatoes

- **Juice pressing:** all fruits

- **Steam juicing:** cherries, apples, or grapes

- **Blender juicing:** watermelon, pineapple, peaches, pears, and berries

Heat juicing

Heat juicing requires just a few pieces of equipment: several pans, a food processor, thick wooden spoon or potato masher/ricer, cheesecloth or a sieve, and jars. Remove the stems and pits from cherries or peaches, and carefully sort out any bad or under ripe pieces. Rinse the fruit well — if you like, you can allow the fruit to soak for a few minutes to make sure it is clean and free from bugs and dirt. After draining the fruit, crush it slightly to get the juice to flow readily. You can pulse the fruit in small batches in a food processor, or place it in a pan and crush it with a heavy spoon or potato masher.

Bring the fruit to a boil in a large covered pot, and simmer about ten minutes, stirring occasionally. Keep mashing the fruit from time to time so that you extract as much juice as possible. This will also extract the color from the skins to make a more attractive juice — but if you spill any juice, wipe it up immediately, because most dark fruits will easily stain counters, appliances, and clothing.

Once you have extracted all the juice from the fruit, allow the mixture to cool. Then strain the juice through a fine sieve or several layers of cheesecloth. This may take several hours, because the juice and pulp will be thick. You can speed up the straining process by squeezing your cheesecloth bag or pressing the pulp in the sieve; however, this will make the juice cloudier. If you prefer clear juice, do not squeeze the pulp. Many cooks will let the juice drain overnight to extract as much as possible from the pulp. Hang the bag of cheesecloth on a nail, or raise it above the bowl collecting the juice, so that gravity does the draining work for you. You can either discard the pulp leftovers, or compost them in the garden.

Juices produced through this method will be thicker and more concentrated than by other methods. Once you taste the result, you may want to dilute the juice with water, or use as syrup. Alternatively, you can freeze or can the juice as a space-saving fruit concentrate, and mix with water when you are ready to drink it.

Juice pressing

Juice pressing is done manually with a fruit press. These presses range in size from a small tabletop press, suitable for juicing citrus fruits, to large barrel-like presses. To use a small citrus press, slice the fruit in half and remove the seeds. Put the fruit half on top of the juicer cone, and pull down the lever to crush the juice from the rind. Some electrical versions will press down the juicing lid when a button is pressed. The juice will run from a spigot or run into a collection container. Citrus juices retain more flavors when frozen rather than canned, but either method is acceptable. If freezing, make sure the juice is sealed in leak-proof freezer bags or sturdy containers.

Spice up your pancakes with different-flavored syrups
— *photo courtesy of Blue Ridge Farms*

For larger batches of fruit, you may want to purchase a hand-crank fruit press. These presses have a barrel-like container for holding the fruit and a flat lid with a crank handle that you slowly screw down to crush the fruit. The juice will run out of a spigot at the bottom of the press, while the pulp and remains of the fruit stay in the barrel. These fruit presses come in many sizes, from a gallon-sized tabletop version to a model that can hold a bushel or more of fruit. These presses can also be used to press other kinds of produce for vegetable juices, as long as tough or large vegetables are sliced before they are placed in the barrel. In addition, large fruits, such as apples or pears, should be chopped or sliced before pressing, because plenty of strength would be needed to crank down the lid otherwise. Juices produced from fruit presses can be preserved by either canning or freezing.

Steam juicing

A steam juicer is a stovetop appliance consisting of a covered double boiler with a spigot or hose that runs from a center pan. The water boils in the bottom pot and releases steam to the prepared fruit in the top pot. The juicer extracts juice from fruit by breaking down the fruit through heat and water; the juice runs to the central pan of the steamer while steam replaces the lost juice in the fruit cells. Steam juicing is quicker than some other methods — small fruits will complete processing in about 30 minutes. Just like any other food that is steam cooked rather than boiled, the produce retains its taste and nutrients better than through boiling. Juice produced by a steam juicer is generally very clear and pure; the resulting juice makes a delicious clear fruit jelly as well as nutritious drinks.

The steam juicer is a popular tool in many parts of Europe. The juicers come in a wide range of prices, mostly based on the material. Enamel steamers will prevent an acid reaction with acidic fruits, but they are subject to cracking on impact or with extreme changes in temperature. Aluminum pans can cause a reaction with acidic fruits, but they are usually the cheapest variety. Stainless steel steamers are very study and non-reactive. Because there are few moving parts, and the pots easily come apart for cleaning, a good steam juicer is simple to maintain and should last for a long time.

Blender juicing

Creating juices from a blender is a quick, easy way to make healthy juice. A medium-duty blender is relatively inexpensive, can quickly make an entire pitcher of juice, and makes it easy to create juice blends and smoothies.

However, the juicing will take more prep time than the other methods described above. Some juicing purists maintain that the blending action introduces oxygen into the juice, thus destroying some of the nutrition. But if you are planning to can or freeze the juice to preserve it, some nutrients might be lost anyway.

A blender will mix all the fruit pulp, fiber, and skins into a thick drink. This can be satisfying as a fresh smoothie, especially when blended with yogurt, fiber supplement, or protein powder. However, if you want a clearer drink, remove as much of the skin, stalks, and tough fibers from the food ahead of time as possible, as well as carefully washing and sorting the produce. Core or pit the fruit and remove the skins, and add some extra water to the blender. Once the juice is blended, let it sit for 30 minutes or so to let the heavy pulp sink to the bottom. Then strain the juice before drinking, freezing, or canning.

Using a juicer

A juicer appliance is all that is needed to produce many raw fruit and veg-etable blends. These appliances will range in price from $50 to several hun-dred dollars. Consider how often you will use it when you purchase it. If you are just beginning to explore juicing, you may want to start out with a mid-range model without many extra bells and whistles.

There are several different types of juicers. Centrifugal juicers spin the juice out of produce, but add oxygen, which will start to break down food nu-trients. If you use this type of juicer, you should drink your juice soon after making it. Masticating juicers mash the produce at a low speed to remove juices. This method introduces less oxygen to the juice and so the juice will store for a longer period of time. High-speed fruit and vegetable juicers can produce quantities of juice more quickly, but they also create heat that can remove some of the juices' nutrients. Hydraulic-press juicers squeeze the juice out of produce, but the process generates very little oxidation and make the best nutritional juice. Make sure you have a juicer that can handle the woody parts of some tough fruits and vegetables, such as celery's tough fibers or the rough roots of beets. When using any juicer, the pulp that remains should be discarded, used for making soup stock, or composted.

To use a juicer, first prepare your fruits or vegetables. Choose produce at the peak of freshness and maturity. Make sure the fruit is not bruised, damaged, or blemished, because the fruits will generally be put into a juicer whole. Wash your produce well. Some people like to use a scrubber pad and a tiny bit of dish soap to scrub the surface of fruits and vegetables before juicing them. If your produce is purchased from a grocery store, this removes dirt, pesticides, and insect debris. If you grow your own, using a scrubber pad removes dirt and pollutants from the environment. After washing, thoroughly rinse all soap from your fruits and vegetables before using. Fruits should be seeded and cored, and vegetables should have the tough rinds and seeds discarded. The juicer will remove the nutrients from thin-skinned fruits and vegetables, but fruits with rinds, such as melons and citrus fruits, should be peeled. Cut your produce into quarters or dice it, and place it into the juicer. Follow the instructions for using the appliance.

Laura uses her juicer to make fresh and nutritious carrot juice

After each use, clean all the parts of your juicer thoroughly, according to the manufacturer's directions. If you notice that the machine is slowing down during use and the juicer does not eject pulp automatically, stop the machine and remove any pith, pulp, or fibers that may be clogging the machine's operation.

Fruit juices

Many people enjoy fruit blends, and creating your own blends during a fruit's season is the most economical way of enjoying juice. Some people have a hard time drinking acidic juices on an empty stomach. Some easily tolerated fruits include berries, melon, apples, and grapes. Your best bet is to use fruit with high juice content; thicker fruits like bananas will become too mushy to juice well. Here are a few easy-to-make, easily-tolerated fruit blends:

Apple Pineapple Ginger Juice

- 1 apple, cored and sliced
- 1 cup pineapple, peeled and diced
- ½ inch fresh gingerroot

Blueberry Grape Juice

- 1 cup of grapes (any variety; does not need to be seeded)
- 1 cup blueberries, fresh or frozen

Apple Kiwi Juice

- 3 kiwis, peeled
- 2 apples, cored and chopped

Pineapple Orange Strawberry

- 1 orange, peeled and sectioned, all white pith removed
- 1 cup pineapple, peeled and diced
- 5 strawberries

Melonade

- 1 lemon, peeled and pith removed
- 5 strawberries
- 1/4 watermelon, without rind

For extra flavor, toss in a few tablespoons of raisins, nuts, or dates while juicing produce. Alternatively, add banana chunks or yogurt while juicing to create a satisfying smoothie.

Vegetable Juices

People are more familiar with drinking fruit juices than vegetable juices. It is easiest to start out with mild vegetables that you already know you like. Always cut vegetables into small pieces and remove hard rinds or seeds. If you use pithy vegetables or ones with fibrous stalks, clean out the juicer often.

Try a combination of the following easily digestible vegetables: celery, fennel stalks, and cucumbers. These three do not have the same nutrient density as leafy green vegetables, but they are a good start. Add cilantro or parsley for additional flavor. Once you get accustomed to these three vegetables, start adding vegetables that are denser in nutrients and stronger-tasting vegetables. Carrots and beets are a good choice, because they contain easily digested sugars, and add taste and color to your drink. Always cut vegetables into pieces and remove stems and tough, woody ends.

To experiment with different vegetable juice tastes, try adding vegetables like bell peppers, tomatoes, red leaf lettuce, green leaf lettuce, romaine, cabbage, endive, escarole, and spinach. You can grow your own wheatgrass, bean, or alfalfa sprouts to add nutrients to your juices. Experiment with the quantities so that you get the taste you enjoy.

Herbs and spices are also an excellent way to add flavor and additional vitamins to your juices. Although fresh herbs provide the best nutritional punch, dried herbs are just as acceptable. Remember, though, that dried herbs are more potent than fresh. You can also add hot sauce, garlic, pepper, and other seasonings to the juice. If you use kale, collard greens, dandelion greens, or mustard greens, which have high nutritional value, add only a small amount, because these leaves can be bitter.

To expand your vegetable repertoire, try some of these vegetable blends:

5-Vegetable Juice

- 4 potatoes
- 4 carrots, sliced
- 6 broccoli florets
- 6 Brussels sprouts, woody stems removed
- 1 cucumber, skin on, chopped
- 1 teaspoon seasoned salt

Celery-Cabbage Combo

- 4 carrots, sliced
- 2 celery stalks, sliced
- 1 cup chopped cabbage
- 1 teaspoon fennel seed

Garden Tonic

- 1 cup baby spinach leaves
- 3 celery stalks, sliced
- 2 stalks of asparagus, sliced
- 1 tomato, quartered
- 1 tablespoon fresh basil leaves

Wheatgrass Tonic

- 2 stalks of celery, sliced
- ½ cucumber, sliced
- 1 cup baby spinach leaves or 4 kohlrabi leaves
- ½ cup parsley
- ½ cup wheatgrass

Powerful Carrot Juice

- 1 beet, sliced
- 1 cucumber, skin on, chopped
- 1 cup baby spinach leaves
- ½ cup of parsley
- 1 green pepper, cored and quartered
- 1 clove garlic
- 1 slice gingerroot
- 6 carrots, sliced

If you want to blend fruits and vegetables, you might find new and interesting combinations you never have considered before. Try some of these blends:

Cucumber Celery Cooler

- 4 medium carrots, tops removed, sliced
- ½ cucumber, skin on, chopped
- 1 stalk celery, sliced
- 1 apple, cored and sliced
- ½ lemon, peeled and pith removed

Calcium Blend

- 6 broccoli florets
- 3 carrots, sliced and greens removed
- ½ cup edamame peas (removed from pods)
- 1 apple, cored and chopped
- ⅓ cup fresh parsley
- ½ lemon, peeled and pith removed

Potassium Blend

- 4 medium carrots, sliced and greens removed
- 1 stalk of celery
- 1 apple
- ½ cup fresh parsley
- ½ cup baby spinach leaves
- ½ lemon, peeled and pith removed

Tomato Spice

- 6 tomatoes, quartered
- ½ cup beet tops, sliced
- ½ lemon, peeled and pith removed
- 1 to 2 drops hot sauce
- ½ teaspoon horseradish
- ½ apple, chopped

Winter Blend

- ½ cup cranberries
- 1 cup apples, seeded and cored
- ½ cup chopped parsnips
- ½ cup beets, sliced
- 2 leaves of kale, cabbage, or escarole
- ½ cup sliced Brussels sprouts
- ¼ cup walnuts

Cabbage/Cherry Juice

- 3 carrots, sliced
- ¼ head of cabbage
- 1 celery stalk, sliced
- ¼ cup fresh cilantro leaves
- 10 pitted cherries

Preserving juices

The best way to preserve your vegetable or fruit blends is to keep them refrigerated, can them, make them into jams or jellies, or to store them in the freezer. Juice can be poured into a plastic bag or freezer-proof plastic container. You can freeze juices such as pure lime or lemon juice in ice cube trays, and then store them in plastic bags in the freezer. When you need citrus juice for a drink or a recipe, simply remove cubes from the bag. Each cube should produce about 1 tablespoon of juice, depending on the size of the cubes. When frozen, juices will last 6 to 9 months in the freezer and will last up to 2 weeks in a refrigerator. Juices can also be canned, though this will damage some of the nutrients. Tomato juice and citrus juices can be canned through boiling water bath processes, but most other low-acid juices must be canned in a pressure canner. Follow the directions in the canning chapter for the proper canning of juices.

Chapter 7

Other Preservation Methods

T his chapter looks at other ways to preserve foods, including ways to preserve dairy products and use your juices to create alcoholic beverages.

Preserving Food in a Root Cellar

Root cellars are used to keep food supplies cool and consistently humid year-round, without freezing in the winter or heating up in the summer.

After the fall harvest, the produce of the gardens can be stored in the root cellar. Some people also store beverages or allow wine or beer to ferment in the root cellar.

The name "root cellar" comes from the main function of storing root or underground vegeta-

Old houses like this one used to have cellar doors

bles like potatoes, parsnips, onions, and carrots. Most root vegetables will keep fresh for at least 2 months, given an environment of low temperature, darkness, and controlled humidity. Other vegetables, like winter squash, pumpkins, cabbages, kohlrabi, apples, and strings of garlic or dried peppers can also be preserved in a root cellar. In addition, a root cellar is also an ideal place to store canned, dried, or salted foods because of the ideal storage conditions.

There are many ways to create root cellars. Some common examples are:

- Digging a pit in the ground and building a shed or lid over the hole (some builders line the hole with wood, straw, or concrete)

- Digging a cave into the side of a hill

- Building a box or shed on the ground and surrounding it with hay bales, earth, or rocks

- Building a storage structure in the basement or crawl space of the house

The one drawback to an outdoor cellar is the lack of control over the climate. A root cellar built in your basement will allow much more room, as well as give you more control over the temperature and humidity. To create a root cellar, choose an out-of the way site next to a window. Build walls with studs and plywood, using foam batting as insulation between walls.

Add a door and then insulate and close off the ceiling. Remove the glass from the window and insert a piece of plywood. This wood will be the gateway for two pipes, one to bring cool air into the room, and one to remove warm air from the room.

A locked, underground root cellar

Site the first pipe towards the top of the room to remove warm air; put a piece of screen over the outdoor end so that insects and mice cannot enter the room. The lower pipe should also be screened, and will be used to draw cool air into the room.

Root cellar storage times

These storage times are based on ideal conditions and produce in excellent condition. However, it is important to check your produce often and remove any decaying produce before it infects other food.

Produce	Approximate Storage Time
Beets	3-4 months
Broccoli	2-3 weeks
Brussels sprouts	3-5 weeks
Carrots	3-4 months
Cauliflower	2-3 weeks
Eggplant	1-2 weeks
Parsnips	1-2 months
Potatoes	4-6 months
Radishes	2-3 months
Rutabagas	2-4 months
Turnips	4-6 months
Winter squash and pumpkins	3-4 months

Pickling and Fermenting Food

Pickling is a method of preserving food by brining or fermentation — and pickles might be the first thing you think of when you think about preserving or canning. Though pickled cucumbers are probably the most popular pickled food, you can

A quaint root cellar at the base of a cliff

actually preserve many fruits, vegetables, meat, and fish this way. This preservation method uses large quantities of vinegar, salt, spices, and herbs to add extraordinary flavor to ordinary foods. However, the process of pickling or fermenting removes most of the vitamins and nutrients from produce, so pickles are usually eaten as condiments, rather than as part of your daily allowance of vegetables.

Fermentation is the process of using an agent, such as yeast, to detoxify the food and create organic acids that preserve the food. Although there are "bad" types of fermentation caused by spoiled food, a controlled fermentation process using specific, beneficial fermenting agents will create delicious, well-preserved food.

Jars of ingredients ready to make pickles

Other types of food also use a type of fermenting for preserving and to create a characteristic flavor. Wine and beer are the result of fermented fruit juices or grains, and have gained popularity in the last 15 years for home brewers and vintners. There are several types of cheese that easily are made at home, and the basic principles of fermenting apply to these, as well. And whenever you use yeast to create a loaf of bread, you are harnessing the power of "good" fermentation.

Types of pickling

There are several different types of pickling. One type of pickling is called brining; this method preserves vegetables such as cabbage by soaking them in a salt solution for a long period of time. The solution begins to ferment, and the salt prevents undesirable bacteria from growing. This method is used to make sauerkraut and kimchee, a traditional Korean fermented dish.

Fresh packing is the process of soaking vegetables in brine and then hot packing them in jars with vinegar and flavorings. These pickles are usually canned for long-term storage or kept refrigerated or frozen. Sweet pickles are fruit or small cucumbers hot-packed with a mixture of sugar, vinegar, pungent spices like coriander and mustard seed, and sweet spices like cloves or cinnamon. The result is a sweet-and-sour combination. Relishes are a chopped mix of vegetables that can be either sweet or sour, depending on the recipe. Relishes are a condiment or salad served with many meals. Finally, herbal vinegars blend fresh herbs with different types of vinegar to produce a fragrant or spicy condiment.

Cucumber pickles are made with a specific type of cucumber bred for pickling; it is a smaller cucumber that remains crisper during the brining and canning process — and the pickle's crunch is a major part of its appeal. Cucumber pickles can be processed whole, sliced, or cut into spears. The crunchiest pickles are ones that are pickled whole.

The pickling process

When harvesting fruit and vegetables for pickling, choose tender, unblemished produce. Make sure you pick cucumbers before they grow too mature — older pickles will become somewhat hollow inside, and the seeds will be large and tough. It is best to process your pickles on the same day you pick your produce, if the produce is coming out of your own garden. If you buy your produce at the store, try to time your visit so you get the pick of the latest produce delivery.

As you begin your pickling season, it is a good idea to replace any old seasonings. Spices and herbs are at their best for a year or two after opening, and old jars will lose much of their flavor. Because the produce may be processing in those seasonings for a long time, it is worth it to use spices with the maximum flavor. When the recipe calls for salt, you must use coarse pickling or kosher salt without additives like iodine or minerals commonly found in sea salt.

Any vinegar can be used for pickling, and some recipes call for a specific kind, such as cider or red wine vinegar. If the recipe does not specify a type, choose white vinegar at 40 to 60 percent acidity. White vinegar has a clean, neutral taste and does not add color to the produce.

Pickling methods require the same equipment that hot water bath canners use:

1. A jar lifter — a set of tongs specially made for canning jars. They have handles coated with rubber so you do not burn your hands when taking jars out of boiling-hot water.

2. A plastic or rubber spatula with a small blade. You use this to remove bubbles from jars — like when canning.

3. An accurate kitchen timer, measuring cups, and spoons.

4. Saucepans to warm lids and cook sauces.

5. Colanders to drain.

6. Knives and cutting boards.

7. Pot holders or mitts.

8. A large spoon.

9. Towels to set hot jars on to cool.

It is best to have all the equipment out and ready to use when you start a recipe; it can be frustrating to stop in the middle to search for a crucial tool or spice. Included in the appendix are several time-tested recipes for different types of pickles, along with processing and canning instructions. Once you create the brine or liquid for the pickles, it is recommended that you taste your concoction before mixing with the pickles. Some recipes could sound more to your taste on paper than they do in the pan. Some herbs and spices are stronger than others are, and you will learn to correct the season-ings. It is better to find that out before you use up your produce, rather than after you open the jar to serve your food.

Sometimes pickling can go wrong. If you find your pickles are hollow, this can mean that the cucumbers were too mature, or the brine was not strong enough to start good fermentation. If the pickles feel slimy, they spoiled in the jar; discard them. Pickles that look unusually dark are safe to eat, but they have been darkened by minerals in the salt or water, overcooked, or had a reaction with the vinegar and metal utensils. Bubbles in the jar or liquid that spurts out when the jar is opened, indicates spoilage, as well as mold found on the inside of the jar. If you notice the produce is an off color or smells funny, it should not be eaten.

If you see signs that your pickles are contaminated, take care with your dis-posal method. Some bacteria are deadly even in small amounts; you could spill a tiny splash on your hand and then wipe your mouth, and then the bacterium has entered your system. It is best to dump bad products down the drain, where the water treatment plants will neutralize contaminants, then scrub your sink and hands, and sterilize the jars. Make sure you *always* discard the self-seal lids after using them. The screw ring can be re-used once it is sterilized. Alternatively, you can boil the jars in a water bath can-ner for 30 minutes to neutralize the contents, and then place the cooled, unopened jars in the trash.

Making vinegar at home

Basic vinegar is the product of fermented fruit juices, although vinegar can be made from any liquid that contains starch and sugar. The process is similar to wine-making, although the extra processing is what gives vinegar the sour, tangy flavor that would be unacceptable in a wine. The vinegar you make at home may have even more flavor and zest than any brand you can buy at a store. In addition, it is a great way to use up any fruit that was too damaged or visually unappealing when canning or drying the produce.

Apple cider vinegar is a popular variety to make at home, but you can also make red or white wine vinegar, or experiment with other fruit juices to create your own signature blend. Plain white vinegar is manufactured from pure acetic acid and is an all-purpose type sold in stores, but it is less flavorful and rich than items made with fresher fruit juices.

Processing vinegar begins with the juice or wine. Press or steam out the fruit juice by following the instructions in this book's chapter on juicing. Once the juice is extracted, strain it through several layers of cheesecloth, without squeezing, until the juice is clear. Remember that juices produced by the heat or steam method will be thicker and more concentrated than by other methods; taste the result and dilute the juice with water until it has the usual juice consistency. If you are making wine vinegar, you can start with either a freshly opened bottle of wine, or the remains of opened wine that you do not want to finish or that has become old. Pour your liquid into a large glass, plastic, or ceramic container (a metal container will cause an acid reaction with the vinegar).

Next, you must add special brewer's yeast, or a bacteria culture called "mother of vinegar" to begin the fermentation process. Brewer's yeast can sometimes be found in grocery or gourmet stores, but you can order it online as well. Mother of vinegar may be a little harder to find, but a quick Internet search will send you in the right direction. During fermentation, the yeast will consume the sugars and, along with "friendly" bacteria, will turn them into alcohol. Place the container in an out-of-the-way place that remains between 60 and 80 degrees, so that the bacteria can multiply without being killed by extreme temperatures. Cover the container with a layer of cheesecloth, and stir the liquid every day to maintain a good level of oxygen in the brew.

Vinegar takes about a month to completely process, although you may process it for longer if desired. After the first few weeks, you will notice a "mat" or bubbly scum forming on the surface of the liquid, and you will start to notice the smell of vinegar. The mat is the formation of mother of vinegar, and you can remove some of this to start a new batch of vinegar, or give some to a friend so he or she can start their own vinegar culture. Eventually this mat will sink to the bottom of the container, but you will usually strain this out when your vinegar is ready to be bottled. You may need to strain the vinegar several times until it is clear and you no longer see the mother of vinegar culture.

Using a funnel, pour the vinegar into sterilized bottles and screw on a cap. You can save old vinegar bottles and re-use them until you see damage or dents in the cap. Vinegar will keep indefinitely in the refrigerator, or several months at room temperature. If you would like to store vinegar for long periods of time in a pantry or outside the refrigerator, pasteurize the vinegar by heating it to 180 degrees Fahrenheit and keeping it at that temperature for at least 10 minutes. Then pour it into your sterilized jars. Like all stored foods, vinegar should be kept in a cool, dark place.

These infused oils and vinegars make tasty salad dressings

Vinegar flavorings

Once you make a basic vinegar, it can be fun to add different herbs and seasonings to create new flavors and condiments. Try some of these combinations:

Red Wine: 1 large sprig of rosemary, 10 black peppercorns, 6 capers or ½ cup crushed raspberries, 1 teaspoon garlic powder, 2 sprigs of marjoram, and 1/2 teaspoon sugar.

Apple Cider Vinegar: ¼ teaspoon cinnamon, ½ cup raisins, 1/8 teaspoon ground cloves, 2 sprigs thyme; or 1 teaspoon chili powder, 1 teaspoon celery salt, and ½ teaspoon honey.

White Vinegar: 1 teaspoon chopped oregano, 1 teaspoon chopped thyme, 1 minced garlic clove, and ½ teaspoon sugar; or 1 teaspoon ground coriander, 3 sprigs of cilantro, 1½ teaspoons sesame seeds, and ½ teaspoon crushed red pepper.

White Wine vinegar: 2 large sprigs tarragon, 1 teaspoon onion powder, and 2 sprigs of lavender; or 1 large sprig of rosemary, ½ teaspoon juniper berries, 1 teaspoon garlic powder, and ½ teaspoon salt.

Making cheese at home

The basic method for making cheese is the same as any other fermentation process — only the ingredients are different. Cheese makers use any kind of raw or pasteurized dairy animal milk (such as cow, sheep, or goat — in Asia, sometimes camel or yak milk is used), add acid or bacteria to convert the milk sugars into lactic acid, and with the removal of some of the milk's moisture, create a curd, which is the basic unit of all cheese. Cheeses are classified into several categories:

- cream, such as sour cream or cream cheese

- soft, such as Neufchatel, Mascarpone, ricotta, or yogurt

- semi-soft, such as Gouda, blue, feta, or Mozzarella

- semi-hard, such as cheddar, Swiss, or Monterey Jack

- hard, such as parmesan or Romano.

The type of animal milk, the fat content, the processing and aging time, and the type of bacteria used in fermentation will all determine the flavor and type of cheese that is made.

Cheese-making begins with the milk. Fat-free milk will produce low fat cheese, but heavy cream will produce only mascarpone cheese, used for desserts. It is crucial to use milk that is as fresh as possible. If the milk is not already pasteurized, put the milk in the top pan of a double boiler and heat it to 160 degrees Fahrenheit, stirring constantly. Remove from heat and allow to cool completely before beginning to make the cheese. Then pour the milk into a large sterilized pot. When you make the cheese, the milk should be kept at about 90 degrees Fahrenheit. Maintain this temperature by putting the pot into a sink of warm water and adding hot water if the temperature falls. Once the temperature is at 90 degrees Fahrenheit, you can move on to the next step.

Next, you must add the cheese-making bacteria to the milk. This can be bought as a "cheese starter mix" — in fact, many places sell an entire cheese making kit that also includes rennet, the ingredient you will add later to form curds in the milk. There are three kinds of bacteria: helvetic, used to make Italian cheeses like provolone or parmesan; lactophilic, a starter that makes a buttery-flavored cheese and forms holes more easily than others; and mesophilic, a general-purpose starter for soft to semi-hard cheeses. Stir in the desired culture and allow it to process for about 45 minutes to an hour (cheese makers call this "ripening" the milk), stirring gently from time to time. You will see the milk start to separate, forming curds between thin liquid, called whey.

When the ripening time is up, according to the specific directions for your cheese recipe, dilute the prescribed amount of rennet with cold water and add to the milk mixture. This will cause the milk to coagulate and thicken into one large curd. Gently stir and then allow to process for about 45 minutes. At the end of this time, the mixture should have hardened into a solid mass.

Using a knife, cut the curd into equal ½-inch pieces inside the pot. This will provide more surface area for the curd to release the whey. Gently stir the pot one time, and then pour the mixture back into the top of the double boiler. On low heat, gradually increase the temperature of the mixture until it reaches the temperature described in the recipe.

Once the mixture has reached the proper temperature and consistency, pour it into a colander lined with cheesecloth. Allow the whey to drain off into a bowl if you plan to use it for cooking. The curds are completely processed when they are shiny and firm and have lost moisture. Then place the curds in a bowl and add one tablespoon of salt for each gallon of milk, stirring until completely mixed. If you would like a flavored cheese, you can add peppers, celery, or caraway seeds, or any herb or flavoring you prefer. Make sure the seasoning is completely mixed with the curds.

The next step is to press the cheese into a mold, causing the curds to connect into a solid block ("knitting" the curds). Experts use a cheese mold that is a large pot or cylinder with holes in the bottom to drain out the whey. However, you can use a colander or strainer if you do not have a cheese mold. Line the bottom of your container with damp cheesecloth, then press in the curds. Fold the cheesecloth over the top of the curds and place a plate and a weight (about 5 to 8 pounds) on top of the curds to press them down into the proper shape. If using a cheese mold, it will come with its own weight, called a follower. Raise the container on a catch plate so that the curds do not come into contact with the whey that will drain from the mold. Follow the recipe's instructions for the length of time the cheese should be pressed (usually 1 to 3 days). Turn the cheese daily.

At the end of the pressing period, package the cheese in thick plastic wrap, or coat it in cheese makers' wax. Then you begin aging your cheese. The length of aging will determine how pungent the end product will be, as well as how dry it will become; the aging time can range from a few days to a year. The cheese should be aged in a cool, dark place. Once the aging is complete, and you break open the wax coating, store the cheese in the refrigerator or freezer.

Cheese and mold

Most people know that some varieties of cheese use a mold culture to create the flavor — and that some cheeses develop mold as they age. Are these safe to eat? Here are the guidelines from the USDA:

Molds are used to make certain kinds of cheeses and can be on the surface of cheese or be developed internally. Blue-veined cheese such as Roquefort, blue, Gorgonzola, and Stilton are created by the introduction of *P. roqueforti* or *Penicillium roqueforti* spores. Cheeses such as Brie and Camembert have white surface molds. Other cheeses have both an internal and a surface mold. The molds used to manufacture these cheeses are safe to eat.

Hard cheese — these are not cheeses where mold is part of the processing

You can use these cheeses if mold is present. Cut off at least 1 inch around and below the mold spot (keep the knife out of the mold itself so it will not cross-contaminate other parts of the cheese). After trimming off the mold, re-cover the cheese in fresh wrap. Mold generally cannot penetrate deep into the product.

Cheese made with mold — these are cheeses such as Roquefort, blue, Gorgonzola, Stilton, Brie, Camembert

Discard soft cheeses such as Brie and Camembert if they contain molds that are not a part of the manufacturing process. If surface mold is on harder cheeses such as Gorgonzola and Stilton, cut off mold at least 1 inch around and below the mold spot and handle like hard cheese, as described above. Molds that are not a part of the manufacturing process can be dangerous.

Soft cheese — such as cottage, cream cheese, Neufchatel, chevre, Bel Paese, among others. And **Crumbled, shredded, and sliced cheeses** (all types)

Discard these cheeses if mold is present. Foods with high moisture content can be contaminated below the surface. Shredded, sliced, or crumbled cheese can be contaminated by the cutting instrument. Moldy, soft cheese can also have bacteria growing along with the mold.

Yogurt and sour cream

Discard these if mold is present. Foods with high moisture content can be contaminated below the surface. Moldy foods may also have bacteria growing along with the mold.

Information courtesy of the USDA Food Safety and Inspection Service, public domain fact sheet at www.fsis.usda.gov/Fact_Sheets/Molds_On_Food/index.asp

Fermenting Beverages

Many do not think of alcoholic beverages as preserved food, but technically they are. Both hobbyists and serious brewers take pride in crafting their own beers and wines. You can create delicious and unique beverages at your home by following these guidelines.

Home brewing beer

One of the world's original fermented beverages is beer. Brewing beer started as a "home brew" process, but over time became a mostly commercial product. More recently, in the past 25 years, home brewing beer has become very popular again. The brewing of beer has been around since ancient times. There is some archeological evidence that indicates the brewing of beer dates back almost 7,000 years ago. This evidence was discovered by archeologists in what is today Iran, China, Mesopotamia, and Egypt. Essentially, the fermentation of grains in the making of beer is a method of preserving the energy or carbohydrates of the grain in a tasty form called beer. The spent grains and yeast from the brewing process make an excellent source of energy and protein for livestock.

It is theorized that the making of beer began accidentally. Barley and barley-related grains was the staple of the diet in ancient Egypt and Mesopotamia.

By letting the grains get wet and then dried quickly, they became more flavorful and sweeter. Today we call this malt. The malted barley was used to improve the bread they made for their daily food. Some scientists and archaeologists believe that it is possible for wild yeast to have contaminated the wet grain. The carbohydrates in the grain, in the form of sugars, were the food for the yeast to grow and multiply. As the mixture of liquid and grain fermented it would have been a bubbly stew. The byproducts of this fermentation were alcohol and brewer's grains, or spent barley. The liquid beer would be separated off and put into jugs. Home brewing was born.

Ears of barley straws

In America, home brewing was declared illegal, along with all other manufacture of alcoholic beverages for consumption, as a result of Prohibition in 1920. Prohibition ended in 1933 when the 21st Amendment to the Constitution was ratified. Apparently there was a clerical error and home brewing beer remained technically illegal. The words "and/or beer" were left out of the 21st Amendment when it was recorded in the Federal Register. This did not apply to the home making of wine, because of the way the amendment was written. The commercial production of beer was now legal, but home brewing remained illegal.

In 1978 this oversight was corrected when Congress passed, and President Carter signed into effect, a law to make the home brewing of beer legal. This law allowed any adult at least 21 years old to brew up to 100 gallons of beer per year, or 200 gallons per household with two or more adults in the household. One hundred gallons is equivalent to 1,100 bottles of beer, or just under 46 cases. The home brewed beer can only be used for personal use, and not sold or distributed for sale. An average batch of home brew beer is around 5 gallons. It is a fairly ambitious home brewer who brews 20 batches of beer per year. There are some areas of the country were local laws and ordinances prohibit home brewing of beer. Check with local and/ or state authorities prior to brewing beer at home.

Today's modern home brewing process is basically similar to the ancient methods. The brewing techniques modernized, and ingredients improved over the centuries. There are four main ingredients in beer, including water, malted barley or other grains, hops, and yeast.

Ingredients

Water is the primary ingredient in the brewing of beer. It is important that clean, pure water is used. Buying commercially purified water usually is not necessary, depending on your local water source. The water will be boiled to purify it and remove any remaining chlorine prior to the next step in the brewing process. You can also use carbon filters to remove chlorine from the water, while leaving the minerals. If your water source is very high in soluble minerals, you may want to consider buying purified water. This can be the case with some well water depending on your local area.

Malted barley usually in the form of malt extract is commercially available today, although some very serious home brewers malt their own barley. This is a time consuming and laborious project. The grains must be soaked, sprouted and germinated, dried, roasted, and milled or cracked. With the abundance of malt extract or malted barley, home malting is not worth it

These malted barley grains are available through brewing suppliers or on the Internet

for most average home brewers. The malt provides the sugars needed for the yeast to eat, producing carbon dioxide and alcohol.

Hops are actually the flowers of the hop plant. The hop plant is a climbing vine that grows well in climates like Washington State, the source of most commercially available hops for brewing. The hops are most commonly used in the form of compressed plugs or pellets. The compressed hops actually hold the bitter flavor from the oils better than the whole flowers. The pellets or plugs have less surface area exposed to the air, and the oil remains inside. This keeps the hops fresher and more flavorful. Hops add bitterness to the beer, giving it a unique taste and balancing the sweet flavor from the malt. Hops also are a natural antimicrobial, helping to preserve the beer and aid in preventing spoilage. The different types of hops give distinct flavors to beer.

Yeast is how the mix of water, grain, and hops become alcoholic. The yeast digests the sugars from the malted barley, producing the alcohol and carbon dioxide. One method of introducing yeast to the mix is allowing naturally occurring yeast to "contaminate" the wort. This method is called lambic brewing and was perfected centuries ago by Belgian monks. It is becoming more popular for serious home brewers to experiment with lambic brewing. For the majority of home brewers, especially beginners,

An oast house, which is a hop kiln, where hops for beer are dried

it is recommended to use commercially available brewer's yeast. There are two primary types of yeast depending on the type of beer you are brewing. Ales are brewed using top fermenting yeast, and brewed at a higher temperature. Bottom fermenting yeast is used for brewing lager style beers, and brewed at lower temperatures for a longer time.

Equipment

There is some basic equipment that is required for home brewing. There are many suppliers that can provide the necessary equipment. You will need a large cooking pot, preferably stainless steel, that can hold 5 gallons of liquid. The beer-specific equipment includes a 6 ½ gallon fermenter with lid, airlock that fits into the fermenter lid, a 6 ½ gallon bucket for bottling, thermometer, hydrometer to determine alcohol level, bottle brush, capping device, caps for bottles, racking tube with a shut-off clip, and a siphoning tube. Always use returnable bottles or bottles that do not have a twist top, because these can break during capping. Optional equipment includes a glass carboy for secondary fermentation, and Cornelius kegs and tapping equipment for keg packaging systems.

Sterilization

A key to successful home brewing is proper sterilization. All of the equipment in the brewing process must be completely sterilized. If unwanted bacteria are introduced into the beer, it can result in off flavors, foul smelling beer, and spoilage. Anything that touches the beer or its ingredients must be completely sterilized and handled with care. Home brewing suppliers can provide sterilization products, such as no rinse cleaners, acid-based beer system cleaners, or even common TSP. Never use chlorine bleach, because it imparts off flavors in the final product.

Getting started

The simplest way to start home brewing is with home brew kits. Most common kits include liquid malt extract, hops (imported or domestic depending on the type of beer being brewed), fresh yeast, and sugar. The simplest kits provide already hopped malt extract that just require adding water and boiling to make the wort. More advanced kits include grains to be cooked with the mash prior to cooling and adding the yeast.

The quality of beer from home brewing kits can be quite good, comparable to more complex brewing recipes. There are kits for almost any type of beer you would like to brew. Kits are much less intimidating for the beginning brewer. When a home brewer is ready to try more complex recipes, ingredients, and brewing methods, there are many resources for advanced home brewing. Check your local home brewing supplier for information.

As you advance in your home brewing skills, you can be creative and experiment with varying the quantity of ingredients or adding various flavoring agents. Recently, flavored beers have become quite popular. Fruits such as raspberry, citrus, plum, apple, and more can be used to create original beer flavors. Different types and larger amounts of hops can be used to brew beer with a hoppier, bitter flavor. Extra malt extract can be used to add to the darkness of the beer and give a sweeter taste. It is fun to experiment and find the beer that meets your individual tastes.

Brewing process

There are several steps in the beer brewing process:

1. Mashing

2. Cooking wort

3. Fermentation

4. Conditioning

5. Packaging (in bottles, kegs, or casks)

6. Consumption

The home brewing process is much like commercial brewing but on a much smaller scale. The malted barley is steeped in hot water to release the sugars in the grains. For most beginner home brewers it is easier to use malt extract that can be boiled immediately without going through the mashing process. This saves time and provides a more consistently flavored beer when just getting started, because the water and malt boil the hops are added to give the bitter flavor. The resulting blend is called the "wort." Wort is basically non-fermented beer. Finishing or flavoring hops can be added to the wort at the end of the cooking process for the particular flavor desired, dependent on the recipe and style of beer being brewed.

After the hopped wort is finished, it is cooled to the temperature required for the type of beer you are brewing. For example, ales are cooled to around 65 to 70 degrees Fahrenheit, and lagers are cooled to 45 to 55 degrees Fahrenheit. Transfer the wort to a fermenter by siphoning with a sterilized tube. The fermenter is essentially a 5 gallon plastic food-grade bucket, or a glass or plastic carboy. The yeast is then added to the cooled wort to begin the fermentation process. The fermenter is sealed and an airlock is used in the top of the lid to allow excess carbon dioxide to escape without allowing air to leak into the fermenter. Air can have naturally occurring airborne bacteria that can contaminate the brew.

The fermentation takes 2 to 3 weeks for ales and up to 6 weeks for certain types of lagers. Because ales are fermented at higher temperatures, the fermenter can be stored in a cool area of the house. The best place is usually in a dark part of the basement or a closet. Lagers ferment at lower temperatures. A second refrigerator set to 45 to 55 degrees is ideal. The cold floor of a basement in winter can be cold enough.

Secondary fermentation is started by adding additional sugar. For most beginners to average home brewers, the primary fermenter container is used for both primary and secondary fermentation. More advanced home brewers will use a separate container for the secondary fermentation. This requires more equipment and careful handling to prevent contamination.

You can tell when the fermentation process has completed when the foam on the surface from the bubbling carbon dioxide has dissipated and there is a layer of sediment on the bottom. If you are using a plastic bucket or plastic carboy, you will not be able to see the foam or sediment. The fermentation has completed when no carbon dioxide is bubbling out of the air lock.

Once the fermentation has completed, it is time for final carbonation. Carbonization is most commonly achieved by adding about 3/4 cup of corn sugar or dextrose to the beer prior to packaging. The beer is then transferred to the final conditioning containers. The containers are usually sterilized bottles or kegs. The beer is carefully siphoned into the containers and then sealed. Bottles are then capped, or kegs are sealed so that the carbonization process can complete. This is a result of the remaining yeast that is in the beer combining with the sugar and the fermentation that occurs carbonates the sealed beer. The carbon dioxide that is produced is dissolved into the beer and goes into suspension. When the beer is opened and poured into a glass, the carbon dioxide is released from suspension and forms the creamy foam or head. This process usually takes 1 to 2 weeks depending on the type of beer brewed.

A more advanced method of carbonization involves pressurizing carbon dioxide into the beer into a special type of keg. Recently, the Cornelius keg has become available for the home brewer. This is the type of canister used for soda pop storage in food service establishments. With the advent of premix soda systems, the Cornelius containers or kegs are more readily available for the home brewer. The advantage of the keg container is less packaging time. Kegs require specialized dispensing equipment and require refrigeration resulting in more upfront costs than bottling.

Home beer brewing safety

Remember that boiling anything on the stovetop has varying degrees of risk for burns or accidents. The equipment used in home brewing is quite large and can be awkward to handle as well. Obviously when you are home brewing, you want to be careful not to let children be close to hot equipment. Be careful for your own safety as well. You are dealing with very hot liquids. The risk of burns from steam is also a possibility. Use protective clothing, hot pads, and safety glasses.

Home wine making

The process of home wine making is very similar to home brewing beer. The basic process is very simple. In its simplest form, wine is made by adding yeast to fruit juices and allowing it to ferment. The yeast combines with the sugars in the fruit juice and the resulting product is a tasty liquid with high alcohol content. The earliest evidence discovered by archaeologists date back to 6,000 to 5,000 BC in present day Georgia, Iran, and Mesopotamia. As with beer, where there is agriculture, there is fermentation for preservation. Wine making began to flourish and became a standard part of culture in ancient Greece and Egypt. The wine making techniques and grape varieties advanced rapidly during the time of the Roman Empire. Today home wine making has not grown as rapidly in popularity as home brewing beer, but home wine makers have been brewing up wine for many years. The popularity of making higher quality grape varietal wines is on the rise.

Just like the home brewing of beer, home wine making became illegal in the United States during prohibition from 1920 to 1933. The 21st Amendment to the Constitution repealed Prohibition and in turn legalized the home making of wine. Unlike beer in which the omission of the words "and/or beer," wine was included in the language of the amendment. Making wine at home can be a great way to save money and can be a very fulfilling hobby. You can also utilize the foods that you are preserving as shown in previous parts of this book.

Ingredients

The basic ingredients for wine are the juice from crushed fruit, usually grapes. Use the juices you made from Chapter 6 of this book as the primary ingredient for you wine. You also need yeast, nutrients for yeast, acid, sugar, water, Campden tablets (sodium metabisulfite), tannins (optional), and finings (optional). Use the Heat Juicing and Juice Pressing sections of Chapter 6 for a good base for your wine. Wine does not have to be made only with grapes, but can be made from almost any type of fruit or even vegetables. Who can forget stories of going to your crazy uncle's house and being forced to try his dandelion wine?

Using quality yeast for wine is important. There are many strains of yeast on the market, such as baker's yeast, active dry yeast, brewer's yeast (from the previous section), and many more. For the best quality wines, it is important to use wine making yeast. Yeast nutrients are added when the yeast is added to your juice. These yeast nutrients are readily available from home wine making suppliers. The nutrients such as vitamins and amino acids supplied provide the yeast with the necessary nutrition to optimize the fermentation process. Sugar is also added as a source of energy and nutrition for the yeast during the fermentation process. There are expensive sugars for wine making that are available, but plain white cane sugar will do just fine.

Water is an important ingredient and should be purified much like in the beer brewing process. Some prefer to use granulated charcoal carbon filtration to remove the chlorine and other chemicals that can affect the flavor of your wine but do not remove the minerals. Water from distillation or reverse osmosis removes all the soluble minerals. These minerals add character to your wine.

The other ingredients are used for balancing flavor, sterilizing, or clarification. The sodium metabisulfite, commonly called Campden tablets, is used for the sanitization of the wine making equipment. Just like in beer making, it is very important to have clean, sterilized equipment that comes into contact with the wine. It is also used to sterilize the wine by killing harmful bacteria that are naturally present in the ingredients. Tannins may be added to give more bite to the wines, especially wines from red grapes. Grape tannins are available from wine making suppliers or simple black tea can be used as a tannin source. Balancing the acidity is important in making wines. Citric acid is often used and there are blends of acids available from your wine making supplier.

Equipment

The equipment is very similar to that used in home brewing beer. The basic equipment is available from home wine making suppliers. You will need

An aged wine barrel

a large pot for preparing the must, preferably stainless steel that can hold 5 gallons of liquid. You will also need 6 ½ gallon fermenter with lid, airlock that fits into the fermenter lid, a 6 ½ gallon bucket for racking, thermometer, hydrometer to determine alcohol level, bottle brush, good quality wine corks, racking tube with a shut-off clip, a siphoning tube, and a wooden barrel for racking (optional). Always use glass bottles for final bottling. Optional equipment includes a glass carboy instead of a plastic bucket for secondary fermentation.

Sterilization

A key to successful home wine making is proper sterilization. All of the equipment in the wine making process must be completely sterilized. If unwanted bacteria are introduced into the wine, it can result in off flavors, foul smelling wine, and spoilage. Anything that touches the wine or its ingredients must be completely sterilized and handled with care. Home brewing suppliers can provide sterilization products, such as Campden tablets or sodium metabisulfite. Never use chlorine bleach, because it imparts off flavors in the final product.

Getting started

The simplest way to start home wine making is using wine making kits. Most common kits include the juice and grape concentrates, fining agents, flavorings, and even labels. This is an easy way to get started, but it does not have the hands-on character of extracting your own juice for your wine. Equipment starter kits are very helpful when beginning. These usually include the basic equipment needed such as the first fermenter, carboy for secondary fermentation, stoppers and airlock, hydrometer, and racking and siphoning tubes. More deluxe kits include everything you need. You do not need to buy fancy kits though. Many of the components can be purchased separately or you may already have them on hand.

Wine making process

The home wine making process begins with sterilizing the equipment. Follow the label directions and use a generous amount of solution made with the Campden tablets to sanitize all of the equipment that comes into contact with the wine and ingredients. After the equipment is thoroughly dried, begin the first phase of the wine making process.

Next you prepare the juice. This is commonly called the "must" in wine making. If you prepared the juice, you are ready to finish preparing the must. If not, you will need to begin with extracting the juice from your fruit by boiling and pressing. Add the must starter to the sterilized primary fermenter. This is usually a 6 ½ gallon food-grade pail or carboy. These are readily available from your home wine making and home brewing supplier. Add the crushed Campden tablets and dissolve completely. Follow your recipe adding the additional ingredients. Do not add the sugar yet. You want to determine the specific gravity using your hydrometer prior to adjusting the must with the proper amount of sugar. Take a starter reading with the hydrometer. Add sugar very slowly while stirring to dissolve it completely. You can also dissolve the sugar in some of the water by boiling and stirring in the sugar. This will ensure that your sugar is completely dissolved before adding it to the must. Take a reading with the hydrometer and adjust the amount of sugar to reach the specific gravity level that your recipe suggests. A good final alcohol level to aim for is 11 percent to 13 percent. A lower alcohol level actually produces a better tasting wine. If you are using a kit or basic recipe and do not have a hydrometer do not worry, just follow the directions. Let this stand for 24 hours so the sulfite can sterilize the wine making ingredients in the must. Cover the fermenter with the lid and leave the airlock out of the hole on top. Plug the hole with a paper towel or cover with a piece of cloth so that bugs do not get in.

The next day, add the yeast and yeast nutrients to the must. This will begin the first fermentation of the must. The must will go through the first fermentation in about 4 to 9 days. It is best to cover the mix with the lid from the primary fermenter and plug or cover the hole. This will keep bugs out and the carbon dioxide can be released. Allow this fermentation to happen in a warm environment of approximately 70 to 75 degrees Fahrenheit. You will know that the fermentation is taking place by the bubbling and formation of foam. A layer of pulp from the fruit can build up on the top of the must. It is a good idea to push this down into the mix. This will help prevent the growth of mold on this layer. Always use a clean, sanitized spoon for pushing this down. It is recommended to use a plastic or stainless steel spoon. Wooden spoons are very difficult to sanitize due to the porous surface of the wood.

After the first fermentation is complete, you need to siphon the liquid out of the fermenter and strain it through cheese cloth to remove the solids. The liquid is poured into a secondary fermenter. As before, it is vital that all of the equipment be thoroughly washed and sanitized with the sulfite. Once all the liquid is strained and in the secondary fermenter, seal with the lid and put in the airlock. This will allow the secondary fermentation to begin and for the carbon dioxide to be released from the container. From time to time, take a reading with the hydrometer, or follow your recipe, to adjust the sugar level to achieve the desired alcohol level. You will know this step is complete when the airlock stops bubbling. Be patient here, because this step can take several weeks to complete.

After the secondary fermentation stops, you will need to fill the container the rest of the way to prevent spoilage. You can fill it with some leftover wine from the first fermentation, or you can use other wine to blend into the mix. Reseal the container with the airlock. Siphon and strain the wine again to remove any remaining sediment and return to the secondary fermenter. Seal the fermenter and allow the fermentation to complete. Once the bubbles have completely stopped, the fermentation is done. This can take a month or more to complete. Again, be patient. Patience in wine making pays off in quality product.

The next step is called "racking." Racking is drawing off the wine from the secondary fermenter into containers for final conditioning and aging. If you have small wooden barrels available, this is ideal for racking grape wines, especially red wines. The wine is siphoned into the barrel, filling it completely, and the hole is plugged with a large cork that is called a bung. If you do not have a barrel or large container available, you can rack the wine directly into the wine bottles and cork the bottles. The advantage of the wooden barrels is the wine will take on some of the flavor and character of the wood. This can really enhance the flavor of red wine especially. The aging should take place in a cool, dark place. Ideally the temperature should be around 65 degrees Fahrenheit. If you are racking directly into bottles, allow them to stand for a few days and then lay them on the side for the racking period. Now is when the patience really begins. You will need to age white wine for 4 to 6 months and red wine for a year or more. Wine continues to improve with age up to a point. While the wine is aging, the flavors and aromas will develop over time. This occurs due to the oxidation that slowly takes place while it is racking or aging.

When the aging or racking is complete you can transfer the wine from the barrel into individual bottles and seal tightly with cork. This will prevent the deterioration of the wine. You can seal the cork with some paraffin wax to prevent the cork top from getting moldy. There may be some sediment that settles to the bottom of the bottles. This is normal and completely harmless. If your bottles have some sediment, you can "candle" the wine when you pour it. This is a technique where you hold a candle or small flashlight under the neck of the bottle while slowly pouring the wine into a decanter. When the sediment at the bottom of the bottle reaches the neck you can stop pouring. There is usually very little sediment and little wine will be wasted. You can also pour the wine though clean cheese cloth. This will strain out the sediment. You are now ready to enjoy your homemade wine.

Homemade cider

Homemade fermented cider, or hard cider as it is also known, is fermented fruit juices for consumption. Many different types of fruits can be used to make cider. Apples are the most common fruit, but you can also make cider from pears, pomegranates, berries, plums, cherries, oranges, and peaches. Use your imagination to come up with interesting cider varieties. Worldwide cider is synonymous with alcoholic or hard cider. In the United States, cider is usually referring to non-alcoholic apple cider, or fresh apple juice. For the rest of this section when cider is referred to, it means fermented and preserved alcoholic cider.

Ingredients

The basic ingredient for cider is the apple juice or other fruit juices. You also need wine or brewer's yeast, nutrients for yeast, acid, sugar, and Campden tablets (sodium metabisulfite).

Equipment

The equipment required is basically the same as for home brewing. There are many suppliers that can provide the necessary equipment. You will need a large cooking pot, preferably stainless steel that can hold 5 gallons of liquid. Starter equipment kits usually include a 6 ½ gallon fermenter with lid, airlock that fits into the fermenter lid, a 6 ½ gallon bucket for bottling, thermometer, hydrometer to determine alcohol level, bottle brush, capping device, caps for bottles, racking tube with a shut-off clip, and a siphoning tube. Always use returnable bottles or bottles that do not have a twist top, because these can break during capping. Optional equipment includes a glass carboy instead of the plastic pail for secondary fermentation.

Sterilization

As in any fermentation process, it is very important to have properly sterilized equipment. Any contamination will spoil your batch of cider. You can use the Campden tablets or sodium metabisulfite to sanitize your equipment. Any surface touching the ingredients or the cider must be sterilized. Always wash your hands thoroughly as well.

Getting started

The simplest way to get started is to use a cider kit. These kits are available from home brewer suppliers. It is more fun at home to make your own juice. *Follow the directions in Chapter 6 for juicing.*

Brewing process

The brewing process is much like that of beer. It is a basic fermentation process. You prepare the apple juice or other fruit juice as you prefer. If you prepared the juice from Chapter 6, you are ready to finish preparing the juice. If not, you will need to begin with extracting the juice from your fruit by boiling and pressing. Add the juice to the sterilized primary fermenter. This is usually a 6 ½ gallon food-grade pail or carboy. These are readily available from your home wine making and home brewing supplier. Add the crushed Campden tablets and dissolve completely. Follow your recipe, adding the additional ingredients. Do not add the sugar yet. Add sugar very slowly while stirring to dissolve it completely or dissolve in hot water prior to adding. This will ensure that your sugar is completely dissolved before adding it to the juice. Let this stand for 24 hours so the sulfite can sterilize the cider ingredients.

Cover the fermenter with the lid and airlock. The next day, add the yeast and yeast nutrients to the juice. This will begin the first fermentation. The juice will go through the first fermentation in about 4 to 9 days. It is best to cover the mix with the lid from the primary fermenter and plug the hole with the airlock. This will keep bugs out and the carbon dioxide can be slowly released. Allow this fermentation to happen in a cool environment of approximately 40 to 55 degrees Fahrenheit, similar to brewing lager beer. You will know that the fermentation is taking place by the bubbling and formation of foam.

After the first fermentation has mostly stopped bubbling and is complete, you need to siphon the liquid out of the fermenter and strain it through cheese cloth to remove the solids. The liquid is poured into a secondary fermenter. As before it, is vital that all of the equipment be thoroughly washed and sanitized with the sulfite. Once all the liquid is strained and in the secondary fermenter, seal with the lid and put in the airlock. This will allow the secondary fermentation to begin and for the carbon dioxide to be released from the container. This should take about 2 weeks and should be kept at a warmer temperature of about 70 to 75 degrees Fahrenheit. You will know this step is completely when the airlock has stopped bubbling.

Preserving food is a timeless hobby

Siphon and strain the cider again into the fermenter container and then rack it back into the secondary fermenter. Seal the fermenter and allow the fermentation to complete for another 10 to 14 days. Once the bubbles have completely stopped, the fermentation is done. The cider is carefully siphoned into the sterilized bottles and then capped. Let the bottles condition for the next 2 weeks. You are now ready to enjoy your home made hard cider.

Fruit and Fruit Product Canning Recipes

— Courtesy of the USDA

General

Adding syrup to canned fruit helps to retain its flavor, color, and shape. It does not prevent spoilage of these foods. The following guidelines for preparing and using syrups offer a new "very light" syrup, which approximates the natural sugar content of many fruits. The sugar content in each of the five syrups is increased by about 10 percent. Quantities of water and sugar to make enough syrup for a canner load of pints or quarts are provided for each syrup type.

Preparing and using syrups						
		Measures of Water and Sugar				
		For 9-Pt Load*		For 7-Qt		
Syrup Type	Approx. % Sugar	Cups Water	Cups Sugar	Cups Water	Cups Sugar	Fruits commonly packed in syrup**
Very Light	10	6-1/2	3/4	10-1/2	1-1/4	Approximates natural sugar levels in most fruits and adds the fewest calories.
Light	20	5-3/4	1-1/2	9	2-1/4	Very sweet fruit. Try a small amount the first time to see if your family likes it.
Medium	30	5-1/4	2-1/4	8-1/4	3-3/4	Sweet apples, sweet cherries, berries, grapes.
Heavy	40	5	3-1/4	7-3/4	5-1/4	Tart apples, apricots, sour cherries, gooseberries, nectarines, peaches, pears, plums.
Very Heavy	50	4-1/4	4-1/4	6-1/2	6-3/4	Very sour fruit. Try a small amount the first time to see if your family likes it.

* This amount is also adequate for a 4-quart load.

** Many fruits that are typically packed in heavy syrup are excellent and tasteful products when packed in lighter syrups. It is recommended that lighter syrups be tried, because they contain fewer calories from added sugar.

Procedure

Heat water and sugar together. Bring to a boil and pour over raw fruits in jars. For hot packs, bring water and sugar to boil, add fruit, reheat to boil, and fill into jars immediately.

Other sweeteners

Light corn syrups or mild-flavored honey may be used to replace up to half the table sugar called for in syrups. See the section, "Canned foods for special diets," for further discussion.

Apple Butter

Use Jonathan, Winesap, Stayman, Golden Delicious, Macintosh, or other tasty apple varieties for good results.

  8 lbs apples
  2 cups cider
  2 cups vinegar
  2-1/4 cups white sugar
  2-1/4 cups packed brown sugar
  2 tbsp ground cinnamon
  1 tbsp ground cloves

Yield: About 8 to 9 pints

Procedure: Wash, remove stems, quarter, and core fruit. Cook slowly in cider and vinegar until soft. Press fruit through a colander, food mill, or strainer. Cook fruit pulp with sugar and spices, stirring frequently. To test if done, remove a spoonful and hold it away from the steam for 2 minutes. It is done if the butter remains mounded on the spoon. Another way to determine when the butter is cooked adequately is to spoon a small quantity onto a plate. When a rim of liquid does not separate around the edge of the butter, it is ready for canning. Fill hot into sterile half-pint or pint jars, leaving 1/4-inch headspace. Quart jars need not be presterilized but should be clean and kept hot until filling. Remove air bubbles and adjust headspace if needed. Wipe rims of jars with a dampened clean paper towel. Adjust lids and process.

Recommended process time for Apple Butter in a boiling-water canner				
		Process Time at Altitudes of		
Style of Pack	Jar Size	0-1,000 ft	1,001-6,000 ft	Above 6,000 ft
Hot	Half-pints or Pints	5 min	10	15
	Quarts	10	15	20

Apple Juice

Quality: Good quality apple juice is made from a blend of varieties. For best results, buy fresh juice from a local cider maker within 24 hours after it has been pressed.

Procedure: Refrigerate juice for 24 to 48 hours. Without mixing, carefully pour off clear liquid and discard sediment. Strain clear liquid through a paper coffee filter or double layers of damp cheesecloth. Heat quickly, stirring occasionally, until juice begins to boil. Fill immediately into sterile pint or quart jars, or fill into clean, hot half-gallon jars, leaving 1/4-inch headspace. Wipe rims of jars with a dampened clean paper towel. Adjust lids and process.

Recommended process time for Apple Juice in a boiling-water canner				
		Process Time at Altitudes of		
Style of Pack	Jar Size	0-1,000 ft	1,001-6,000 ft	Above 6,000 ft
Hot	Half-pints or Pints	5 min	10	15
	Quarts	10	15	20

Apples — Sliced

Quantity: An average of 19 pounds is needed per canner load of 7 quarts; an average of 12-1/4 pounds is needed per canner load of 9 pints. A bushel weighs 48 pounds and yields 16 to 1 9 quarts — an average of 2-3/4 pounds per quart.

Quality: Select apples that are juicy, crispy, and preferably both sweet and tart.

Procedure: Wash, peel, and core apples. To prevent discoloration, slice apples into water containing ascorbic acid. Raw packs make poor quality products. Place drained slices in large saucepan and add 1 pint water or very light, light, or medium syrup per 5 pounds of sliced apples. Boil 5 minutes, stirring occasionally to prevent burning. Fill hot jars with hot slices and hot syrup or water, leaving 1/2-inch headspace. Remove air bubbles and adjust headspace if needed. Wipe rims of jars with a dampened clean paper towel. Adjust lids and process.

Processing directions for canning sliced apples in a dial- or weighted-gauge canner are given later in this chapter.

Recommended process time for Apples, sliced in a boiling-water canner					
		Process Time at Altitudes of			
Style of Pack	Jar Size	0-1,000 ft	1,001-3,000 ft	3,001-6,000 ft	Above 6,000 ft
Hot	Pints or Quarts	20 min	25	30	15

Applesauce

Quantity: An average of 21 pounds is needed per canner load of 7 quarts; an average of 13-1/2 pounds is needed per canner load of 9 pints. A bushel weighs 48 pounds and yields 14 to 19 quarts of sauce — an average of 3 pounds per quart.

Quality: Select apples that are sweet, juicy, and crisp. For a tart flavor, add 1 to 2 pounds of tart apples for each 3 pounds of sweeter fruit.

Procedure: Wash, peel, and core apples. If desired, slice apples into water containing ascorbic acid to prevent browning. Placed drained slices in an 8 to 10-quart pot. Add 1/2 cup water. Stirring occasionally to prevent burning, heat quickly until tender (5 to 20 minutes, depending on maturity and variety). Press through a sieve or food mill, or skip the pressing step if you prefer chunk-style sauce. Sauce may be packed without sugar. If desired, add 1/8 cup sugar per quart of sauce. Taste and add more, if preferred. Reheat sauce to a rolling boil. Fill hot jars with hot sauce, leaving 1/2-inch headspace. Remove air bubbles and adjust headspace if needed. Wipe rims of jars with a dampened clean paper towel. Adjust lids and process.

Recommended process time for Applesauce in a boiling-water canner					
		Process Time at Altitudes of			
Style of Pack	Jar Size	0-1,000 ft	1,001-3,000 ft	3,001-6,000 ft	Above 6,000 ft
Hot	Pints	15 min	20	20	25
	Quarts	20	25	30	35

Spiced Apple Rings

12 lbs firm tart apples (maximum diameter, 2-1/2 inches)

12 cups sugar

6 cups water

1 -1/4 cups white vinegar (5%)

3 tbsp whole cloves

3/4 cup red hot cinnamon candies or

   8 cinnamon sticks and 1 tsp red food coloring (optional)

Yield: About 8 to 9 pints

Procedure: Wash apples. To prevent discoloration, peel and slice one apple at a time. Immediately cut crosswise into 1/2-inch slices, remove core area with a melon bailer, and immerse in ascorbic acid solution. To make flavored syrup, combine sugar, water, vinegar, cloves, cinnamon candies, or cinnamon sticks and food coloring in a 6-qt saucepan. Stir, heat to boil, and simmer 3 minutes. Drain apples, add to hot syrup, and cook 5 minutes. Fill hot jars (preferably wide-mouth) with apple rings and hot flavored syrup, leaving 1/2-inch headspace. Remove air bubbles and adjust headspace if needed. Wipe rims of jars with a dampened clean paper towel. Adjust lids and process.

Recommended process time for Spiced Apple Rings in a boiling-water canner				
		Process Time at Altitudes of		
Style of Pack	Jar Size	0-1,000 ft	1,001- 6,000 ft	Above 6,000 ft
Hot	Half-pints or Pints	10 min	15	20

Spiced Crab Apples

5 lbs crab apples

4-1/2 cups apple cider vinegar (5%)

3-3/4 cups water

7-1/2 cups sugar

4 tsp whole cloves

4 sticks cinnamon

Six 1/2-inch cubes of fresh ginger root

Yield: About 9 pints

Procedure: Remove blossom petals and wash apples, but leave stems attached. Puncture the skin of each apple 4 times with an ice pick or toothpick. Mix vinegar, water, and sugar and bring to a boil. Add spices tied in a spice bag or cheesecloth. Using a blancher basket or sieve, immerse 1/3 of the apples at a time in the boiling vinegar/syrup solution for 2 minutes. Place cooked apples and spice bag in a clean 1- or 2-gallon crock and add hot syrup. Cover and let stand overnight. Remove spice bag, drain syrup into a large saucepan, and reheat to boiling. Fill hot pint jars with apples and hot syrup, leaving 1/2-inch headspace. Remove air bubbles and adjust headspace if needed. Wipe rims of jars with a dampened clean paper towel. Adjust lids and process.

Recommended process time for Spiced Crab Apples in a boiling-water canner					
		Process Time at Altitudes of			
Style of Pack	Jar Size	0-1,000 ft	1,001-3,000 ft	3,001-6,000 ft	Above 6,000 ft
Hot	Pints	20 min	25	30	35

Apricots — Halved or Sliced

Quantity: An average of 16 pounds is needed per canner load of 7 quarts; an average of 10 pounds is needed per canner load of 9 pints. A bushel weighs 50 pounds and yields 20 to 25 quarts — an average of 2-1/4 pounds per quart.

Quality: Select firm, well-colored mature fruit of ideal quality for eating fresh.

Procedure: Follow directions for peaches. The boiling water dip and removal of skin process is optional. Wash fruit well if skins are not removed; use either hot or raw pack, and use the same process time.

Berries — Whole

The following directions can be applied to blackberries, blueberries, currants, dewberries, elderberries, gooseberries, huckleberries, loganberries, mulberries, and raspberries.

Quantity: An average of 12 pounds is needed per canner load of 7 quarts; an average of 8 pounds is needed per canner load of 9 pints. A 24-quart crate weighs 36 pounds and yields 18 to 24 quarts — an average of 1-3/4 pounds per quart.

Quality: Choose ripe, sweet berries with uniform color.

Procedure: Wash 1 or 2 quarts of berries at a time. Drain, cap, and stem if necessary. For gooseberries, snip off heads and tails with scissors. Prepare and boil your preferred syrup if desired. Add 1/2 cup syrup, juice, or water to each clean jar.

Hot pack — For blueberries, currants, elderberries, gooseberries, and huckleberries. Heat berries in boiling water for 30 seconds and drain. Fill hot jars and cover with hot juice, leaving 1/2-inch headspace.

Raw pack — Fill hot jars with any of the raw berries, shaking down gently while filling. Cover with hot syrup, juice, or water, leaving 1/2-inch headspace.

Remove air bubbles and adjust headspace if needed. Wipe rims of jars with a dampened, clean paper towel. Adjust lids and process.

Recommended process time for Berries in a boiling-water canner					
		Process Time at Altitudes of			
Style of Pack	Jar Size	0-1,000 ft	1,001-3,000 ft	3,001-6,000 ft	Above 6,000 ft
Hot	Pints or Quarts	15 min	20	20	25
Raw	Pints	15	20	20	25

Recommended process time for Berries in a boiling-water canner					
		Process Time at Altitudes of			
Style of Pack	Jar Size	0-1,000 ft	1,001-3,000 ft	3,001-6,000 ft	Above 6,000 ft
Raw	Quarts	20	25	30	35

Berry Syrup

Juices from fresh or frozen blueberries, cherries, grapes, raspberries (black or red), and strawberries are easily made into toppings for use on ice cream and pastries.

Yield: About 9 half-pints.

Procedure: Select 6-1/2 cups of fresh or frozen fruit of your choice. Wash, cap, and stem fresh fruit and crush in a saucepan. Heat to boiling and simmer until soft (5 to 10 minutes). Strain hot through a colander and drain until cool enough to handle. Strain the collected juice through a double layer of cheesecloth or jelly bag. Discard the dry pulp. The yield of the pressed juice should be about 4-1/2 to 5 cups. Combine the juice with 6-3/4 cups of sugar in a large saucepan, bring to boil, and simmer 1 minute. To make a syrup with whole fruit pieces, save 1 or 2 cups of the fresh or frozen fruit, combine these with the sugar, and simmer as in making regular syrup. Remove from heat, skim off foam, and fill into hot half-pint or pint jars, leaving 1/2-inch headspace. Remove air bubbles and adjust headspace if needed. Wipe rims of jars with a dampened clean paper towel. Adjust lids and process.

Recommended process time for Berry Syrup in a boiling-water canner				
		Process Time at Altitudes of		
Style of Pack	Jar Size	0-1,000 ft	1,001-6,000 ft	Above 6,000 ft
Hot	Half-pint/Pint	10 min	15	20

Cantaloupe Pickles

5 lbs of 1-inch cantaloupe cubes (about 2 medium underripe* cantaloupe)
1 tsp crushed red pepper flakes
2 one-inch cinnamon sticks
2 tsp ground cloves
1 tsp ground ginger
4-1/2 cups cider vinegar (5%)
2 cups water
1 -1/2 cups white sugar
1 -1/2 cups packed light brown sugar

*Select cantaloupe that are full size but almost fully green and firm to the touch in all areas including the stem area.

Yield: About 4 pint jars

Procedure:

Day One: Wash cantaloupe and cut into halves; remove seeds. Cut into 1-inch slices and peel. Cut strips of flesh into 1 inch cubes. Weigh out 5 pounds of pieces and place in large glass bowl. Place red pepper flakes, cinnamon sticks, cloves, and ginger in a spice bag and tie the ends firmly. Combine vinegar and water in a 4-quart stockpot. Bring to a boil, then turn heat off. Add spice bag to the vinegar-water mixture and let steep for 5 minutes, stirring occasionally. Pour hot vinegar solution and spice bag over melon pieces in the bowl. Cover with a food-grade plastic lid or wrap and let stand overnight in the refrigerator (about 18 hours).

Day Two: Carefully pour off vinegar solution into a large 8- to 10-quart saucepan and bring to a boil. Add sugar; stir to dissolve. Add cantaloupe and bring back to a boil. Lower heat and simmer until cantaloupe pieces turn translucent (about 1 to 1-1/4 hours). Remove cantaloupe pieces into a medium-sized stockpot, cover, and set aside. Bring remaining liquid to a boil and boil an additional 5 minutes. Return cantaloupe to the liquid syrup, and bring back to a boil. With a slotted spoon, fill hot cantaloupe pieces into hot pint jars, leaving 1-inch headspace. Cover with boiling hot syrup, leaving 1/2-inch headspace. Remove air bubbles and adjust headspace if needed. Wipe rims of jars with a dampened clean paper towel. Adjust lids and process.

Recommended process time for Cantaloupe Pickles in a boiling-water canner				
		Process Time at Altitudes of		
Style of Pack	Jar Size	0-1,000 ft	1,001- 6,000 ft	Above 6,000 ft
Hot	Pints	15 min	20	25

Cantaloupe Pickles, No Sugar Added

> 6 lbs of 1-inch cantaloupe cubes (about 3 medium
>   underripe* cantaloupe)
> 7 tsp crushed red pepper flakes
> 2 one-inch cinnamon sticks
> 2 tsp ground cloves
> 1 tsp ground ginger
> 4-1/2 cups cider vinegar (5%)
> 2 cups water
> 3 cups Splenda®

*Select cantaloupes that are full size but almost fully green and firm to the touch in all areas including the stem area.

Yield: About 4 pint jars

Procedure: Follow the directions for Cantaloupe Pickles, weighing out 6 pounds of prepared cantaloupe cubes instead and substituting Splenda® when sugar would be added.

Cherries — Whole, Sweet or Sour

Quantity: An average of 17-1/2 pounds is needed per canner load of 7 quarts; an average of 11 pounds is needed per canner load of 9 pints. A lug weighs 25 pounds and yields 8 to 12 quarts — an average of 2-1/2 pounds per quart.

Quality: Select bright, uniformly colored cherries that are mature (of ideal quality for eating fresh or cooking).

Procedure: Stem and wash cherries. Remove pits if desired. If pitted, place cherries in water containing ascorbic acid to prevent stem-end discoloration. If canned unpitted, prick skins on opposite sides with a clean needle to prevent splitting. Cherries may be canned in water, apple juice, white grape juice, or syrup.

Hot pack — In a large saucepan add 1/2 cup water, juice, or syrup for each quart of drained fruit and bring to boil. Fill hot jars with cherries and cooking liquid, leaving 1/2-inch headspace.

Raw pack — Add 1/2 cup hot water, juice, or syrup to each jar. Fill hot jars with drained cherries, shaking down gently as you fill. Add more hot liquid, leaving 1/2-inch headspace.

Remove air bubbles and adjust headspace if needed. Wipe rims of jars with a dampened clean paper towel. Adjust lids and process.

Recommended process time for Cherries, whole in a boiling-water canner					
		Process Time at Altitudes of			
Style of Pack	Jar Size	0-1,000 ft	1,001-3,000 ft	3,001-6,000 ft	Above 6,000 ft
Hot	Pints	15 min	20	20	25
	Quarts	20	25	30	35
Raw	Pints or Quarts	25	30	35	40

Cranberry Orange Chutney

24 ounces fresh whole cranberries

2 cups chopped white onion

2 cups golden raisins

7 -1/2 cups white sugar

7 -1/2 cups packed brown sugar

2 cups white distilled vinegar (5%)

7 cup orange juice

4 tsp peeled, grated fresh ginger

3 sticks cinnamon

Yield: About 8 half-pint jars

Procedure: Rinse cranberries well. Combine all ingredients in a large Dutch oven. Bring to a boil over high heat; reduce heat and simmer gently for 15 minutes or until cranberries are tender. Stir often to prevent scorching. Remove cinnamon sticks and discard. Fill the hot chutney into hot half-pint jars, leaving 1/2-inch headspace. Remove air bubbles and adjust headspace if needed. Wipe rims of jars with a dampened, clean paper towel. Adjust lids and process.

Recommended process time for Cranberry Orange Chutney in a boiling-water canner				
		Process Time at Altitudes of		
Style of Pack	Jar Size	0-1,000 ft	1,001-6,000 ft	Above 6,000 ft
Hot	Half-pints	10 min	15	20

Note: Other dried spices can be added to taste (for example, cloves, dry mustard, or cayenne pepper). Add or adjust spices during the simmering period.

Figs

Important: All home-canned figs must be acidified before canning in a boiling water canner to make them safe from the microorganism that causes botulism.

Quantity: An average of 16 pounds is needed per canner load of 7 quarts; an average of 11 pounds is needed per canner load of 9 pints — an average of 2-1/2 pounds yields 1 quart.

Quality: Select firm, ripe, uncracked figs. The mature color depends on the variety. Avoid overripe figs with very soft flesh.

Procedure: Wash figs thoroughly in clean water. Drain. Do not peel or remove stems. Cover figs with water and boil 2 minutes. Drain. Gently boil figs in light syrup for 5 minutes. Add 2 tablespoons bottled lemon juice per quart or 1 tablespoon per pint to the jars; or add 1/2 teaspoon citric acid per quart or 1/4 teaspoon per pint to the jars. Fill hot jars with hot figs and cooking syrup, leaving 1/2-inch headspace. Remove air bubbles and adjust head-space if needed. Wipe rims of jars with a dampened, clean paper towel. Adjust lids and process.

Recommended process time for Figs in a boiling-water canner					
		Process Time at Altitudes of			
Style of Pack	Jar Size	0-1,000 ft	1,001-3,000 ft	3,001-6,000 ft	Above 6,000 ft
Hot	Pints	45 min	50	55	60
	Quarts	50	55	60	65

Fruit Purees

Important: These recommendations should not be used with figs, tomatoes, cantaloupe and other melons, papaya, ripe mango, or coconut. There are no home canning recommendations available for purees of these products.

Procedure: Stem, wash, drain, peel, and remove pits if necessary. Measure fruit into large saucepan, crushing slightly if desired. Add 1 cup hot water for each quart of fruit. Cook slowly until fruit is soft, stirring frequently. Press through sieve or food mill. If desired for flavor, add sugar to taste. Reheat pulp to boil, or until sugar dissolves if added. Fill hot into hot jars, leaving 1/4-inch headspace. Remove air bubbles and adjust headspace if needed. Wipe rims of jars with a dampened clean paper towel. Adjust lids and process.

Recommended process time for Fruit Purees in a boiling-water canner				
		Process Time at Altitudes of		
Style of Pack	Jar Size	0-1,000 ft	1,001-6,000 ft	Above 6,000 ft
Hot	Pints or Quarts	15 min	20	25

Grapefruit and Orange Sections

Quantity: An average of 15 pounds is needed per canner load of 7 quarts; an average of 13 pounds is needed per canner load of 9 pints — an average of about 2 pounds yields 1 quart.

Quality: Select firm, mature, sweet fruit of ideal quality for eating fresh. The flavor of orange sections is best if the sections are canned with equal parts of grapefruit. Grapefruit may be canned without oranges. Sections may be packed in your choice of water, citrus juice, or syrup.

Procedure: Wash and peel fruit and remove white tissue to prevent a bitter taste. If you use syrup, prepare a very light, light, or medium syrup and bring to boil. Fill hot jars with sections and water, juice, or hot syrup, leaving 1/2-inch headspace. Remove air bubbles and adjust headspace if needed. Wipe rims of jars with a dampened clean paper towel. Adjust lids and process.

Recommended process time for Grapefruit and Orange Sections in a boiling-water canner				
		Process Time at Altitudes of		
Style of Pack	Jar Size	0-1,000 ft	1,001-6,000 ft	Above 6,000 ft
Hot	Pints or Quarts	10 min	15	20

Grape Juice

Quantity: An average of 24-1/2 pounds is needed per canner load of 7 quarts; an average of 16 pounds per canner load of 9 pints. A lug weighs 26 pounds and yields 7 to 9 quarts of juice — an average of 3-1/2 pounds per quart.

Quality: Select sweet, well-colored, firm, mature fruit of ideal quality for eating fresh or cooking.

Procedure: Wash and stem grapes. Place grapes in a saucepan and add boiling water to cover grapes. Heat and simmer slowly until skin is soft. Strain through a damp jelly bag or double layers of cheesecloth. Refrigerate juice for 24 to 48 hours. Without mixing, carefully pour off clear liquid and save; discard sediment. If desired, strain through a paper coffee filter for a clearer juice. Add juice to a saucepan and sweeten to taste. Heat and stir until sugar is dissolved. Continue heating with occasional stirring until juice begins to boil. Fill into hot or presterilized jars immediately, leaving 1/4-inch headspace. (*To sterilize empty pint and quart jars, see Chapter 1.*) Wipe rims of jars with a dampened, clean paper towel. Adjust lids and process.

Recommended process time for Grape Juice in a boiling-water canner				
		Process Time at Altitudes of		
Style of Pack	Jar Size	0-1,000 ft	1,001-6,000 ft	Above 6,000 ft
Hot	Pints or Quarts	5 min	10	15
	Half-gallons	10	15	20

Grapes — Whole

Quantity: An average of 14 pounds is needed per canner load of 7 quarts; an average of 9 pounds is needed per canner load of 9 pints. A lug weighs 26 pounds and yields 12 to 14 quarts of whole grapes — an average of 2 pounds per quart.

Quality: Choose unripe, tight-skinned, preferably green seedless grapes harvested 2 weeks before they reach optimum eating quality.

Procedure: Stem, wash, and drain grapes. Prepare very light, or light syrup.

Hot pack — Blanch grapes in boiling water for 30 seconds. Drain, and proceed as for raw pack.

Raw pack — Fill hot jars with grapes and hot syrup, leaving 1-inch headspace.

Remove air bubbles and adjust headspace if needed. Wipe rims of jars with a dampened, clean paper towel. Adjust lids and process.

Recommended process time for Grapes, whole in a boiling-water canner					
		Process Time at Altitudes of			
Style of Pack	Jar Size	0-1,000 ft	1,001–3,000 ft	3,001–6,000 ft	Above 6,000 ft
Hot	Pints or Quarts	10 min	15	15	20
Raw	Pints	15	20	20	25
	Quarts	20	25	30	35

Mango Chutney

11 cups or 4 lbs chopped unripe (hard) mango, either Tommy Atkins or Kent varieties

2-1/2 cups or 3/4 lb finely chopped yellow onion

2-1/2 tbsp grated fresh ginger

1 -1/2 tbsp finely chopped fresh garlic

4-1/2 cups sugar

3 cups white distilled vinegar (5%)

2-1/2 cups golden raisins

1-1/2 tsp canning salt

4 tsp chili powder

Caution: Handling green mangoes may irritate the skin of some people in the same way as poison ivy. (They belong to the same plant family.) To avoid this reaction, wear plastic or rubber gloves when working with raw green mango. Do not touch your face, lips, or eyes after touching or cutting raw green mangoes until all traces are washed away.

Yield: About 6 pint jars

Procedure: Wash all produce well. Peel, core, and chop mangoes into 3/4-inch cubes. Chop mango cubes in food processor, using 6 one-second pulses per food processor batch. (Do not puree or chop too finely.) By hand, peel and dice onion, finely chop garlic, and grate ginger. Mix sugar and vinegar in an 8- to 10-quart stockpot. Bring to a boil, and boil 5 minutes. Add all other ingredients and bring back to a boil. Reduce heat and simmer 25 minutes, stirring occasionally. Fill hot chutney into hot pint or half-pint jars, leaving 1/2-inch headspace. Remove air bubbles and adjust headspace if needed. Wipe rims of jars with a dampened, clean paper towel. Adjust lids and process.

Recommended process time for **Mango Chutney** in a boiling-water canner				
		Process Time at Altitudes of		
Style of Pack	**Jar Size**	**0-1,000 ft**	**1,001- 6,000 ft**	**Above 6,000 ft**
Hot	**Half-pints or Pints**	10 min	15	20

Mango Sauce

> 5-1/2 cups or 3-1/4 lbs mango puree
>   (use slightly underripe to just-ripe mango)
> 6 tbsp honey
> 4 tbsp bottled lemon juice
> 3/4 cup sugar
> 2-1/2 tsp (7500 milligrams) ascorbic acid
> 1/8 tsp ground cinnamon
> 1/8 tsp ground nutmeg

Caution: Handling green mangoes may irritate the skin of some people in the same way as poison ivy. (They belong to the same plant family.) To avoid this reaction, wear plastic or rubber gloves while working with raw green mango. Do not touch your face, lips, or eyes after touching or cutting raw green mangoes until all traces are washed away.

Yield: About 6 half-pint jars

Storage Notes: Store in a dark place, away from direct light, to preserve the color of the canned sauce. This sauce is best used within 4 to 6 months; otherwise, discoloration may occur.

Procedure: Wash, peel, and separate mango flesh from seed. Chop mango flesh into chunks and puree in blender or food processor until smooth. Combine all ingredients in a 6- to 8-quart Dutch oven or stockpot and heat on medium-high heat, with continuous stirring, until the mixture reaches 200 degrees F. The mixture will sputter as it is being heated, so be sure to wear gloves or oven mitts to avoid burning skin. Fill hot sauce into hot half-pint jars, leaving 1/4-inch headspace. Remove air bubbles and adjust headspace if needed. Wipe rims of jars with a dampened, clean paper towel. Adjust lids and process.

Recommended process time for Mango Sauce in a boiling-water canner				
		Process Time at Altitudes of		
Style of Pack	Jar Size	0-1,000 ft	1,001- 6,000 ft	Above 6,000 ft
Hot	Half-pints	15 min	20	25

Mixed Fruit Cocktail

3 lbs peaches
3 lbs pears
1 -1/2 lbs slightly underripe seedless green grapes
10-oz jar of maraschino cherries
3 cups sugar
4 cups water

Yield: About 6 pints

210 The Complete Guide to Food Preservation

Procedure: Stem and wash grapes, and keep in ascorbic acid solution. Dip ripe but firm peaches, a few at a time, in boiling water for 1 to 1-1/2 minutes to loosen skins. Dip in cold water and slip off skins. Cut in half, remove pits, cut into 1/2-inch cubes and keep in solution with grapes. Peel, halve, and core pears. Cut into 1/2-inch cubes, and keep in solution with grapes and peaches. Combine sugar and water in a saucepan and bring to boil. Drain mixed fruit. Add 1/2 cup of hot syrup to each hot jar. Then add a few cherries and gently fill the jar with mixed fruit and more hot syrup, leaving 1/2-inch headspace. Remove air bubbles and adjust headspace if needed. Wipe rims of jars with a dampened clean paper towel. Adjust lids and process.

Recommended process time for Mixed Fruit Cocktail in a boiling-water canner					
		Process Time at Altitudes of			
Style of Pack	Jar Size	0-1,000 ft	1,001-3,000 ft	3,001-6,000 ft	Above 6,000 ft
Raw	Half-pints or Pints	20 min	25	30	35

Nectarines — Halved or Sliced

Quantity: An average of 17-1/2 pounds is needed per canner load of 7 quarts; an average of 11 pounds is needed per canner load of 9 pints. A bushel weighs 48 pounds and yields 16 to 24 quarts—an average of 2-1/2 pounds per quart.

Quality: Choose ripe, mature fruit of ideal quality for eating fresh or cooking.

Procedure: Follow directions for peaches, except do not dip in hot water or remove skins. Wash fruit and use either hot or raw pack, and use the same process time.

Peaches — Halved or Sliced

Quantity: An average of 17-1/2 pounds is needed per canner load of 7 quarts; an average of 11 pounds is needed per canner load of 9 pints. A bushel weighs 48 pounds and yields 16 to 24 quarts — an average of 2-1/2 pounds per quart.

Quality: Choose ripe, mature fruit of ideal quality for eating fresh or cooking.

Procedure: Dip fruit in boiling water for 30 to 60 seconds until skins loosen. Dip quickly in cold water and slip off skins. Cut in half, remove pits, and slice if desired. To prevent darkening, keep peeled fruit in ascorbic acid solution. Prepare and boil a very light, light or medium syrup or pack peaches in water, apple juice, or white grape juice. Raw packs make poor quality peaches.

Hot pack — In a large saucepan place drained fruit in syrup, water, or juice and bring to boil. Fill hot jars with hot fruit and cooking liquid, leaving 1/2-inch headspace. Place halves in layers, cut side down.

Raw pack — Fill hot jars with raw fruit, cut side down, and add hot water, juice, or syrup, leaving 1/2-inch headspace.

Remove air bubbles and adjust headspace if needed. Wipe rims of jars with a dampened, clean paper towel. Adjust lids and process.

Recommended process time for Peaches, halved or sliced in a boiling-water canner					
		Process Time at Altitudes of			
Style of Pack	Jar Size	0-1,000 ft	1,001-3,000 ft	3,001-6,000 ft	Above 6,000 ft
Hot	Pints	20 min	25	30	35
	Quarts	25	30	35	40
Raw	Pints	25	30	35	40

Recommended process time for Peaches, halved or sliced in a boiling-water canner					
		Process Time at Altitudes of			
Style of Pack	Jar Size	0-1,000 ft	1,001-3,000 ft	3,001-6,000 ft	Above 6,000 ft
Raw	Quarts	30	35	40	45

Pears — Halved

Quantity: An average of 17-1/2 pounds is needed per canner load of 7 quarts; an average of 11 pounds is needed per canner load of 9 pints. A bushel weighs 50 pounds and yields 16 to 25 quarts — an average of 2-1/2 pounds per quart.

Quality: Choose ripe, mature fruit of ideal quality for eating fresh or cooking.

Procedure: Wash and peel pears. Cut lengthwise in halves and remove core. A melon baller or metal measuring spoon is suitable for coring pears. To prevent discoloration, keep pears in an ascorbic acid solution. Prepare a very light, light, or medium syrup or pack pears in apple juice, white grape juice, or water. Raw packs make poor quality pears. Boil drained pears 5 minutes in syrup, juice, or water. Fill hot jars with hot fruit and cooking liquid, leaving 1/2-inch headspace. Remove air bubbles and adjust headspace if needed. Wipe rims of jars with a dampened, clean paper towel. Adjust lids and process.

Recommended process time for Pears, halved in a boiling-water canner					
		Process Time at Altitudes of			
Style of Pack	Jar Size	0-1,000 ft	1,001-3,000 ft	3,001-6,000 ft	Above 6,000 ft
Hot	Pints	20 min	25	30	35
	Quarts	25	30	35	40

Pears, Asian — Halved or Sliced

Important: All home-canned Asian pears must be acidified before canning in a boiling water canner to make them safe from the microorganism that causes botulism.

Quantity: An average of 17 to 19 pounds is needed per canner load of 7 quarts; an average of 11 to 13 pounds is needed per canner load of 9 pints.

Quality: Choose ripe, mature fruit of ideal quality for eating fresh or cooking.

Procedure: Wash and peel pears. Cut lengthwise in halves and remove cores. Slice, if desired. To prevent discoloration, keep pears in an ascorbic acid solution. Prepare a very light, light, or medium syrup, or pack pears in apple juice, white grape juice, or water.

Hot pack — Boil drained pears 5 minutes in syrup, juice, or water. Fill hot jars with hot fruit and cover with boiling cooking liquid, leaving 1/2-inch headspace. Add 1 tablespoon bottled lemon juice per pint jar or 2 tablespoons per quart jar. Remove air bubbles and adjust headspace if needed. Wipe rims of jars with a dampened, clean paper towel. Adjust lids and process.

Recommended process time for Asian Pears, halved or sliced in a boiling-water canner					
		Process Time at Altitudes of			
Style of Pack	Jar Size	0-1,000 ft	1,001-3,000 ft	3,001-6,000 ft	Above 6,000 ft
Hot	Pints	20 min	25	30	35
	Quarts	25	30	35	40

Pineapple

Quantity: An average of 21 pounds is needed per canner load of 7 quarts; an average of 13 pounds is needed per canner load of 9 pints — an average of 3 pounds per quart.

Quality: Select firm, ripe pineapples.

Procedure: Wash pineapple. Peel and remove eyes and tough fiber. Slice or cube. Pineapple may be packed in water, apple juice, white grape juice, or in very light, light, or medium syrup. In a large saucepan, add pineapple to syrup, water, or juice, and simmer 10 minutes. Fill hot jars with hot pieces and cooking liquid, leaving 1/2-inch headspace. Remove air bubbles and adjust headspace if needed. Wipe rims of jars with a dampened, clean paper towel. Adjust lids and process.

Recommended process time for Pineapple in a boiling-water canner					
		Process Time at Altitudes of			
Style of Pack	Jar Size	0-1,000 ft	1,001-3,000 ft	3,001-6,000 ft	Above 6,000 ft
Hot	Pints	15 min	20	20	25
	Quarts	20	25	30	35

Plums — Halved or Whole

Quantity: An average of 14 pounds is needed per canner load of 7 quarts; an average of 9 pounds is needed per canner load of 9 pints. A bushel weighs 56 pounds and yields 22 to 36 quarts — an average of 2 pounds per quart.

Quality: Select deep-colored, mature fruit of ideal quality for eating fresh or cooking. Plums may be packed in water or syrup.

Procedure: Stem and wash plums. Plums may be packed in water or syrup. To can whole, prick skins on two sides of plums with fork to prevent splitting. Freestone varieties may be halved and pitted. If you use syrup, prepare very light, light, or medium syrup according to directions.

Hot pack — Add plums to hot water or hot syrup and boil 2 minutes. Cover saucepan and let stand 20 to 30 minutes. Fill hot jars with hot plums and cooking liquid or syrup, leaving 1/2-inch headspace.

Raw pack — Fill hot jars with raw plums, packing firmly. Add hot water or syrup, leaving 1/2-inch headspace.

Remove air bubbles and adjust headspace if needed. Wipe rims of jars with a dampened, clean paper towel. Adjust lids and process.

Recommended process time for Plums, halved or whole in a boiling-water canner					
		Process Time at Altitudes of			
Style of Pack	Jar Size	0-1,000 ft	1,001-3,000 ft	3,001-6,000 ft	Above 6,000 ft
Hot and Raw	Pints	20 min	25	30	35
	Quarts	25	30	35	40

Rhubarb — Stewed

Quantity: An average of 10-1/2 pounds is needed per canner load of 7 quarts; an average of 7 pounds is needed per canner load of 9 pints. A lug weighs 28 pounds and yields 14 to 28 quarts — an average of 1-1/2 pounds per quart.

Quality: Select young, tender, well-colored stalks from the spring or late fall crop.

Procedure: Trim off leaves. Wash stalks and cut into 1/2-inch to 1-inch pieces. In a large saucepan add 1/2 cup sugar for each quart of fruit. Let stand until juice appears. Heat gently to boiling. Fill hot jars without delay, leaving 1/2-inch headspace. Remove air bubbles and adjust headspace if needed. Wipe rims of jars with a dampened, clean paper towel. Adjust lids and process.

Recommended process time for Rhubarb, stewed in a boiling-water canner				
		Process Time at Altitudes of		
Style of Pack	Jar Size	0-1,000 ft	1,001-6,000 ft	Above 6,000 ft
Hot	Pints or Quarts	15 min	20	25

Zucchini-Pineapple

4 qts cubed or shredded zucchini

46 oz canned unsweetened pineapple juice

1-1/2 cups bottled lemon juice

3 cups sugar

Yield: About 8 to 9 pints

Procedure: Peel zucchini and either cut into 1/2-inch cubes or shred. Mix zucchini with other ingredients in a large saucepan and bring to a boil. Simmer 20 minutes. Fill hot jars with hot mixture and cooking liquid, leaving 1/2-inch headspace. Remove air bubbles and adjust headspace if needed. Wipe rims of jars with a dampened, clean paper towel. Adjust lids and process.

Recommended process time for Zucchini-Pineapple in a boiling-water canner				
		Process Time at Altitudes of		
Style of Pack	Jar Size	0-1,000 ft	1,001-6,000 ft	Above 6,000 ft
Hot	Half-pints or Pints	15 min	20	25

Fruit Salsas

Spicy Cranberry Salsa

> *6 cups chopped red onion*
> *4 finely chopped large Serrano peppers**
> *1-1/2 cups water*
> *1-1/2 cups cider vinegar (5%)*
> *1 tbsp canning salt*
> *1-1/3 cups sugar*
> *6 tbsp clover honey*
> *12 cups (2-3/4 lbs) rinsed, fresh whole cranberries*

*Caution: Wear plastic or rubber gloves when handling and cutting hot peppers or wash hands thoroughly with soap and water before touching your face or eyes.

Yield: About 6 pint jars

Procedure: Combine all ingredients except cranberries in a large Dutch oven. Bring to a boil over high heat; reduce heat slightly and boil gently for 5 minutes. Add cranberries, reduce heat slightly and simmer mixture for 20 minutes, stirring occasionally to prevent scorching. Fill the hot mixture into hot pint jars, leaving 1/4-inch headspace. Leave saucepot over low heat while filling jars. Remove air bubbles and adjust headspace if needed. Wipe rims of jars with a dampened, clean paper towel. Adjust lids and process.

Recommended process time for Spicy Cranberry Salsa in a boiling-water canner				
		Process Time at Altitudes of		
Style of Pack	Jar Size	0-1,000 ft	1,001-6,000 ft	Above 6,000 ft
Hot	Half-pints or Pints	10 min	15	20

Mango Salsa

6 cups diced unripe mango (about 3 to 4 large, hard green mangoes)
1-1/2 cups diced red bell pepper
1/2 cup finely chopped yellow onion
1/2 tsp crushed red pepper flakes
2 tsp finely chopped garlic
2 tsp finely chopped ginger
1 cup light brown sugar
1-1/4 cups cider vinegar (5%)
1/2 cup water

Caution: Handling green mangoes may irritate the skin of some people in the same way as poison ivy. (They belong to the same plant family.) To avoid this reaction, wear plastic or rubber gloves while working with raw green mango. Do not touch your face, lips, or eyes after touching or cutting raw green mangoes until all traces are washed away.

Yield: About 6 half-pint jars

Procedure: Wash all produce well. Peel and chop mango into 1/2-inch cubes. Dice bell pepper into 1/2-inch pieces. Finely chop yellow onions. Combine all ingredients in an 8-quart Dutch oven or stockpot. Bring to a boil over high heat, stirring to dissolve sugar. Reduce to simmering, and simmer 5 minutes. Fill hot solids into hot half-pint jars, leaving 1/2-inch headspace. Cover with hot liquid, leaving 1/2-inch headspace. Remove air bubbles and adjust headspace if needed. Wipe rims of jars with a dampened, clean paper towel. Adjust lids and process.

Recommended process time for Mango Salsa in a boiling-water canner				
		Process Time at Altitudes of		
Style of Pack	Jar Size	0-1,000 ft	1,001- 6,000 ft	Above 6,000 ft
Hot	Half-pints	10 min	15	20

Peach Salsa

Procedure: Follow directions for Mango Salsa using diced, hard, underripe but yellow peaches in place of the mango

Peach Apple Salsa

> *6 cups chopped Roma tomatoes*
> *2-1/2 cups diced yellow onions*
> *2 cups chopped green bell peppers*
> *10 cups chopped hard, unripe peaches*
> *2 cups chopped Granny Smith apples*
> *4 tbsp mixed pickling spice*
> *1 tbsp canning salt*
> *2 tsp crushed red pepper flakes*
> *3-3/4 cups (1-1/4 pounds) packed light brown sugar*
> *2-1/4 cups cider vinegar (5%)*

Yield: About 7 pint jars

Procedure: Place pickling spice on a clean, double-layered, 6-inch-square piece of 100 percent cheesecloth. Bring corners together and tie with a clean string. (Or use a purchased muslin spice bag). Wash and peel tomatoes (place washed tomatoes in boiling water for 1 minute, immediately place in cold water, and slip off skins). Chop into 1/2-inch pieces. Peel, wash and dice onions into 1/4-inch pieces. Wash, core, and seed bell peppers; chop into 1/4-inch pieces. Combine chopped tomatoes, onions, and peppers in an 8- or 10- quart Dutch oven or saucepot. Wash, peel, and pit peaches; cut into halves and soak for 10 minutes in an ascorbic acid solution (1500 mg in half gallon water). Wash, peel, and core apples; cut into halves and soak for 10 minutes in ascorbic acid solution. Quickly chop peaches and apples into 1/2-inch cubes to prevent browning. Add chopped peaches and apples to the saucepot with the vegetables. Add the pickling spice bag to the saucepot; stir in the salt, red pepper flakes, brown sugar and vinegar. Bring to boiling, stirring gently to mix ingredients. Reduce heat and simmer 30 minutes, stirring occasionally. Remove spice bag from pan and discard. With a slotted spoon, fill salsa solids into hot pint jars, leaving 1-1/4-inch headspace (about 3/4 pound solids in each jar). Cover with cooking liquid, leaving 1/2-inch headspace. Remove air bubbles and adjust headspace if needed. Wipe rims of jars with a dampened, clean paper towel. Adjust lids and process.

Recommended process time for Peach Apple Salsa in a boiling-water canner				
		Process Time at Altitudes of		
Style of Pack	Jar Size	0-1,000 ft	1,001-6,000 ft	Above 6,000 ft
Hot	Pints	15 min	20	25

Pie Fillings

General: The following fruit fillings are excellent and safe products. Each canned quart makes one 8-inch to 9-inch pie. The filling may be used as toppings on dessert or pastries. "Clearjel®" is a chemically modified corn starch that produces excellent sauce consistency even after fillings are canned and baked. Other available starches break down when used in these pie fillings, causing a runny sauce consistency. Clearjel® is available only through a few supply outlets and is not currently available in grocery stores. Find out about its availability prior to gathering other ingredients to make these pie fillings. If you cannot find it, ask your county extension family and consumer sciences educator about sources for Clearjel®.

Because the variety of fruit may alter the flavor of the fruit pie, it is suggested that you first make a single quart, make a pie with it, and serve. Then adjust the sugar and spices in the recipe to suit your personal preferences. The amount of lemon juice should not be altered, because it aids in controlling the safety and storage stability of the fillings.

When using frozen cherries and blueberries, select unsweetened fruit. If sugar has been added, rinse it off while fruit is frozen. Thaw fruit, then collect, measure, and use juice from fruit to partially replace the water specified in the recipe. Use only 1/4 cup Clearjel® per quart, or 1-3/4 cups for 7 quarts. Use fresh fruit in the apple and peach pie filling recipes.

Apple Pie Filling

	Quantities of Ingredients Needed for:	
	1 Quart	**7 Quarts**
Blanched, sliced fresh apples	3-1/2 cups	6 quarts
Granulated sugar	3/4 cups + 2 tbsp	5-1/2 cups
Clearjel®	1/4 cup	1-1/2 cups
Cinnamon	1/2 tsp	1 tbsp
Cold water	1/2 cup	2-1/2 cups
Apple juice	3/4 cups	5 cups
Bottled lemon juice	2 tbsp	3/4 cup
Nutmeg (optional)	1/8 tsp	1 tsp
Yellow food coloring (optional)	1 drop	7 drops

Quality: Use firm, crisp apples. Stayman, Golden Delicious, Rome, and other varieties of similar quality are suitable. If apples lack tartness, use an additional 1/4 cup of lemon juice for each 6 quarts of slices.

Yield: 1 quart *or* 7 quarts

Procedure: Wash, peel, and core apples. Prepare slices 1/2-inch wide and place in water containing ascorbic acid to prevent browning. For fresh fruit, place 6 cups at a time in 1 gallon of boiling water. Boil each batch 1 minute after the water returns to a boil. Drain but keep heated fruit in a covered bowl or pot. Combine sugar, Clearjel®, and cinnamon in a large kettle with water and apple juice. If desired, food coloring and nutmeg may be added. Stir and cook on medium high heat until mixture thickens and begins to bubble. Add lemon juice and boil 1 minute, stirring constantly. Fold in drained apple slices immediately and fill hot jars with mixture without delay, leaving 1-inch headspace. Remove air bubbles and adjust headspace if needed. Wipe rims of jars with a dampened, clean paper towel. Adjust lids and process immediately.

Recommended process time for Apple Pie Filling in a boiling-water canner					
		Process Time at Altitudes of			
Style of Pack	**Jar Size**	**0-1,000 ft**	**1,001-3,000 ft**	**3,001-6,000 ft**	**Above 6,000 ft**
Hot	Pints or Quarts	25 min	30	35	40

Blueberry Pie Filling

	Quantities of Ingredients Needed for:	
	1 Quart	**7 Quarts**
Fresh berries or thawed	*3-1/2 cups*	*6 quarts*
Granulated sugar	*3/4 cup + 2 tbsp*	*6 cups*
Clearjel®	*1/4 cup + 1 tbsp*	*2-1/4 cups*
Cold water	*1 cup*	*7 cups*
Bottled lemon juice	*3 tbsp*	*1/2 cup*
Blue food coloring (optional)	*3 drops*	*20 drops*
Red food coloring (optional)	*1 drop*	*7 drops*

Quality: Select fresh, ripe, and firm blueberries. Unsweetened frozen blueberries may be used. If sugar has been added, rinse it off while fruit is still frozen.

Yield: 1 quart *or* 7 quarts

Procedure: Wash and drain fresh blueberries. For fresh fruit, place 6 cups at a time in 1-gallon boiling water. Boil each batch 1 minute after the water returns to a boil. Drain, but keep heated fruit in a covered bowl or pot. Combine sugar and Clearjel® in a large kettle. Stir. Add water and, if desired, food coloring. Cook on medium high heat until mixture thickens and begins to bubble. Add lemon juice and boil 1 minute, stirring constantly. Fold in drained berries immediately and fill hot jars with mixture without delay, leaving 1-inch headspace. Remove air bubbles and adjust headspace if needed. Wipe rims of jars with a dampened, clean paper towel. Adjust lids and process immediately.

Recommended process time for Blueberry Pie Filling in a boiling-water canner					
		Process Time at Altitudes of			
Style of Pack	Jar Size	0-1,000 ft	1,001-3,000 ft	3,001-6,000 ft	Above 6,000 ft
Hot	Pints or Quarts	30 min	35	40	45

Cherry Pie Filling

	Quantities of Ingredients Needed for:	
	1 Quart	**7 Quarts**
Fresh or thawed sour cherries	*3-1/3 cups*	*6 quarts*
Granulated sugar	*1 cup*	*7 cups*
Clearjel®	*1/4 cup + 1 tbsp*	*1-3/4 cups*
Cold water	*1-1/3 cups*	*9-1/3 cups*
Bottled lemon juice	*1 tbsp + 1 tsp*	*1/2 cups*

Cinnamon (optional)	*1/8 tsp*	*1 tsp*
Almond extract (optional)	*1/4 tsp*	*2 tsp*
Red food coloring (optional)	*6 drops*	*1/4 tsp*

Quality: Select fresh, very ripe, and firm cherries. Unsweetened frozen cherries may be used. If sugar has been added, rinse it off while the fruit is still frozen.

Yield: 1 quart or 7 quarts

Procedure: Rinse and pit fresh cherries, and hold in cold water. To prevent stem end browning, use ascorbic acid solution. For fresh fruit, place 6 cups at a time in 1 gallon boiling water. Boil each batch 1 minute after the water returns to a boil. Drain but keep heated in a covered bowl or pot. Combine sugar and Clearjel® in a large saucepan and add water. If desired, add cinnamon, almond extract, and food coloring. Stir mixture and cook over medium high heat until mixture thickens and begins to bubble. Add lemon juice and boil 1 minute, stirring constantly. Fold in drained cherries immediately and fill hot jars with mixture without delay, leaving 1-inch headspace. Remove air bubbles and adjust headspace if needed. Wipe rims of jars with a dampened, clean paper towel. Adjust lids and process immediately.

Recommended process time for Cherry Pie Filling in a boiling-water canner					
		Process Time at Altitudes of			
Style of Pack	**Jar Size**	**0-1,000 ft**	**1,001-3,000 ft**	**3,001-6,000 ft**	**Above 6,000 ft**
Hot	Pints or Quarts	30 min	35	40	45

Festive Mincemeat Pie Filling

2 cups finely chopped suet
4 lbs ground beef or 4 lb ground venison and 1 lb sausage
5 qts chopped apples

2 lbs dark seedless raisins

1 lb white raisins

2 qts apple cider

2 tbsp ground cinnamon

2 tsp ground nutmeg

5 cups sugar

2 tbsp salt

Yield: About 7 quarts

Procedure: Cook meat and suet in water to avoid browning. Peel, core, and quarter apples. Put meat, suet, and apples through food grinder using a medium blade. Combine all ingredients in a large saucepan, and simmer 1 hour or until slightly thickened. Stir often. Fill hot jars with mixture without delay, leaving 1-inch headspace. Remove air bubbles and adjust headspace if needed. Wipe rims of jars with a dampened, clean paper towel. Adjust lids and process.

Recommended process time for Festive Mincemeat Pie Filling in a dial-gauge pressure canner						
			Canner Pressure (PSI) at Altitudes of			
Style of Pack	Jar Size	Process Time	0-2,000 ft	2,001-4,000 ft	4,001-6,000 ft	6,001-8,000 ft
Hot	Quarts	90 min	11 lb	12 lb	13 lb	14 lb

Recommended process time for Festive Mincemeat Pie Filling in a weighted-gauge pressure canner				
			Canner Pressure (PSI) at Altitudes of	
Style of Pack	Jar Size	Process Time	0-1,000 ft	Above 1,000 ft
Hot	Quarts	90 min	10 lb	15 lb

Green Tomato Pie Filling

4 qts chopped green tomatoes

3 qts peeled and chopped tart apples

1 lb dark seedless raisins

1 lb white raisins

1/4 cup minced citron, lemon, or orange peel

2 cups water

2-1/2 cups brown sugar

2-1/2 cups white sugar

1/2 cup vinegar (5%)

1 cup bottled lemon juice

2 tbsp ground cinnamon

1 tsp ground nutmeg

1 tsp ground cloves

Yield: About 7 quarts

Procedure: Combine all ingredients in a large saucepan. Cook slowly, stirring often, until tender and slightly thickened (about 35 to 40 minutes). Fill hot jars with hot mixture, leaving 1/2-inch headspace. Remove air bubbles and adjust headspace if needed. Wipe rims of jars with a dampened, clean paper towel. Adjust lids and process.

Recommended process time for Green Tomato Pie Filling in a boiling-water canner				
		Process Time at Altitudes of		
Style of Pack	Jar Size	0-1,000 ft	1,001-6,000 ft	Above 6,000 ft
Hot	Quarts	15 min	20	25

Peach Pie Filling

	Quantities of Ingredients Needed for:	
	1 Quart	**7 Quarts**
Sliced fresh peaches	*3-1/2 cups*	*6 quarts*
Granulated sugar	*1 cup*	*7 cups*
Clearjel®	*1/4 cup + 1 tbsp*	*2 cups + 3 tbsp*
Cold water	*3/4 cup*	*5-1/4 cups*
Cinnamon (optional)	*1/8 tsp*	*1 tsp*
Almond extract (optional)	*1/8 tsp*	*1 tsp*
Bottled lemon juice	*1/4 cup*	*1-3/4 cups*

Quality: Select ripe but firm fresh peaches. Red Haven, Redskin, Sun High, and other varieties of similar quality are suitable.

Yield: 1 quart *or* 7 quarts

Procedure: Peel peaches. To loosen skins, submerge peaches in boiling water for approximately 30 to 60 seconds, and then place in cold water for 20 seconds. Slip off skins and prepare slices 1/2-inch thick. Place slices in water containing 1/2 tsp of ascorbic acid crystals or six 500-milligram vitamin C tablets in 1 gallon of water to prevent browning. For fresh fruit, place 6 cups at a time in 1 gallon boiling water. Boil each batch 1 minute after the water returns to a boil. Drain but keep heated fruit in a covered bowl or pot. Combine water, sugar, Clearjel®, and, if desired, cinnamon and/or almond extract in a large kettle. Stir and cook over medium high heat until mixture thickens and begins to bubble. Add lemon juice and boil sauce 1 minute more, stirring constantly. Fold in drained peach slices and continue to heat mixture for 3 minutes. Fill hot jars without delay, leaving 1-inch headspace. Remove air bubbles and adjust headspace if needed. Wipe rims of jars with a dampened, clean paper towel. Adjust lids and process immediately.

Recommended process time for Peach Pie Filling in a boiling-water canner					
		Process Time at Altitudes of			
Style of Pack	**Jar Size**	**0-1,000 ft**	**1,001-3,000 ft**	**3,001-6,000 ft**	**Above 6,000 ft**
Hot	Pints or Quarts	30 min	35	40	45

Process times for some acid foods in a dial-gauge pressure canner							
				Canner Pressure (PSI) at Altitudes of			
Type of Fruit	**Style of Pack**	**Jar Size**	**Process Time (Min)**	**0-2,000 ft**	**2,001-4,000 ft**	**4,001-6,000 ft**	**6,001-8,000 ft**
Applesauce	Hot	Pints	8	6 lb	7 lb	8 lb	9 lb
Applesauce	Hot	Quarts	10	6	7	8	9
Apples, sliced	Hot	Pints or Quarts	8	6	7	8	9
Berries, whole	Hot	Pints or Quarts	8	6	7	8	9
	Raw	Pints	8	6	7	8	9
	Raw	Quarts	10	6	7	8	9
Cherries, sweet	Hot	Pints	8	6	7	8	9
	Hot	Quarts	10	6	7	8	9
	Raw	Pints or Quarts	10	6	7	8	9
Fruit Purees	Hot	Pints or Quarts	8	6	7	8	9
Grapefruit and Orange Sections	Hot	Pints or Quarts	8	6	7	8	9
	Raw	Pints	8	6	7	8	9
	Raw	Quarts	10	6	7	8	9

Process times for some acid foods in a dial-gauge pressure canner				Canner Pressure (PSI) at Altitudes of			
Type of Fruit	Style of Pack	Jar Size	Process Time (Min)	0-2,000 ft	2,001-4,000 ft	4,001-6,000 ft	6,001-8,000 ft
Peaches, Apricots, and Nectarines	Hot and Raw	Pints or Quarts	10	6	7	8	9
Pears	Hot	Pints or Quarts	10	6	7	8	9
Plums	Hot and Raw	Pints or Quarts	10	6	7	8	9
Rhubarb	Hot	Pints or Quarts	8	6	7	8	9

Process times for some acid foods in a weighted-gauge pressure canner				Canner Pressure (PSI) at Altitudes of	
Type of Fruit	Style of Pack	Jar Size	Process Time (Min)	0-1,000 ft	Above 1,000 ft
Applesauce	Hot	Pints	8	5 lb	10 lb
	Hot	Quarts	10	5	10
Apples, sliced	Hot	Pints or Quarts	8	5	10
Berries, whole	Hot	Pints or Quarts	8	5	10
	Raw	Pints	8	5	10
	Raw	Quarts	10	5	10
Cherries, sweet	Hot	Pints	8	5	10
	Hot	Quarts	10	5	10
	Raw	Pints or Quarts	10	5	10
Fruit Purees	Hot	Pints or Quarts	8	5	10

Process times for some acid foods in a weighted-gauge pressure canner					
				Canner Pressure (PSI) at Altitudes of	
Type of Fruit	Style of Pack	Jar Size	Process Time (Min)	0- 1,000 ft	Above 1,000 ft
Grapefruit and Orange Sections	Hot	Pints or Quarts	8	5	10
	Raw	Pints	8	5	10
	Raw	Quarts	10	5	10
Peaches, Apricots, and Nectarines	Hot and Raw	Pints or Quarts	10	5	10
Pears	Hot	Pints or Quarts	10	5	10
Plums	Hot and Raw	Pints or Quarts	10	5	10
Rhubarb	Hot	Pints or Quarts	8	5	10

Appendix B

Canning Tomatoes and Tomato Products

— Courtesy of the USDA

General

Quality: Select only disease-free, preferably vine-ripened, firm fruit for canning.

Caution: Do not can tomatoes from dead or frost-killed vines. Green tomatoes are more acidic than ripened fruit and can be canned safely with any of the following recommendations.

Acidification: To ensure safe acidity in whole, crushed, or juiced tomatoes, add 2 tablespoons of bottled lemon juice or 1/2 teaspoon of citric acid per quart of tomatoes. For pints, use 1 tablespoon bottled lemon juice or 1/4 teaspoon citric acid. Acid can be added directly to the jars before filling with product. Add sugar to offset acid taste, if desired. Four tablespoons of a 5 percent acidity vinegar per quart may be used instead of lemon juice or citric acid. However, vinegar may cause undesirable flavor changes.

When a procedure in this guide for canning tomatoes offers both boiling water and pressure canning options, all steps in the preparation ("Procedure") are still required even if the pressure processing option is chosen. This includes acidification. The boiling water and pressure alternatives are equal processes with different time/temperature combinations calculated for these products.

Recommendation: Use of a pressure canner will result in higher quality and more nutritious canned tomato products. If your pressure canner cannot be operated above 15 PSI, select a process time at a lower pressure.

Tomato Juice

Quantity: An average of 23 pounds is needed per canner load of 7 quarts, or an average of 14 pounds per canner load of 9 pints. A bushel weighs 53 pounds and yields 15 to 18 quarts of juice — an average of 3-1/4 pounds per quart.

Procedure: Wash, remove stems, and trim off bruised or discolored portions. To prevent juice from separating, quickly cut about 1 pound of fruit into quarters and put directly into saucepan. Heat immediately to boiling while crushing. Continue to slowly add and crush freshly cut tomato quarters to the boiling mixture. Make sure the mixture boils constantly and vigorously while you add the remaining tomatoes. Simmer 5 minutes after you add all pieces.

If you are not concerned about juice separation, simply slice or quarter tomatoes into a large saucepan. Crush, heat, and simmer for 5 minutes before juicing.

Press both types of heated juice through a sieve or food mill to remove skins and seeds. Add bottled lemon juice or citric acid to jars. See acidification instructions on page 231. Heat juice again to boiling. Add 1 teaspoon of salt per quart to the jars, if desired. Fill hot jars with hot tomato juice, leaving 1/2-inch headspace. Wipe rims of jars with a dampened clean paper towel. Adjust lids and process. (Acidification is still required for the pressure canning options; follow all steps in the procedures above for any of the processing options.)

Recommended process time for Tomato Juice in a boiling-water canner					
		Process Time at Altitudes of			
Style of Pack	Jar Size	0-1,000 ft	1,001- 3,000 ft	3,001- 6,000 ft	Above 6,000 ft
Hot	Pints	35 min	40	45	50
	Quarts	40	45	50	55

Recommended process time for Tomato Juice in a dial-gauge pressure canner						
			Canner Pressure (PSI) at Altitudes of			
Style of Pack	Jar Size	Process Time	0-2,000 ft	2,001- 4,000 ft	4,001- 6,000 ft	6,001- 8,000 ft
Hot	Pints or Quarts	20 min	6 lb	7 lb	8 lb	9 lb
		15	11	12	13	14

Recommended process time for Tomato Juice in a weighted-gauge pressure canner				
			Canner Pressure (PSI) at Altitudes of	
Style of Pack	Jar Size	Process Time	0-1,000 ft	Above 1,000 ft
Hot	Pints or Quarts	20 min	5 lb	10 lb
		15	10	15
		10	15	Not recommended

Tomato and Vegetable Juice Blend

Quantity: An average of 22 pounds of tomatoes is needed per canner load of 7 quarts. No more than 3 cups of other vegetables may be added for each 22 pounds of tomatoes.

Procedure: Crush and simmer tomatoes as for making tomato juice (see page 232). Add no more than 3 cups of any combination of finely chopped celery, onions, carrots, and peppers for each 22 lbs of tomatoes. Simmer mixture 20 minutes. Press hot, cooked tomatoes and vegetables through a sieve or food mill to remove skins and seeds. Add bottled lemon juice or citric acid to jars. See acidification directions on page 231. Add 1 teaspoon of salt per quart to the jars, if desired. Reheat tomato-vegetable juice blend to boiling and fill immediately into hot jars, leaving 1/2-inch headspace. Wipe rims of jars with a dampened clean paper towel. Adjust lids and process. (Acidification is still required for the pressure canning options; follow all steps in the procedures above for any of the processing options.)

Recommended process time for Tomato-Vegetable Blend in a boiling-water canner					
		Process Time at Altitudes of			
Style of Pack	Jar Size	0-1,000 ft	1,001-3,000 ft	3,001-6,000 ft	Above 6,000 ft
Hot	Pints	35 min	40	45	50
	Quarts	40	45	50	55

Recommended process time for Tomato-Vegetable Blend in a dial-gauge pressure canner						
			Canner Pressure (PSI) at Altitudes of			
Style of Pack	Jar Size	Process Time	0-2,000 ft	2,001-4,000 ft	4,001-6,000 ft	6,001-8,000 ft
Hot	Pints or Quarts	20 min	6 lb	7 lb	8 lb	9 lb
		15	11	12	13	14

			Canner Pressure (PSI) at Altitudes of	
Style of Pack	Jar Size	Process Time	0-1,000 ft	Above 1,000 ft
Hot	Pints or Quarts	20 min	5 lb	10 lb
		15	10	15
		10	15	Not recommended

Recommended process time for Tomato-Vegetable Blend in a weighted-gauge pressure canner

Tomatoes — Crushed (with no added liquid)

A high-quality product, ideally suited for use in soups, stews, and casseroles. This recipe is similar to that formerly referred to as "Quartered Tomatoes."

Quantity: An average of 22 pounds is needed per canner load of 7 quarts; an average of 14 fresh pounds is needed per canner load of 9 pints. A bushel weighs 53 pounds and yields 17 to 20 quarts of crushed tomatoes — an average of 2-3/4 pounds per quart.

Procedure: Wash tomatoes and dip in boiling water for 30 to 60 seconds or until skins split. Then dip in cold water, slip off skins, and remove cores. Trim off any bruised or discolored portions and quarter. Heat 1/6 of the quarters quickly in a large pot, crushing them with a wooden mallet or spoon as they are added to the pot. This will exude juice. Continue heating the tomatoes, stirring to prevent burning. Once the tomatoes are boiling, gradually add remaining quartered tomatoes, stirring constantly. These remaining tomatoes do not need to be crushed. They will soften with heating and stirring. Continue until all tomatoes are added. Then boil gently 5 minutes. Add bottled lemon juice or citric acid to jars. See acidification directions on page 231. Add 1 teaspoon of salt per quart to the jars, if desired. Fill hot jars immediately with hot tomatoes, leaving 1/2-inch headspace. Remove air bubbles and adjust headspace if needed. Wipe rims of jars with a dampened clean paper towel. Adjust lids and process. (Acidification is still required for the pressure canning options; follow all steps in the procedures above for any of the processing options.)

Recommended process time for Crushed Tomatoes in a boiling-water canner					
		Process Time at Altitudes of			
Style of Pack	Jar Size	0-1,000 ft	1,001-3,000 ft	3,001-6,000 ft	Above 6,000 ft
Hot	Pints	35 min	40	45	50
	Quarts	45	50	55	60

Recommended process time for Crushed Tomatoes in a dial-gauge pressure canner						
			Canner Pressure (PSI) at Altitudes of			
Style of Pack	Jar Size	Process Time	0-2,000 ft	2,001-4,000 ft	4,001-6,000 ft	6,001-8,000 ft
Hot	Pints or Quarts	20 min	6 lb	7 lb	8 lb	9 lb
		15	11	12	13	14

Recommended process time for Crushed Tomatoes in a weighted-gauge pressure canner				
			Canner Pressure (PSI) at Altitudes of	
Style of Pack	Jar Size	Process Time	0-1,000 ft	Above 1,000 ft
Hot	Pints or Quarts	20 min	5 lb	10 lb
		15	10	15
		10	15	Not recommended

Standard Tomato Sauce

Quantity: For thin sauce — an average of 35 pounds is needed per canner load of 7 quarts; an average of 21 pounds is needed per canner load of 9 pints. A bushel weighs 53 pounds and yields 10 to 12 quarts of sauce — an average of 5 pounds per quart. For thick sauce — an average of 46 pounds is needed per canner load of 7 quarts; an average of 28 pounds is needed per canner load of 9 pints. A bushel weighs 53 pounds and yields 7 to 9 quarts of thick sauce — an average of 6-1/2 pounds per quart.

Procedure: Prepare and press as for making tomato juice. Simmer in large-diameter saucepan until sauce reaches desired consistency. Boil until volume is reduced by about 1/3 for thin sauce, or by 1/2 for thick sauce. Add bottled lemon juice or citric acid to jars. See acidification directions on page 231. Add 1 teaspoon of salt per quart to the jars, if desired. Fill hot jars, leaving 1/4-inch headspace. Remove air bubbles and adjust headspace if needed. Wipe rims of jars with a dampened clean paper towel. Adjust lids and process. (Acidification is still required for the pressure canning options; follow all steps in the procedures above for any of the processing options.)

Recommended process time for Standard Tomato Sauce in a boiling-water canner					
		Process Time at Altitudes of			
Style of Pack	Jar Size	0-1,000 ft	1,001-3,000 ft	3,001-6,000 ft	Above 6,000 ft
Hot	Pints	35 min	40	45	50
	Quarts	40	45	50	55

Recommended process time for Standard Tomato Sauce in a dial-gauge pressure canner						
			Canner Pressure (PSI) at Altitudes of			
Style of Pack	Jar Size	Process Time	0-2,000 ft	2,001-4,000 ft	4,001-6,000 ft	6,001-8,000 ft
Hot	Pints or Quarts	20 min	6 lb	7 lb	8 lb	9 lb
		15	11	12	13	14

Recommended process time for Standard Tomato Sauce in a weighted-gauge pressure canner				
			Canner Pressure (PSI) at Altitudes of	
Style of Pack	Jar Size	Process Time	0-1,000 ft	Above 1,000 ft
Hot	Pints or Quarts	20 min	5 lb	10 lb
		15	10	15
		10	15	Not recommended

Tomatoes — Whole or Halved (packed in water)

Quantity: An average of 21 pounds is needed per canner load of 7 quarts; an average of 13 pounds is needed per canner load of 9 pints. A bushel weighs 53 pounds and yields 15 to 21 quarts — an average of 3 pounds per quart.

Procedure for hot or raw tomatoes filled with water in jars: Wash tomatoes. Dip in boiling water for 30 to 60 seconds or until skins split; then dip in cold water. Slip off skins and remove cores. Leave whole or halve. Add bottled lemon juice or citric acid to jars. Add 1 teaspoon of salt per quart to the jars, if desired. For hot pack products, add enough water to cover the tomatoes and boil them gently for 5 minutes. Fill hot jars with hot tomatoes or with raw peeled tomatoes. Add the hot cooking liquid to the hot pack, or hot water for raw pack to cover, leaving 1/2-inch headspace. Remove air bubbles and adjust headspace if needed. Wipe rims of jars with a dampened clean paper towel. Adjust lids and process. (Acidification is still required for the pressure canning options; follow all steps in the procedures above for any of the processing options.)

Recommended process time for Water-Packed Whole Tomatoes in a boiling-water canner					
		Process Time at Altitudes of			
Style of Pack	Jar Size	0-1,000 ft	1,001-3,000 ft	3,001-6,000 ft	Above 6,000 ft
Hot and Raw	Pints	40 min	45	50	55
	Quarts	45	50	55	60

Recommended process time for Water-Packed Whole Tomatoes in a dial-gauge pressure canner						
			Canner Pressure (PSI) at Altitudes of			
Style of Pack	Jar Size	Process Time	0-2,000 ft	2,001-4,000 ft	4,001-6,000 ft	6,001-8,000 ft
Hot and Raw	Pints or Quarts	15 min	6 lb	7 lb	8 lb	9 lb
		10	11	12	13	14

Recommended process time for Water-Packed Whole Tomatoes in a weighted-gauge pressure canner				
			Canner Pressure (PSI) at Altitudes of	
Style of Pack	Jar Size	Process Time	0-1,000 ft	Above 1,000 ft
Hot or Raw	Pints or Quarts	15 min	5 lb	10 lb
		10	10	15
		1	15	Not recommended

Tomatoes — Whole or Halved (packed in tomato juice)

Quantity: See whole tomatoes packed in water.

Procedure: Wash tomatoes. Dip in boiling water for 30 to 60 seconds or until skins split, then dip in cold water. Slip off skins and remove cores.

Leave whole or halve. Add bottled lemon juice or citric acid to the jars. Add 1 teaspoon of salt per quart to the jars, if desired.

Raw pack — Heat tomato juice in a saucepan. Fill hot jars with raw tomatoes, leaving 1/2-inch headspace. Cover tomatoes in the jars with hot tomato juice, leaving 1/2-inch headspace.

Hot pack — Put tomatoes in a large saucepan and add enough tomato juice to completely cover them. Boil tomatoes and juice gently for 5 minutes. Fill hot jars with hot tomatoes, leaving 1/2-inch headspace. Add hot tomato juice to the jars to cover the tomatoes, leaving 1/2-inch headspace.

Remove air bubbles and adjust headspace if needed. Wipe rims of jars with a dampened clean paper towel. Adjust lids and process. (Acidification is still required for the pressure canning options; follow all steps in the procedures above for any of the processing options.)

Recommended process time for Tomato Juice-Packed Whole Tomatoes in a boiling-water canner					
		Process Time at Altitudes of			
Style of Pack	Jar Size	0-1,000 ft	1,001-3,000 ft	3,001-6,000 ft	Above 6,000 ft
Hot and Raw	Pints or Quarts	85 min	90	95	100

Recommended process time for Tomato Juice-Packed Whole Tomatoes in a dial-gauge pressure canner						
			Canner Pressure (PSI) at Altitudes of			
Style of Pack	Jar Size	Process Time	0-2,000 ft	2,001-4,000 ft	4,001-6,000 ft	6,001-8,000 ft
Hot and Raw	Pints or Quarts	40 min	6 lb	7 lb	8 lb	9 lb
		25	11	12	13	14

Recommended process time for Tomato Juice-Packed Whole Tomatoes in a weighted-gauge pressure canner				
			Canner Pressure (PSI) at Altitudes of	
Style of Pack	Jar Size	Process Time	0-1,000 ft	Above 1,000 ft
Hot or Raw	Pints or Quarts	40 min	5 lb	10 lb
		25	10	15
		15	15	Not recommended

Tomatoes — Whole or Halved (packed raw without added liquid)

Quantity: See whole tomatoes packed in water.

Procedure: Wash tomatoes. Dip in boiling water for 30 to 60 seconds or until skins split, then dip in cold water. Slip off skins and remove cores. Leave whole or halve. Add bottled lemon juice or citric acid to the jars. Add 1 teaspoon of salt per quart to the jars, if desired.

Fill hot jars with raw tomatoes, leaving 1/2-inch headspace. Press tomatoes in the jars until spaces between them fill with juice. Leave 1/2-inch headspace. Remove air bubbles and adjust headspace if needed. Wipe rims of jars with a dampened clean paper towel. Adjust lids and process. (Acidification is still required for the pressure canning options; follow all steps in the procedures above for any of the processing options.)

Recommended process time for Raw Whole Tomatoes Without Added Liquid in a boiling-water canner					
		Process Time at Altitudes of			
Style of Pack	Jar Size	0-1,000 ft	1,001- 3,000 ft	3,001- 6,000 ft	Above 6,000 ft
Raw	Pints or Quarts	85 min	90	95	100

Recommended process time for Raw Whole Tomatoes Without Added Liquid in a dial-gauge pressure canner						
			Canner Pressure (PSI) at Altitudes of			
Style of Pack	Jar Size	Process Time	0-2,000 ft	2,001-4,000 ft	4,001-6,000 ft	6,001-8,000 ft
Hot and Raw	Pints or Quarts	40 min	6 lb	7 lb	8 lb	9 lb
		25	11	12	13	14

Recommended process time for Raw Whole Tomatoes Without Added Liquid in a weighted-gauge pressure canner				
			Canner Pressure (PSI) at Altitudes of	
Style of Pack	Jar Size	Process Time	0-1,000 ft	Above 1,000 ft
Hot or Raw	Pints or Quarts	40 min	5 lb	10 lb
		25	10	15
		15	15	Not recommended

Tomatoes with Okra or Zucchini

Quantity: An average of 12 pounds of tomatoes and 4 pounds of okra or zucchini is needed per canner load of 7 quarts. An average of 7 pounds of tomatoes and 2-1/2 pounds of okra or zucchini is needed per canner load of 9 pints. (Use about 3 pounds tomatoes to 1 pound vegetable.)

Procedure: Wash tomatoes and okra or zucchini. Dip tomatoes in boiling water 30 to 60 seconds or until skins split. Then dip in cold water, slip off skins and remove cores, and quarter. Trim stems from okra and slice into 1-inch pieces or leave whole. Slice or cube zucchini if used. Bring tomatoes to a boil and simmer 10 minutes. Add okra or zucchini and boil gently 5 minutes. Add 1 teaspoon of salt for each quart to the jars, if desired. Fill hot jars with mixture, leaving 1-inch headspace. Remove air bubbles and adjust headspace if needed. Wipe rims of jars with a dampened clean paper towel. Adjust lids and process.

Variation: You may add 4 or 5 pearl onions or 2 onion slices to each jar.

Recommended process time for Tomatoes with Okra or Zucchini in a dial-gauge pressure canner						
			Canner Pressure (PSI) at Altitudes of			
Style of Pack	Jar Size	Process Time	0-2,000 ft	2,001-4,000 ft	4,001-6,000 ft	6,001-8,000 ft
Hot	Pints	30 min	11 lb	12 lb	13 lb	14 lb
	Quarts	35	11	12	13	14

Recommended process time for Tomatoes with Okra or Zucchini in a weighted-gauge pressure canner				
			Canner Pressure (PSI) at Altitudes of	
Style of Pack	Jar Size	Process Time	0-1,000 ft	Above 1,000 ft
Hot	Pints	30 min	10 lb	15 lb
	Quarts	35	10	15

Tomatillos

Quantity: An average of 14 pounds is needed per canner load of 7 quarts; an average of 9 pounds is needed per canner load of 9 pints. A bushel weighs 32 pounds and yields 14 to 16 quarts — an average of 2 pounds per quart.

Quality: Select unblemished, firm, deep, bright green tomatillos with a dry papery husk.

Procedure: Remove the dry outer husks entirely from the tomatillos and wash the fruit well. Leave whole; do not peel or remove seeds. Add bottled lemon juice or citric acid to jars. Follow the acidification amounts for tomatoes on page 231. Add enough water to cover the tomatillos in a large saucepan and boil them gently until tender, about 5 to 10 minutes. Drain and fill hot tomatillos loosely into hot jars, leaving 1/2-inch headspace. Fill hot jars with boiling water, leaving 1/2-inch headspace. Remove air bubbles and adjust headspace if needed. Wipe rims of jars with a dampened clean paper towel. Adjust lids and process.

Process the same as Water-Packed Whole Tomatoes, hot pack, on page 238.

Spaghetti Sauce without Meat

30 lbs tomatoes
1 cup chopped onions
5 cloves garlic, minced
1 cup chopped celery or green peppers
1 lb fresh mushrooms, sliced (optional)
4-1/2 tsp salt
2 tbsp oregano
4 tbsp minced parsley
2 tsp black pepper
1/4 cup brown sugar
1/4 cup vegetable oil

Yield: About 9 pints

Procedure: Caution: Do not increase the proportion of onions, peppers, or mushrooms. Wash tomatoes and dip in boiling water for 30 to 60 seconds or until skins split. Dip in cold water and slip off skins. Remove cores and quarter tomatoes. Boil 20 minutes, uncovered, in large saucepan. Put through food mill or sieve. Saute onions, garlic, celery or peppers, and mushrooms (if desired) in vegetable oil until tender. Combine sauteed vegetables and tomatoes and add remainder of spices, salt, and sugar. Bring to a boil. Simmer, uncovered, until thick enough for serving. At this time, the initial volume will have been reduced by nearly one-half. Stir frequently to avoid burning. Fill hot jars, leaving 1-inch headspace. Remove air bubbles and adjust headspace if needed. Wipe rims of jars with a dampened clean paper towel. Adjust lids and process.

Recommended process time for Spaghetti Sauce Without Meat in a dial-gauge pressure canner						
			Canner Pressure (PSI) at Altitudes of			
Style of Pack	Jar Size	Process Time	0-2,000 ft	2,001-4,000 ft	4,001-6,000 ft	6,001-8,000 ft
Hot	Pints	20 min	11 lb	12 lb	13 lb	14 lb
	Quarts	25	11	12	13	14

Recommended process time for Spaghetti Sauce Without Meat in a weighted-gauge pressure canner				
			Canner Pressure (PSI) at Altitudes of	
Style of Pack	Jar Size	Process Time	0-1,000 ft	Above 1,000 ft
Hot	Pints	20 min	10 lb	15 lb
	Quarts	25	10	15

Spaghetti Sauce with Meat

30 lbs tomatoes

2-1/2 lbs ground beef or sausage

5 cloves garlic, minced

1 cup chopped onions

1 cup chopped celery or green peppers

1 lb fresh mushrooms, sliced (optional)

4-1/2 tsp salt

2 tbsp oregano

4 tbsp minced parsley

2 tsp black pepper

1/4 cup brown sugar

Yield: About 9 pints

Procedure: To prepare tomatoes, follow directions for Spaghetti Sauce without Meat. Saute beef or sausage until brown. Add garlic, onion, celery or green pepper, and mushrooms, if desired. Cook until vegetables are tender. Combine with tomato pulp in large saucepan. Add spices, salt, and sugar. Bring to a boil. Simmer, uncovered, until thick enough for serving. At this time initial volume will have been reduced by nearly one-half. Stir frequently to avoid burning. Fill hot jars, leaving 1-inch headspace. Remove air bubbles and adjust head-space if needed. Wipe rims of jars with a dampened clean paper towel. Adjust lids and process.

Recommended process time for Spaghetti Sauce With Meat in a dial-gauge pressure canner						
			Canner Pressure (PSI) at Altitudes of			
Style of Pack	Jar Size	Process Time	0-2,000 ft	2,001-4,000 ft	4,001-6,000 ft	6,001-8,000 ft
Hot	Pints	60 min	11 lb	12 lb	13 lb	14 lb
	Quarts	70	11	12	13	14

Recommended process time for Spaghetti Sauce With Meat in a weighted-gauge pressure canner				
			Canner Pressure (PSI) at Altitudes of	
Style of Pack	Jar Size	Process Time	0-1,000 ft	Above 1,000 ft
Hot	Pints	60 min	10 lb	15 lb
	Quarts	70	10	15

Mexican Tomato Sauce

2-1/2 to 3 lbs chile peppers

18 lbs tomatoes

3 cups chopped onions

1 tbsp salt

1 tbsp oregano

1/2 cup vinegar

Yield: About 7 quarts

Procedure: Caution: Wear plastic or rubber gloves and do not touch your face while handling or cutting hot peppers. If you do not wear gloves, wash hands thoroughly with soap and water before touching your face or eyes. Wash and dry chiles. Slit each pepper along the side to allow steam to escape. Blister skins using one of these two methods:

Oven or broiler method to blister skins: Place peppers in a hot oven (400 degrees F) or under a broiler for 6 to 8 minutes until skins blister.

Range-top method to blister skins: Cover hot burner (either gas or electric) with heavy wire mesh. Place peppers on burner for several minutes until skins blister.

After blistering skins, place peppers in a pan and cover with a damp cloth. (This will make peeling the peppers easier.) Cool several minutes; peel off skins. Discard seeds and chop peppers. Wash tomatoes and dip in boiling water for 30 to 60 seconds or until skins split. Dip in cold water, slip off skins, and remove cores. Coarsely chop tomatoes and combine chopped peppers and remaining ingredients in large saucepan. Bring to a boil. Cover. Reduce heat and simmer 10 minutes. Fill hot jars, leaving 1-inch headspace. Remove air bubbles and adjust headspace if needed. Wipe rims of jars with a dampened clean paper towel. Adjust lids and process.

Recommended process time for Mexican Tomato Sauce in a dial-gauge pressure canner						
			Canner Pressure (PSI) at Altitudes of			
Style of Pack	Jar Size	Process Time	0-2,000 ft	2,001- 4,000 ft	4,001- 6,000 ft	6,001- 8,000 ft
Hot	Pints	20 min	11 lb	12 lb	13 lb	14 lb
	Quarts	25	11	12	13	14

Recommended process time for Mexican Tomato Sauce in a weighted-gauge pressure canner				
			Canner Pressure (PSI) at Altitudes of	
Style of Pack	Jar Size	Process Time	0-1,000 ft	Above 1,000 ft
Hot	Pints	20 min	10 lb	15 lb
	Quarts	25	10	15

Easy Hot Sauce

8 cups (64 ounces) canned, diced tomatoes, undrained

1-1/2 cups seeded, chopped Serrano peppers

4 cups distilled white vinegar (5%)

2 tsp canning salt

2 tbsp whole mixed pickling spices

Yield: About 4 half-pints

Procedure: Caution: Wear plastic or rubber gloves and do not touch your face while handling or cutting hot peppers. If you do not wear gloves, wash hands thoroughly with soap and water before touching your face or eyes. Place mixed pickling spices in a spice bag and tie the ends firmly. Mix all ingredients in a Dutch oven or large saucepot. Bring to a boil, stirring occasionally. Simmer another 20 minutes, until tomatoes are soft. Press mixture through a food mill. Return the liquid to the stockpot, heat to boiling and boil for another 15 minutes. Fill hot sauce into hot half-pint jars, leaving 1/4-inch headspace. Remove air bubbles and adjust headspace if needed. Wipe rims of jars with a dampened clean paper towel. Adjust lids and process.

Recommended process time for Easy Hot Sauce in a boiling-water canner				
		Process Time at Altitudes of		
Style of Pack	Jar Size	0-1,000 ft	1,001-6,000 ft	Above 6,000 ft
Hot	Half-pints	10 min	15	20

Cayenne Pepper Sauce

3 lbs hot peppers (for example, Anaheim, Hungarian, Jalapenos)

1/3 cup minced garlic

4 cups sliced onion

1/3 cup stemmed, chopped cilantro

3 cans (28 ounces each) diced tomatoes

3 cups cider vinegar (5%)

2-1/2 cups water

Yield: About 5 pints

Procedure: Caution: Wear plastic or rubber gloves and do not touch your face while handling or cutting hot peppers. If you do not wear gloves, wash hands thoroughly with soap and water before touching your face or eyes. Wash, trim, and slice peppers and onions into rings, using a mandolin slicer or a food processor. In a 10-quart Dutch oven or stockpot, mix together all ingredients. Bring to a boil and boil 1 hour. Reduce heat slightly and simmer 1 additional hour. Turn heat off, and cool mixture slightly. Puree vegetables in a blender about 2 minutes per blender batch. Return pureed mixture to stockpot and bring carefully just to a boil. (The mixture will start to spatter as it gets close to boiling; heat slowly while stirring constantly, being careful not to get burned by splashing sauce.) Turn off heat. Fill hot sauce into hot pint jars, leaving 1/2-inch headspace. Remove air bubbles and adjust headspace if needed. Wipe rims of jars with a dampened clean paper towel. Adjust lids and process.

Recommended process time for Cayenne Pepper Sauce in a boiling-water canner				
		Process Time at Altitudes of		
Style of Pack	Jar Size	0-1,000 ft	1,001-6,000 ft	Above 6,000 ft
Hot	Pints	10 min	15	20

Tomato Ketchup

24 lbs ripe tomatoes

3 cups chopped onions

3/4 tsp ground red pepper (cayenne)

3 cups cider vinegar (5%)

4 tsp whole cloves

3 sticks cinnamon, crushed

1-1/2 tsp whole allspice

3 tbsp celery seeds

1-1/2 cups sugar

1/4 cup salt

Yield: 6 to 7 pints

Procedure: Wash tomatoes. Dip in boiling water for 30 to 60 seconds or until skins split. Dip in cold water. Slip off skins and remove cores. Quarter tomatoes into 4-gallon stockpot or a large kettle. Add onions and red pepper. Bring to a boil and simmer 20 minutes, uncovered. Cover, turn off heat and let stand for 20 minutes. Combine spices in a spice bag and add to vinegar in a 2-quart saucepan. Bring to boil. Remove spice bag and combine vinegar and tomato mixture. Boil about 30 minutes. Put boiled mixture through a food mill or sieve. Return to pot. Add sugar and salt, boil gently, and stir frequently until volume is reduced by one-half or until mixture rounds up on spoon without separation. Fill hot pint jars, leaving 1/8-inch headspace. Remove air bubbles and adjust headspace if needed.

Wipe rims of jars with a dampened clean paper towel. Adjust lids and process.

Recommended process time for Tomato Ketchup in a boiling-water canner				
		Process Time at Altitudes of		
Style of Pack	Jar Size	0-1,000 ft	1,001-6,000 ft	Above 6,000 ft
Hot	Pints	15 min	20	25

Country Western Ketchup

24 lbs ripe tomatoes

5 chile peppers, sliced and seeded

1/4 cup salt

2-2/3 cups vinegar (5%)

1-1/4 cups sugar

1/2 tsp ground red pepper (cayenne)

4 tsp paprika

4 tsp whole allspice

4 tsp dry mustard

1 tbsp whole peppercorns

1 tsp mustard seeds

1 tbsp bay leaves

Yield: 6 to 7 pints

Procedure: Follow procedure and process time for regular tomato ketchup.

Blender Ketchup

Use an electric blender and eliminate the need for pressing or sieving.

> *24 lbs ripe tomatoes*
> *2 lbs onions*
> *1 lb sweet red peppers*
> *1 lb sweet green peppers*
> *9 cups vinegar (5%)*
> *9 cups sugar*
> *1/4 cup canning or pickling salt*
> *3 tbsp dry mustard*
> *1-1/2 tbsp ground red pepper*
> *1-1/2 tsp whole allspice*
> *1-1/2 tbsp whole cloves*
> *3 sticks cinnamon*

Yield: About 9 pints

Procedure: Wash tomatoes and dip in boiling water for 30 to 60 seconds or until skins split. Then dip in cold water, slip off skins, core, and quarter. Remove seeds from peppers and slice into strips. Peel and quarter onions. Blend tomatoes, peppers, and onions at high speed for 5 seconds in an electric blender. Pour into a 3- to 4-gallon stock pot or large kettle and heat. Boil gently for 60 minutes, stirring frequently. Add vinegar, sugar, salt, and a spice bag containing dry mustard, red pepper, and other spices. Continue boiling and stirring until volume is reduced by one-half and ketchup rounds up on a spoon with no separation of liquid and solids. Remove spice bag and fill hot jars, leaving 1/8-inch headspace. Remove air bubbles and adjust head-space if needed. Wipe rims of jars with a dampened clean paper towel. Adjust lids and follow process times for regular ketchup.

Salsa Recipes

The salsas in this guide, as well as most salsas, are mixtures of low-acid foods, such as onions and peppers, with acid foods, such as tomatoes. It is important that ingredients be carefully measured and that the salsas be made as described to be processed safely in a boiling water canner.

Selection and Preparation of Ingredients

Acids

The acid ingredients help preserve canned salsas. You must add the acid to these salsas processed in a boiling water canner, because the natural acidity of the mixture without it may not be high enough. The acids are usually commercially bottled lemon juice or vinegar so the acidity level will be standardized. Use only vinegar that is at least 5% acidity; do not use home-made vinegar or fresh squeezed lemon juice, because the acidity can vary and will be unknown.

The amounts of vinegar or lemon juice in these recipes cannot be reduced for safe boiling water canning. Sugar can be used to offset the tartness of the acid. An equal amount of bottled lemon juice may be substituted for vinegar in recipes, but do not substitute vinegar for lemon juice. This substitution will result in a less acidic and potentially unsafe canned salsa.

Tomatoes

The type of tomato will affect the consistency of the salsa. Paste tomatoes, such as Roma, have more, and usually firmer, flesh than slicing tomatoes. They will produce thicker salsas than large slicing tomatoes which usually yield a thinner, more watery salsa.

Canning is not a way to use overripe or spoiling tomatoes. Use only high quality, disease-free, preferably vine-ripened, firm tomatoes for canning salsa or any other tomato product. **Do not use tomatoes from dead or frost-killed vines.** Poor quality or overripe tomatoes will yield a thin salsa and one that may spoil. Green tomatoes or tomatillos may be used instead of ripe tomatoes in these recipes, but the flavor of the recipe will change.

When recipes call for peeled tomatoes, remove the skin by dipping washed tomatoes into boiling water for 30 to 60 seconds or until skins split. Dip immediately into cold water, then slip skins off and core the tomato.

Tomatillos

Tomatillos are also known as Mexican husk tomatoes. The dry outer husk must be removed, but they do not need to be peeled or have the seeds removed. They will need to be washed well after the husk is removed.

Peppers

Peppers range from mild to scorching in taste. It is this "heat" factor that makes many salsa fans want to experiment with recipes. Use only high quality peppers, unblemished and free of decay. You may substitute one type of pepper for another, including bell peppers (mild) for some or all of the chiles. Canned chiles may be used in place of fresh. **However, do not increase the total amount (pounds or cups) of peppers in any recipe.** Do not substitute the same number of whole peppers of a large size for the number of peppers of a smaller size (for example, do not use 6 bell peppers or long chiles in place of 6 jalapenos or serranos). This will result in changing the final acidity of the mixture and could lead to potentially unsafe canned salsa.

Milder varieties of peppers include Anaheim, Ancho, College, Colorado and Hungarian Yellow Wax. When the recipe calls for "long green chiles" choose a mild pepper. Jalapeno is a *very* popular hot pepper. Other hot varieties include Cayenne, Habanera, Serrano, and Tabasco. Do not touch your face, particularly the area around your eyes, when you are handling or cutting hot chiles. **Caution: Wear plastic or rubber gloves and do not touch your face while handling or cutting hot peppers. If you do not wear gloves, wash hands thoroughly with soap and water before touching your face or eyes.**

Usually when peppers are finely chopped in a salsa, they do not need to be peeled. However, many recipes say to peel the chiles, and the skin of long green chiles in particular may be tough after canning. If you choose to peel chiles, or procedures with a recipe direct you to peel the peppers, use the following instructions.

Peeling peppers: Wash and dry peppers; slit each pepper along the side to allow steam to escape. Blister skins using one of these two methods :

Oven or broiler method to blister skins: Place peppers in a hot oven (400 degrees F) or under a broiler for 6 to 8 minutes until skins blister.

Range-top method to blister skins: Cover hot burner (either gas or electric) with heavy wire mesh. Place peppers on burner for several minutes until skins blister.

To peel, after blistering skins, place peppers in a pan and cover with a damp cloth. (This will make peeling the peppers easier.) Cool several minutes; peel off skins. Discard seeds and chop.

Spices and Herbs

Spices and herbs add unique flavoring to salsas. The amounts of dried spices and herbs in the following recipes (black pepper, salt, dried oregano leaves, and ground cumin) may be altered or left out. For a stronger cilantro flavor in recipes that list cilantro, it is best to add fresh cilantro just before serving instead of adding more before canning.

Other

Red, yellow, or white onions may be substituted for each other. Do not increase the total amount of onions in any recipe.

Important: You may change the amount of spices, if desired. Do not can salsas that do not follow these or other research-tested recipes. (They may be frozen or stored in the refrigerator.)

Important: Follow the directions carefully for each recipe. Use the amounts of each vegetable (peppers, onions, tomatoes, tomatillos, etc.) listed in the recipe. If the procedures call for chopped tomatoes, use the whole tomato after peeling and coring. Do not drain the tomato or remove all the liquid and juices. Add the amount of vinegar or lemon juice as listed. The only changes you can safely make in these salsa recipes are to substitute bottled lemon juice for vinegar and to change the amount of dried spices and herbs. Do not alter the proportions of vegetables to acid and tomatoes, because it might make the salsa unsafe. Do not thicken salsas with flour, cornstarch, or other starches before canning. If a thicker salsa is desired, you can pour off some of the liquid or add these thickening ingredients after opening.

Chile Salsa (Hot Tomato-Pepper Sauce)

5 lbs tomatoes
2 lbs chile peppers
1 lb onions
7 cup vinegar (5%)
3 tsp salt
1/2 tsp pepper

Yield: About 6 to 8 pints

Procedure: Caution: Wear plastic or rubber gloves and do not touch your face while handling or cutting hot peppers. If you do not wear

gloves, wash hands thoroughly with soap and water before touching your face or eyes. Peel and prepare chile peppers. Wash tomatoes and dip in boiling water for 30 to 60 seconds or until skins split. Dip in cold water, slip off skins, and remove cores. Coarsely chop tomatoes and combine them with chopped peppers, onions, and remaining ingredients in a large saucepan. Heat to a boil, reduce heat, and simmer 10 minutes. Fill hot jars, leaving 1/2-inch headspace. Remove air bubbles and adjust headspace if needed. Wipe rims of jars with a dampened clean paper towel. Adjust lids and process.

Recommended process time for Chile Salsa in a boiling-water canner				
		Process Time at Altitudes of		
Style of Pack	Jar Size	0-1,000 ft	1,001-6,000 ft	Above 6,000 ft
Hot	Pints	15 min	20	25

Chile Salsa II

10 cups peeled, cored, chopped tomatoes
6 cups seeded, chopped chile peppers (use mixture of mild and hot peppers)
4 cups chopped onions
1 cup vinegar (5%)
3 tsp salt
1/2 tsp pepper

Yield: About 7 to 9 pints

Procedure: Caution: Wear plastic or rubber gloves and do not touch your face while handling or cutting hot peppers. If you do not wear gloves, wash hands thoroughly with soap and water before touching your face or eyes. Peel and prepare chile peppers as described on page 255, if desired. Wash tomatoes and dip in boiling water for 30 to 60 seconds or until skins split. Dip in cold water, slip off skins, and remove cores.

Combine ingredients in a large saucepan. Heat to a boil and simmer 10 minutes. Fill hot salsa into hot pint jars, leaving 1/2-inch headspace. Remove air bubbles and adjust headspace if needed. Wipe rims of jars with a dampened clean paper towel. Adjust lids and process.

Recommended process time for Chile Salsa II in a boiling-water canner				
		Process Time at Altitudes of		
Style of Pack	Jar Size	0-1,000 ft	1,001- 6,000 ft	Above 6,000 ft
Hot	Pints	15 min	20	25

Tomatillo Green Salsa

5 cups chopped tomatillos (or green tomatoes may be used)
1-1/2 cups seeded, chopped long green chiles
1/2 cup seeded, finely chopped jalapeno peppers
4 cups chopped onions
1 cup bottled lemon juice
6 cloves garlic, finely chopped
1 tbsp ground cumin (optional)
3 tbsp oregano leaves (optional)
1 tbsp salt
1 tsp black pepper

Yield: About 5 pints

Procedure: Caution: Wear plastic or rubber gloves and do not touch your face while handling or cutting hot peppers. If you do not wear gloves, wash hands thoroughly with soap and water before touching your face or eyes. Peel and prepare chile peppers. Combine all ingredients in a large saucepan and stir frequently over high heat until mixture begins to boil, then reduce heat and simmer for 20 minutes, stirring occasionally. Ladle hot salsa into hot pint jars, leaving 1/2-inch headspace. Remove air bubbles and adjust headspace if needed. Wipe rims of jars with a dampened clean paper towel. Adjust lids and process.

Recommended process time for Tomatillo Green Salsa in a boiling-water canner				
			Process Time at Altitudes of	
Style of Pack	Jar Size	0-1,000 ft	1,001- 6,000 ft	Above 6,000 ft
Hot	Pints	15 min	20	25

Tomato Salsa (Using Paste Tomatoes)

*7 qts peeled, cored, chopped tomatoes**

4 cups seeded, chopped long green chiles

5 cups chopped onion

1/2 cup seeded, finely chopped jalapeno peppers

6 cloves garlic, finely chopped

2 cups bottled lemon or lime juice

2 tbsp salt

1 tbsp black pepper

2 tbsp ground cumin (optional)

3 tbsp oregano leaves (optional)

2 tbsp fresh cilantro (optional)

*This recipe works best with paste tomatoes. Slicing tomatoes require a much longer cooking time to achieve a desirable consistency.

Yield: About 16 to 18 pints

Procedure: Caution: Wear plastic or rubber gloves and do not touch your face while handling or cutting hot peppers. If you do not wear gloves, wash hands thoroughly with soap and water before touching your face or eyes. Peel and prepare chile peppers. Wash tomatoes and dip in boiling water for 30 to 60 seconds or until skins split. Dip in cold water, slip off skins, and remove cores. Combine all ingredients except cumin, oregano, and cilantro in a large pot and bring to a boil, stirring frequently, then reduce heat and simmer 10 minutes. Add spices and simmer for another 20 minutes, stirring occasionally. Fill hot salsa into hot pint jars, leaving 1/2-inch headspace. Remove air bubbles and adjust headspace if needed. Wipe rims of jars with a dampened clean paper towel. Adjust lids and process.

Recommended process time for Tomato Salsa Using Paste Tomatoes in a boiling-water canner				
		Process Time at Altitudes of		
Style of Pack	Jar Size	0-1,000 ft	1,001-6,000 ft	Above 6,000 ft
Hot	Pints	15 min	20	25

Tomato Salsa (Using Slicing Tomatoes)

4 cups peeled, cored, chopped tomatoes

2 cups seeded, chopped long green chiles

1/2 cup seeded, chopped jalapeno peppers

3/4 cup chopped onion

4 cloves garlic, finely chopped

2 cups vinegar (5%)

1 tsp ground cumin (optional)

1 tbsp oregano leaves (optional)

1 tbsp fresh cilantro (optional)

1-1/2 tsp salt

Yield: About 4 pints

Procedure: Caution: Wear plastic or rubber gloves and do not touch your face while handling or cutting hot peppers. If you do not wear gloves, wash hands thoroughly with soap and water before touching your face or eyes. Peel and prepare chile peppers. Wash tomatoes and dip in boiling water for 30 to 60 seconds or until skins split. Dip in cold water, slip off skins, and remove cores. Combine all ingredients in a large pot and bring to a boil, stirring frequently. Reduce heat and simmer 20 minutes, stirring occasionally. Fill hot salsa into hot pint jars, leaving 1/2-inch headspace. Remove air bubbles and adjust headspace if needed. Wipe rims of jars with a dampened clean paper towel. Adjust lids and process.

Recommended process time for Tomato Salsa Using Slicing Tomatoes in a boiling-water canner				
		Process Time at Altitudes of		
Style of Pack	Jar Size	0-1,000 ft	1,001- 6,000 ft	Above 6,000 ft
Hot	Pints	15 min	20	25

Tomato/Green Chile Salsa

3 cups peeled, cored, chopped tomatoes

3 cups seeded, chopped long green chiles

3/4 cup chopped onions

1 jalapeno pepper, seeded, finely chopped

6 cloves garlic, finely chopped

1-1/2 cups vinegar (5%)

1/2 tsp ground cumin (optional)

2 tsp oregano leaves (optional)

1-1/2 tsp salt

Yield: About 3 pints

Procedure: Caution: Wear plastic or rubber gloves and do not touch your face while handling or cutting hot peppers. If you do not wear gloves, wash hands thoroughly with soap and water before touching your face or eyes. Peel and prepare chile peppers. Wash tomatoes and dip in boiling water for 30 to 60 seconds or until skins split. Dip in cold water, slip off skins, and remove cores. Combine all ingredients in a large saucepan and heat, stirring frequently, until mixture boils. Reduce heat and simmer for 20 minutes, stirring occasionally. Fill hot salsa into hot pint jars, leaving 1/2-inch headspace. Remove air bubbles and adjust headspace if needed. Wipe rims of jars with a dampened clean paper towel. Adjust lids and process.

Recommended process time for Tomato Green Chile Salsa in a boiling-water canner				
		Process Time at Altitudes of		
Style of Pack	Jar Size	0-1,000 ft	1,001-6,000 ft	Above 6,000 ft
Hot	Pints	15 min	20	25

Tomato/Tomato Paste Salsa

3 qts peeled, cored, chopped slicing tomatoes

3 cups chopped onions

6 jalapeno peppers, seeded, finely chopped

4 long green chiles, seeded, chopped

4 cloves garlic, finely chopped

2 cans (12-ounce) tomato paste

2 cups bottled lemon or lime juice

1 tbsp salt

1 tbsp sugar

1 tbsp ground cumin (optional)

2 tbsp oregano leaves (optional)

1 tsp black pepper

Yield: About 7 to 9 pints

Procedure: Caution: Wear plastic or rubber gloves and do not touch your face while handling or cutting hot peppers. If you do not wear gloves, wash hands thoroughly with soap and water before touching your face or eyes. Peel and prepare chile peppers. Wash tomatoes and dip in boiling water for 30 to 60 seconds or until skins split. Dip in cold water, slip off skins, and remove cores. Combine all ingredients in a large saucepan. Bring to a boil. Reduce heat and simmer for 30 minutes, stirring occasionally. Fill hot salsa into hot pint jars, leaving 1/2-inch headspace. Remove air bubbles and adjust headspace if needed. Wipe rims of jars with a dampened clean paper towel. Adjust lids and process.

Recommended process time for Tomato/Tomato Paste Salsa in a boiling-water canner				
		Process Time at Altitudes of		
Style of Pack	Jar Size	0-1,000 ft	1,001- 6,000 ft	Above 6,000 ft
Hot	Pints	15 min	20	25

Tomato Taco Sauce

> 8 qts peeled, cored, finely chopped paste tomatoes*
> 2 cloves garlic, crushed
> 5 cups chopped onions
> 4 jalapeno peppers, seeded, chopped
> 4 long green chiles, seeded, chopped
> 2-1/2 cups vinegar
> 2 tbsp salt
> 1-1/2 tbsp black pepper
> 1 tbsp sugar
> 2 tbsp oregano leaves (optional)
> 7 tsp ground cumin (optional)

*This recipe works best with paste tomatoes, because slicing tomatoes will yield a thin watery salsa. If you only have slicing tomatoes available, use the Tomato/Tomato Paste Salsa recipe.

Yield: About 16 to 18 pints

Procedure: Caution: Wear plastic or rubber gloves and do not touch your face while handling or cutting hot peppers. If you do not wear gloves, wash hands thoroughly with soap and water before touching your face or eyes. Peel and prepare chile peppers. Wash tomatoes and dip in boiling water for 30 to 60 seconds or until skins split. Dip in cold water, slip off skins, and remove cores. Combine ingredients in a large saucepan. Bring to a boil, then reduce heat and simmer, stirring frequently until thick (about 1 hour). Fill hot sauce into hot pint jars, leaving 1/2-inch headspace. Remove air bubbles and adjust headspace if needed. Wipe rims of jars with a dampened clean paper towel. Adjust lids and process.

Recommended process time for Tomato Taco Sauce in a boiling-water canner				
		Process Time at Altitudes of		
Style of Pack	Jar Size	0-1,000 ft	1,001-6,000 ft	Above 6,000 ft
Hot	Pints	15 min	20	25

Appendix C

Canning Vegetables and Vegetable Products

— Courtesy of the USDA

Asparagus — Spears or Pieces

Quantity: An average of 24-1/2 pounds is needed per canner load of 7 quarts; an average of 16 pounds is needed per canner load of 9 pints. A crate weighs 31 pounds and yields 7 to 12 quarts—an average of 3-1/2 pounds per quart.

Quality: Use tender, tight-tipped spears, 4 to 6 inches long.

Procedure: Wash asparagus and trim off tough scales. Break off tough stems and wash again. Cut into 1-inch pieces or can whole.

Hot pack — Cover asparagus with boiling water. Boil 2 or 3 minutes. Loosely fill hot jars with hot asparagus, leaving 1-inch headspace.

Raw pack — Fill hot jars with raw asparagus, packing as tightly as possible without crushing, leaving 1-inch headspace.

Add 1 teaspoon of salt per quart to the jars, if desired. Add boiling water, leaving 1-inch headspace. Remove air bubbles and adjust headspace if needed. Wipe rims of jars with a dampened clean paper towel. Adjust lids and process.

Recommended process time for Asparagus in a dial-gauge pressure canner						
			Canner Pressure (PSI) at Altitudes of			
Style of Pack	Jar Size	Process Time	0- 2,000 ft	2,001- 4,000 ft	4,001- 6,000 ft	6,001- 8,000 ft
Hot and Raw	Pints	30 min	11 lb	12 lb	13 lb	14 lb
	Quarts	40	11	12	13	14

Recommended process time for Asparagus in a weighted-gauge pressure canner				
			Canner Pressure (PSI) at Altitudes of	
Style of Pack	Jar Size	Process Time	0-1,000 ft	Above 1,000 ft
Hot and Raw	Pints	30 min	10 lb	15 lb
	Quarts	40	10	15

Beans or Peas — Shelled, Dried

All varieties

Quantity: An average of 5 pounds is needed per canner load of 7 quarts; an average of 3-1/4 pounds is needed per canner load of 9 pints — an average of 3/4 pound per quart.

Quality: Select mature, dry seeds. Sort out and discard discolored seeds.

Procedure: Place dried beans or peas in a large pot and cover with water. Soak 12 to 18 hours in a cool place. Drain water. To quickly hydrate beans, you may cover sorted and washed beans with boiling water in a saucepan.

Boil 2 minutes, remove from heat, soak 1 hour and drain. Cover beans soaked by either method with fresh water and boil 30 minutes. Add 1/2 teaspoon of salt per pint or 1 teaspoon per quart to the jar, if desired. Fill hot jars with beans or peas and cooking water, leaving 1-inch headspace. Remove air bubbles and adjust headspace if needed. Wipe rims of jars with a dampened clean paper towel. Adjust lids and process.

Recommended process time for Beans or Peas in a dial-gauge pressure canner						
			Canner Pressure (PSI) at Altitudes of			
Style of Pack	Jar Size	Process Time	0-2,000 ft	2,001-4,000 ft	4,001-6,000 ft	6,001-8,000 ft
Hot	Pints	75 min	11 lb	12 lb	13 lb	14 lb
	Quarts	90	11	12	13	14

Recommended process time for Beans or Peas in a weighted-gauge pressure canner				
			Canner Pressure (PSI) at Altitudes of	
Style of Pack	Jar Size	Process Time	0-1,000 ft	Above 1,000 ft
Hot	Pints	75 min	10 lb	15 lb
	Quarts	90	10	15

Beans, Baked

Procedure: Soak and boil beans and prepare molasses sauce according to directions for beans with sauce on page 268. Place seven 3/4-inch pieces of pork, ham, or bacon in an earthenware crock, a large casserole, or a pan. Add beans and enough molasses sauce to cover beans. Cover and bake 4 to 5 hours at 350 degrees F. Add water as needed-about every hour. Fill hot jars, leaving 1-inch headspace. Remove air bubbles and adjust headspace if needed. Wipe rims of jars with a dampened clean paper towel. Adjust lids and process like beans with sauce described next.

Beans, Dry, With Tomato or Molasses Sauce

Quantity: An average of 5 pounds of beans is needed per canner load of 7 quarts; an average of 3-1/4 pounds is needed per canner load of 9 pints — an average of 3/4 pound per quart.

Quality: Select mature, dry seeds. Sort out and discard discolored seeds.

Procedure: Sort and wash dry beans. Add 3 cups of water for each cup of dried beans or peas. Boil 2 minutes, remove from heat, and soak 1 hour and drain. Heat to boiling in fresh water, and save liquid for making sauce. Make your choice of the following sauces:

Tomato Sauce — Either mix 1 quart tomato juice, 3 tablespoons sugar, 2 teaspoons salt, 1 tablespoon chopped onion, and 1/4 teaspoon each of ground cloves, allspice, mace, and cayenne pepper; or, mix 1 cup tomato ketchup with 3 cups of cooking liquid from beans. Heat to boiling.

Molasses Sauce — Mix 4 cups water or cooking liquid from beans, 3 tablespoons dark molasses, 1 tablespoon vinegar, 2 teaspoons salt, and 3/4 teaspoon powdered dry mustard. Heat to boiling.

Fill hot jars 3/4 full with hot beans. Add a 3/4-inch cube of pork, ham, or bacon to each jar, if desired. Fill jars with heated sauce, leaving 1-inch headspace. Remove air bubbles and adjust headspace if needed. Wipe rims of jars with a dampened clean paper towel. Adjust lids and process.

Recommended process time for Beans, Dry, with Tomato or Molasses Sauce in a dial-gauge pressure canner						
			Canner Pressure (PSI) at Altitudes of			
Style of Pack	Jar Size	Process Time	0-2,000 ft	2,001-4,000 ft	4,001-6,000 ft	6,001-8,000 ft
Hot	Pints	65 min	11 lb	12 lb	13 lb	14 lb
	Quarts	75	11	12	13	14

			Canner Pressure (PSI) at Altitudes of	
Style of Pack	Jar Size	Process Time	0-1,000 ft	Above 1,000 ft
Hot	Pints	65 min	10 lb	15 lb
	Quarts	75	10	15

Recommended process time for Beans, Dry, with Tomato or Molasses Sauce in a weighted-gauge pressure canner

Beans, Fresh Lima — Shelled

Quantity: An average of 28 pounds is needed per canner load of 7 quarts; an average of 18 pounds is needed per canner load of 9 pints. A bushel weighs 32 pounds and yields 6 to 10 quarts — an average of 4 pounds per quart.

Quality: Select well-filled pods with green seeds. Discard insect-damaged and diseased seeds.

Procedure: Shell beans and wash thoroughly.

Hot pack — Cover beans with boiling water and heat to a boil. Fill hot jars loosely, leaving 1-inch headspace.

Raw pack — Fill hot jars with raw beans. Do not press or shake down.

Note: Small beans — leave 1-inch of headspace for pints and 1-1/2 inches for quarts. Large beans — leave 1-inch of headspace for pints and 1-1/4 inches for quarts.

Add 1 teaspoon of salt per quart to the jar, if desired. Add boiling water, leaving the same headspaces listed above. Remove air bubbles and adjust headspace if needed. Wipe rims of jars with a dampened clean paper towel. Adjust lids and process.

Recommended process time for Lima Beans in a dial-gauge pressure canner						
			Canner Pressure (PSI) at Altitudes of			
Style of Pack	Jar Size	Process Time	0-2,000 ft	2,001-4,000 ft	4,001-6,000 ft	6,001-8,000 ft
Hot and Raw	Pints	40 min	11 lb	12 lb	13 lb	14 lb
	Quarts	50	11	12	13	14

Recommended process time for Lima Beans in a weighted-gauge pressure canner				
			Canner Pressure (PSI) at Altitudes of	
Style of Pack	Jar Size	Process Time	0-1,000 ft	Above 1,000 ft
Hot and Raw	Pints	40 min	10 lb	15 lb
	Quarts	50	10	15

Beans, Snap and Italian Pieces

Quantity: An average of 14 pounds is needed per canner load of 7 quarts; an average of 9 pounds is needed per canner load of 9 pints. A bushel weighs 30 pounds and yields 12 to 20 quarts — an average of 2 pounds per quart.

Quality: Select filled but tender, crisp pods. Remove and discard diseased and rusty pods.

Procedure: Wash beans and trim ends. Leave whole or cut or snap into 1-inch pieces.

Hot pack — Cover with boiling water; boil 5 minutes. Fill hot jars loosely, leaving 1-inch head-space.

Raw pack — Fill hot jars tightly with raw beans, leaving 1-inch headspace.

Add 1 teaspoon of canning salt per quart to the jar, if desired. Add boiling water, leaving 1-inch headspace. Remove air bubbles and adjust headspace if needed. Wipe rims of jars with a dampened clean paper towel. Adjust lids and process.

Recommended process time for Snap and Italian Beans in a dial-gauge pressure canner						
			Canner Pressure (PSI) at Altitudes of			
Style of Pack	Jar Size	Process Time	0-2,000 ft	2,001-4,000 ft	4,001-6,000 ft	6,001-8,000 ft
Hot and Raw	Pints	20 min	11 lb	12 lb	13 lb	14 lb
	Quarts	25	11	12	13	14

Recommended process time for Snap and Italian Beans in a weighted-gauge pressure canner				
			Canner Pressure (PSI) at Altitudes of	
Style of Pack	Jar Size	Process Time	0-1,000 ft	Above 1,000 ft
Hot and Raw	Pints	20 min	10 lb	15 lb
	Quarts	25	10	15

Beets — Whole, Cubed, or Sliced

Quantity: An average of 21 pounds (without tops) is needed per canner load of 7 quarts; an average of 13-1/2 pounds is needed per canner load of 9 pints. A bushel (without tops) weighs 52 pounds and yields 15 to 20 quarts — an average of 3 pounds per quart.

Quality: Beets with a diameter of 1 to 2 inches are preferred for whole packs. Beets larger than 3 inches in diameter are often fibrous.

Procedure: Trim off beet tops, leaving an inch of stem and roots to reduce bleeding of color. Scrub well. Cover with boiling water. Boil until skins slip off easily, about 15 to 25 minutes depending on size. Cool, remove skins, and trim off stems and roots. Leave baby beets whole. Cut medium or large beets into 1/2-inch cubes or slices. Halve or quarter very large slices. Add 1 teaspoon of salt per quart to the jar, if desired. Fill hot jars with hot beets and fresh hot water, leaving 1-inch headspace. Remove air bubbles and adjust headspace if needed. Wipe rims of jars with a dampened clean paper towel. Adjust lids and process.

Recommended process time for Beets in a dial-gauge pressure canner						
			Canner Pressure (PSI) at Altitudes of			
Style of Pack	Jar Size	Process Time	0-2,000 ft	2,001-4,000 ft	4,001-6,000 ft	6,001-8,000 ft
Hot	Pints	30 min	11 lb	12 lb	13 lb	14 lb
	Quarts	35	11	12	13	14

Recommended process time for Beets in a weighted-gauge pressure canner				
			Canner Pressure (PSI) at Altitudes of	
Style of Pack	Jar Size	Process Time	0-1,000 ft	Above 1,000 ft
Hot	Pints	30 min	10 lb	15 lb
	Quarts	35	10	15

Carrots — Sliced or Diced

Quantity: An average of 17-1/2 pounds (without tops) is needed per canner load of 7 quarts; an average of 11 pounds is needed per canner load of 9 pints. A bushel (without tops) weighs 50 pounds and yields 17 to 25 quarts — an average of 2-1/2 pounds per quart.

Quality: Select small carrots, preferably 1 to 1-1/4 inches in diameter. Larger carrots are often too fibrous.

Procedure: Wash, peel, and rewash carrots. Slice or dice.

Hot pack — Cover with boiling water; bring to boil and simmer for 5 minutes. Fill hot jars, leaving 1-inch of headspace.

Raw pack — Fill hot jars tightly with raw carrots, leaving 1-inch headspace.

Add 1 teaspoon of salt per quart to the jar, if desired. Add hot cooking liquid or water, leaving 1-inch headspace. Remove air bubbles and adjust headspace if needed. Wipe rims of jars with a dampened clean paper towel. Adjust lids and process.

Recommended process time for Carrots in a dial-gauge pressure canner						
			Canner Pressure (PSI) at Altitudes of			
Style of Pack	Jar Size	Process Time	0-2,000 ft	2,001-4,000 ft	4,001-6,000 ft	6,001-8,000 ft
Hot	Pints	25 min	11 lb	12 lb	13 lb	14 lb
	Quarts	30	11	12	13	14

Recommended process time for Carrots in a weighted-gauge pressure canner				
			Canner Pressure (PSI) at Altitudes of	
Style of Pack	Jar Size	Process Time	0-1,000 ft	Above 1,000 ft
Hot	Pints	25 min	10 lb	15 lb
	Quarts	30	10	15

Corn — Cream Style

Quantity: An average of 20 pounds (in husks) of sweet corn is needed per canner load of 9 pints. A bushel weighs 35 pounds and yields 12 to 20 pints — an average of 2-1/4 pounds per pint.

Quality: Select ears containing slightly immature kernels or ears of ideal quality for eating fresh.

Procedure: Husk corn, remove silk, and wash ears. Blanch ears 4 minutes in boiling water. Cut corn from cob at about the center of kernel. Scrape remaining corn from cobs with a table knife.

Hot pack — For each quart of corn and scrapings, in a saucepan, add two cups of boiling water. Heat to boiling. Add 1/2 teaspoon salt to each jar, if desired. Fill hot pint jar with hot corn mixture, leaving 1-inch headspace. Remove air bubbles and adjust headspace if needed. Wipe rims of jars with a dampened clean paper towel. Adjust lids and process.

Recommended process time for Cream Style Corn in a dial-gauge pressure canner						
			Canner Pressure (PSI) at Altitudes of			
Style of Pack	Jar Size	Process Time	0-2,000 ft	2,001-4,000 ft	4,001-6,000 ft	6,001-8,000 ft
Hot	Pints	85 min	11 lb	12 lb	13 lb	14 lb

Recommended process time for Cream Style Corn in a weighted-gauge pressure canner				
			Canner Pressure (PSI) at Altitudes of	
Style of Pack	Jar Size	Process Time	0-1,000 ft	Above 1,000 ft
Hot	Pints	85 min	10 lb	15 lb

Corn — Whole Kernel

Quantity: An average of 31-1/2 pounds (in husks) of sweet corn is needed per canner load of 7 quarts; an average of 20 pounds is needed per canner load of 9 pints. A bushel weighs 35 pounds and yields 6 to 11 quarts — an average of 4-1/2 pounds per quart.

Quality: Select ears containing slightly immature kernels or of ideal quality for eating fresh. Canning of some sweeter varieties or too immature kernels may cause browning. Can a small amount first; check color and flavor before canning large quantities.

Procedure: Husk corn, remove silk, and wash. Blanch 3 minutes in boiling water. Cut corn from cob at about 3/4 the depth of kernel.

Caution: Do not scrape cob.

Hot pack — For each clean quart of kernels in a saucepan, add 1 cup of hot water, heat to boiling and simmer 5 minutes. Add 1 teaspoon of salt per quart to the jar, if desired. Fill hot jars with corn and cooking liquid, leaving 1-inch headspace.

Raw pack — Fill hot jars with raw kernels, leaving 1-inch headspace. Do not shake or press down. Add 1 teaspoon of salt per quart to the jar, if desired.

Add fresh boiling water, leaving 1-inch headspace. Remove air bubbles and adjust headspace if needed. Wipe rims of jars with a dampened clean paper towel. Adjust lids and process.

Recommended process time for Whole Kernel Corn in a dial-gauge pressure canner						
			Canner Pressure (PSI) at Altitudes of			
Style of Pack	Jar Size	Process Time	0-2,000 ft	2,001-4,000 ft	4,001-6,000 ft	6,001-8,000 ft
Hot and Raw	Pints	55 min	11 lb	12 lb	13 lb	14 lb
	Quarts	85	11	12	13	14

Recommended process time for Whole Kernel Corn in a weighted-gauge pressure canner				
			Canner Pressure (PSI) at Altitudes of	
Style of Pack	Jar Size	Process Time	0-1,000 ft	Above 1,000 ft
Hot and Raw	Pints	55 min	10 lb	15 lb
	Quarts	85	10	15

Mixed Vegetables

6 cups sliced carrots

6 cups cut, whole kernel sweet corn

6 cups cut green beans

6 cups shelled lima beans

4 cups whole or crushed tomatoes

4 cups diced zucchini

Yield: 7 quarts

Optional mix — You may change the suggested proportions or substitute other favorite vegetables except leafy greens, dried beans, cream-style corn, squash, and sweet potatoes.

Procedure: Except for zucchini, wash and prepare vegetables as described previously for each vegetable. Wash, trim, and slice or cube zucchini; combine all vegetables in a large pot or kettle, and add enough water to cover pieces. Add 1 teaspoon salt per quart to the jar, if desired. Boil 5 minutes and fill hot jars with hot pieces and liquid, leaving 1-inch headspace. Remove air bubbles and adjust headspace if needed. Wipe rims of jars with a dampened clean paper towel. Adjust lids and process.

Recommended process time for Mixed Vegetables in a dial-gauge pressure canner						
			Canner Pressure (PSI) at Altitudes of			
Style of Pack	Jar Size	Process Time	0-2,000 ft	2,001-4,000 ft	4,001-6,000 ft	6,001-8,000 ft
Hot	Pints	75 min	11 lb	12 lb	13 lb	14 lb
	Quarts	90	11	12	13	14

Recommended process time for Mixed Vegetables in a weighted-gauge pressure canner				
			Canner Pressure (PSI) at Altitudes of	
Style of Pack	Jar Size	Process Time	0-1,000 ft	Above 1,000 ft
Hot	Pints	75 min	10 lb	15 lb
	Quarts	90	10	15

Mushrooms — Whole or Sliced

Quantity: An average of 14-1/2 pounds is needed per canner load of 9 pints; an average of 7-1/2 pounds is needed per canner load of 9 half-pints — an average of 2 pounds per pint.

Quality: Select only brightly colored, small to medium-size domestic mushrooms with short stems, tight veils (unopened caps), and no discoloration. **Caution: Do not can wild mushrooms.**

Procedure: Trim stems and discolored parts. Soak in cold water for 10 minutes to remove dirt. Wash in clean water. Leave small mushrooms whole; cut large ones. Cover with water in a saucepan and boil 5 minutes. Fill hot jars with hot mushrooms, leaving 1-inch headspace. Add 1/2 teaspoon of salt per pint to the jar, if desired. For better color, add 1/8 teaspoon of ascorbic acid powder, or a 500-milligram tablet of vitamin C. Add fresh hot water, leaving 1-inch headspace. Remove air bubbles and adjust headspace if needed. Wipe rims of jars with a dampened clean paper towel. Adjust lids and process.

Recommended process time for Mushrooms in a dial-gauge pressure canner						
			Canner Pressure (PSI) at Altitudes of			
Style of Pack	Jar Size	Process Time	0-2,000 ft	2,001-4,000 ft	4,001-6,000 ft	6,001-8,000 ft
Hot	Half-pints	45 min	11 lb	12 lb	13 lb	14 lb

Recommended process time for Mushrooms in a weighted-gauge pressure canner				
			Canner Pressure (PSI) at Altitudes of	
Style of Pack	Jar Size	Process Time	0-1,000 ft	Above 1,000 ft
Hot	Half-pints	45 min	10 lb	15 lb

Okra

Quantity: An average of 11 pounds is needed per canner load of 7 quarts; an average of 7 pounds is needed per canner load of 9 pints. A bushel weighs 26 pounds and yields 16 to 18 quarts — an average of 1-1/2 pounds per quart.

Quality: Select young, tender pods. Remove and discard diseased and rust-spotted pods.

Procedure: Wash pods and trim ends. Leave whole or cut into 1-inch pieces. Cover with hot water in a saucepan, boil 2 minutes and drain. Fill hot jars with hot okra and cooking liquid, leaving 1-inch headspace. Add 1 teaspoon of salt per quart to the jar, if desired. Remove air bubbles and adjust headspace if needed. Wipe rims of jars with a dampened clean paper towel. Adjust lids and process.

Recommended process time for Okra in a dial-gauge pressure canner						
			Canner Pressure (PSI) at Altitudes of			
Style of Pack	Jar Size	Process Time	0-2,000 ft	2,001-4,000 ft	4,001-6,000 ft	6,001-8,000 ft
Hot	Pints	25 min	11 lb	12 lb	13 lb	14 lb
	Quarts	40	11	12	13	14

Recommended process time for Okra in a weighted-gauge pressure canner				
			Canner Pressure (PSI) at Altitudes of	
Style of Pack	Jar Size	Process Time	0-1,000 ft	Above 1,000 ft
Hot	Pints	25 min	10 lb	15 lb
	Quarts	40	10	15

Peas, Green or English — Shelled

It is recommended that sugar snap and Chinese edible pods be frozen for best quality.

Quantity: An average of 31-1/2 pounds (in pods) is needed per canner load of 7 quarts; an average of 20 pounds is needed per canner load of 9 pints. A bushel weighs 30 pounds and yields 5 to 10 quarts—an average of 4-1/2 pounds per quart.

Quality: Select filled pods containing young, tender, sweet seeds. Discard diseased pods.

Procedure: Shell and wash peas. Add 1 teaspoon of salt per quart to the jar, if desired.

Hot pack — Cover with boiling water. Bring to a boil in a saucepan, and boil 2 minutes. Fill hot jars loosely with hot peas, and add cooking liquid, leaving 1-inch headspace.

Raw pack — Fill hot jars with raw peas, add boiling water, leaving 1-inch headspace. Do not shake or press down peas.

Remove air bubbles and adjust headspace if needed. Wipe rims of jars with a dampened clean paper towel. Adjust lids and process.

Recommended process time for Peas, Green or English in a dial-gauge pressure canner						
			Canner Pressure (PSI) at Altitudes of			
Style of Pack	Jar Size	Process Time	0-2,000 ft	2,001-4,000 ft	4,001-6,000 ft	6,001-8,000 ft
Hot and Raw	Pints or Quarts	40 min	11 lb	12 lb	13 lb	14 lb

Recommended process time for Peas, Green or English in a weighted-gauge pressure canner				
			Canner Pressure (PSI) at Altitudes of	
Style of Pack	Jar Size	Process Time	0-1,000 ft	Above 1,000 ft
Hot and Raw	Pints or Quarts	40 min	10 lb	15 lb

Peppers

Hot or sweet, including chiles, jalapeno, and pimiento

Quantity: An average of 9 pounds is needed per canner load of 9 pints. A bushel weighs 25 pounds and yields 20 to 30 pints — an average of 1 pound per pint.

Quality: Select firm yellow, green, or red peppers. Do not use soft or diseased peppers.

Procedure: Select your favorite pepper(s). **Caution: If you choose hot peppers, wear plastic or rubber gloves and do not touch your face while handling or cutting hot peppers. If you do not wear gloves, wash**

hands thoroughly with soap and water before touching your face or eyes. Small peppers may be left whole. Large peppers may be quartered. Remove cores and seeds. Slash 2 or 4 slits in each pepper, and either blanch in boiling water or blister skins using one of these two methods:

Oven or broiler method to blister skins: Place peppers in a hot oven (400 degrees F) or broiler for 6 to 8 minutes until skins blister.

Range-top method to blister skins: Cover hot burner, either gas or electric, with heavy wire mesh. Place peppers on burner for several minutes until skins blister.

After blistering skins, place peppers in a pan and cover with a damp cloth. (This will make peeling the peppers easier.) Cool several minutes; peel off skins. Flatten whole peppers. Add 1/2 teaspoon of salt to each pint jar, if desired. Fill hot jars loosely with peppers and add fresh boiling water, leaving 1-inch headspace. Remove air bubbles and adjust headspace if needed. Wipe rims of jars with a dampened clean paper towel. Adjust lids and process.

Recommended process time for Peppers in a dial-gauge pressure canner						
			Canner Pressure (PSI) at Altitudes of			
Style of Pack	Jar Size	Process Time	0-2,000 ft	2,001-4,000 ft	4,001-6,000 ft	6,001-8,000 ft
Hot	Half-pints or Pints	35 min	11 lb	12 lb	13 lb	14 lb

Recommended process time for Peppers in a weighted-gauge pressure canner				
			Canner Pressure (PSI) at Altitudes of	
Style of Pack	Jar Size	Process Time	0-1,000 ft	Above 1,000 ft
Hot	Half-pints or Pints	35	10 lb	15 lb

Potatoes, Sweet — Pieces Or Whole

It is not recommended to dry pack sweet potatoes.

Quantity: An average of 17-1/2 pounds is needed per canner load of 7 quarts; an average of 11 pounds is needed per canner load of 9 pints. A bushel weighs 50 pounds and yields 17 to 25 quarts — an average of 2-1/2 pounds per quart.

Quality: Choose small to medium-sized potatoes. They should be mature and not too fibrous. Can within 1 to 2 months after harvest.

Procedure: Wash potatoes and boil or steam until partially soft (15 to 20 minutes). Remove skins. Cut medium potatoes, if needed, so that pieces are uniform in size. **Caution: Do not mash or puree pieces.** Fill hot jars, leaving 1-inch headspace. Add 1 teaspoon salt per quart to the jar, if desired. Cover with your choice of fresh boiling water or syrup, leaving 1-inch headspace. Remove air bubbles and adjust headspace if needed. Wipe rims of jars with a dampened clean paper towel. Adjust lids and process.

Recommended process time for Sweet Potatoes in a dial-gauge pressure canner						
			Canner Pressure (PSI) at Altitudes of			
Style of Pack	Jar Size	Process Time	0-2,000 ft	2,001-4,000 ft	4,001-6,000 ft	6,001-8,000 ft
Hot	Pints	65 min	11 lb	12 lb	13 lb	14 lb
	Quarts	90	11	12	13	14

Recommended process time for Sweet Potatoes in a weighted-gauge pressure canner				
			Canner Pressure (PSI) at Altitudes of	
Style of Pack	Jar Size	Process Time	0-1,000 ft	Above 1,000 ft
Hot	Pints	65 min	10 lb	15 lb
	Quarts	90	10	15

Potatoes, White — Cubed or Whole

Quantity: An average of 20 pounds is needed per canner load of 7 quarts; an average of 13 pounds is needed per canner load of 9 pints. A bag weighs 50 pounds and yields 18 to 22 quarts — an average of 2-1/2 to 3 pounds per quart.

Quality: Select small to medium-size mature potatoes of ideal quality for cooking. Tubers stored below 45 degrees F might discolor when canned. Choose potatoes 1 to 2 inches in diameter if they are to be packed whole.

Procedure: Wash and peel potatoes. Place in ascorbic acid solution to prevent darkening. If desired, cut into 1/2-inch cubes. Drain. Cook 2 minutes in boiling water and drain again. For whole potatoes, boil 10 minutes and drain. Add 1 teaspoon of salt per quart to the jar, if desired. Fill hot jars with hot potatoes and fresh hot water, leaving 1-inch headspace. Remove air bubbles and adjust headspace if needed. Wipe rims of jars with a dampened clean paper towel. Adjust lids and process.

Recommended process time for White Potatoes in a dial-gauge pressure canner						
			Canner Pressure (PSI) at Altitudes of			
Style of Pack	Jar Size	Process Time	0-2,000 ft	2,001-4,000 ft	4,001-6,000 ft	6,001-8,000 ft
Hot	Pints	35 min	11 lb	12 lb	13 lb	14 lb
	Quarts	40	11	12	13	14

Recommended process time for White Potatoes in a weighted-gauge pressure canner				
			Canner Pressure (PSI) at Altitudes of	
Style of Pack	Jar Size	Process Time	0-1,000 ft	Above 1,000 ft
Hot	Pints	35 min	10 lb	15 lb
	Quarts	40	10	15

Pumpkins and Winter Squash — Cubed

Quantity: An average of 16 pounds is needed per canner load of 7 quarts; an average of 10 pounds is needed per canner load of 9 pints — an average of 2-1/4 pounds per quart.

Quality: Pumpkins and squash should have a hard rind and stringless, mature pulp of ideal quality for cooking fresh. Small size pumpkins (sugar or pie varieties) make better products.

Procedure: Wash, remove seeds, cut into 1-inch-wide slices, and peel. Cut flesh into 1-inch cubes. Boil 2 minutes in water. **Caution: Do not mash or puree.** Fill hot jars with cubes and cooking liquid, leaving 1-inch headspace. Remove air bubbles and adjust headspace if needed. Wipe rims of jars with a dampened clean paper towel. Adjust lids and process.

For making pies, drain jars and strain or sieve the cubes at preparation time.

Recommended process time for Pumpkin and Winter Squash in a dial-gauge pressure canner						
			Canner Pressure (PSI) at Altitudes of			
Style of Pack	Jar Size	Process Time	0-2,000 ft	2,001-4,000 ft	4,001-6,000 ft	6,001-8,000 ft
Hot	Pints	55 min	11 lb	12 lb	13 lb	14 lb
	Quarts	90	11	12	13	14

Recommended process time for Pumpkin and Winter Squash in a weighted-gauge pressure canner				
			Canner Pressure (PSI) at Altitudes of	
Style of Pack	Jar Size	Process Time	0-1,000 ft	Above 1,000 ft
Hot	Pints	55 min	10 lb	15 lb
	Quarts	90	10	15

Soups

Caution: Do not add noodles or other pasta, rice, flour, cream, milk or other thickening agents to home canned soups. If dried beans or peas are used, they must be fully rehydrated first.

Procedure: Select, wash, and prepare vegetables, meat, and seafoods as described for the specific foods. Cover meat with water and cook until tender. Cool meat and remove bones. Cook vegetables. For each cup of dried beans or peas, add 3 cups of water, boil 2 minutes, remove from heat, soak 1 hour, and heat to boil.

Drain all foods and combine with meat broth, tomatoes, or water to cover. Boil 5 minutes. **Caution: Do not thicken.** Salt to taste, if desired.

Fill hot jars only halfway with mixture of solids. Add and cover with remaining liquid, leaving 1-inch headspace. Remove air bubbles and adjust headspace if needed. Wipe rims of jars with a dampened clean paper towel. Adjust lids and process.

Recommended process time for Soups in a dial-gauge pressure canner						
			Canner Pressure (PSI) at Altitudes of			
Style of Pack	Jar Size	Process Time	0- 2,000 ft	2,001- 4,000 ft	4,001- 6,000 ft	6,001- 8,000 ft
Hot	Pints	60* min	11 lb	12 lb	13 lb	14 lb
	Quarts	75*	11	12	13	14

*Caution: Process 100 minutes if soup contains seafoods.

Recommended process time for Soups in a weighted-gauge pressure canner				
			Canner Pressure (PSI) at Altitudes of	
Style of Pack	Jar Size	Process Time	0-1,000 ft	Above 1,000 ft
Hot	Pints	60* min	10 lb	15 lb
	Quarts	75*	10	15

*Caution: Process 100 minutes if soup contains seafoods.

Spinach and other Greens

Quantity: An average of 28 pounds is needed per canner load of 7 quarts; an average of 18 pounds is needed per canner load of 9 pints. A bushel weighs 18 pounds and yields 3 to 9 quarts — an average of 4 pounds per quart.

Quality: Can only freshly harvested greens. Discard any wilted, discolored, diseased, or insect-damaged leaves. Leaves should be tender and attractive in color.

Procedure: Wash only small amounts of greens at a time. Drain water and continue rinsing until water is clear and free of grit. Cut out tough stems and midribs. Place 1 pound of greens at a time in cheesecloth bag or blancher basket and steam 3 to 5 minutes or until well wilted. Add 1/2 teaspoon of salt to each quart jar, if desired. Fill hot jars loosely with greens and add fresh boiling water, leaving 1-inch headspace. Remove air bubbles and adjust headspace if needed. Wipe rims of jars with a dampened clean paper towel. Adjust lids and process.

Recommended process time for Spinach and Other Greens in a dial-gauge pressure canner						
			Canner Pressure (PSI) at Altitudes of			
Style of Pack	Jar Size	Process Time	0-2,000 ft	2,001-4,000 ft	4,001-6,000 ft	6,001-8,000 ft
Hot	Pints	70 min	11 lb	12 lb	13 lb	14 lb
	Quarts	90	11	12	13	14

Recommended process time for Spinach and Other Greens in a weighted-gauge pressure canner				
			Canner Pressure (PSI) at Altitudes of	
Style of Pack	Jar Size	Process Time	0-1,000 ft	Above 1,000 ft
Hot	Pints	70 min	10 lb	15 lb
	Quarts	90	10	15

Succotash

15 lbs unhusked sweet corn or 3 qts cut whole kernels

14 lbs mature green podded lima beans or 4 qts shelled limas

2 qts crushed or whole tomatoes (optional)

Yield: 7 quarts

Procedure: Wash and prepare fresh produce as described previously for specific vegetables.

Hot pack — Combine all prepared vegetables in a large kettle with enough water to cover the pieces. Add 1 teaspoon salt to each hot quart jar, if desired. Boil succotash gently for 5 minutes and fill hot jars with pieces and cooking liquid, leaving 1-inch headspace.

Raw pack — Fill hot jars with equal parts of all prepared vegetables, leaving 1-inch headspace. Do not shake or press down pieces. Add 1 teaspoon salt to each quart jar, if desired. Add fresh boiling water, leaving 1-inch headspace.

Remove air bubbles and adjust headspace if needed. Wipe rims of jars with a dampened clean paper towel. Adjust lids and process.

Recommended process time for Succotash in a dial-gauge pressure canner						
			Canner Pressure (PSI) at Altitudes of			
Style of Pack	Jar Size	Process Time	0-2,000 ft	2,001-4,000 ft	4,001-6,000 ft	6,001-8,000 ft
Hot and Raw	Pints	60 min	11 lb	12 lb	13 lb	14 lb
	Quarts	85	11	12	13	14

Recommended process time for Succotash in a weighted-gauge pressure canner				
			Canner Pressure (PSI) at Altitudes of	
Style of Pack	Jar Size	Process Time	0-1,000 ft	Above 1,000 ft
Hot and Raw	Pints	60 min	10 lb	15 lb
	Quarts	85	10	15

Appendix D

Canning Poultry, Red Meats, and Seafood

— Courtesy of the USDA

Chicken or Rabbit

Procedure: Choose freshly killed and dressed, healthy animals. Large chickens are more flavorful than fryers. Dressed chicken should be chilled for 6 to 12 hours before canning. Dressed rabbits should be soaked 1 hour in water containing 1 tablespoon of salt per quart, and then rinsed. Remove excess fat. Cut the chicken or rabbit into suitable sizes for canning. Can with or without bones.

Hot pack — Boil, steam, or bake meat until about two-thirds done. Add 1 teaspoon salt per quart to the jar, if desired. Fill hot jars with pieces and hot broth, leaving 1-1/4 inch head-space. Remove air bubbles and adjust headspace if needed.

Raw pack — Add 1 teaspoon salt per quart, if desired. Fill hot jars loosely with raw meat pieces, leaving 1-1/4-inch headspace. Do not add liquid.

Wipe rims of jars with a dampened clean paper towel. Adjust lids and process.

Recommended process time for Chicken or Rabbit in a dial-gauge pressure canner						
			Canner Pressure (PSI) at Altitudes of			
Style of Pack	Jar Size	Process Time	0-2,000 ft	2,001-4,000 ft	4,001-6,000 ft	6,001-8,000 ft
Without Bones:						
Hot and Raw	Pints	75 min	11 lb	12 lb	13 lb	14 lb
	Quarts	90	11	12	13	14
With Bones:						
Hot and Raw	Pints	65 min	11 lb	12 lb	13 lb	14 lb
	Quarts	75	11	12	13	14

Recommended process time for Chicken or Rabbit in a weighted-gauge pressure canner				
			Canner Pressure (PSI) at Altitudes of	
Style of Pack	Jar Size	Process Time	0-1,000 ft	Above 1,000 ft
Without Bones:				
Hot and Raw	Pints	75 min	10 lb	15 lb
	Quarts	90	10	15
With Bones:				
Hot and Raw	Pints	65 min	10 lb	15 lb
	Quarts	75	10	15

Ground or Chopped Meat

Bear, beef, lamb, pork, sausage, veal, venison

Procedure: Choose fresh, chilled meat. With venison, add 1 part high-quality pork fat to 3 or 4 parts venison before grinding. Use freshly made sausage, seasoned with salt and cayenne pepper (sage may cause a bitter off-flavor). Shape chopped meat into patties or balls or cut cased sausage into 3- to 4-inch links. Cook until lightly browned. Ground meat may be sauteed without shaping. Remove excess fat. Fill hot jars with pieces. Add boiling meat broth, tomato juice, or water, leaving 1-inch headspace. Remove air bubbles and adjust headspace if needed. Add 1 teaspoon of salt per quart to the jars, if desired. Wipe rims of jars with a dampened clean paper towel. Adjust lids and process.

Recommended process time for Ground or Chopped Meat in a dial-gauge pressure canner						
			Canner Pressure (PSI) at Altitudes of			
Style of Pack	Jar Size	Process Time	0-2,000 ft	2,001-4,000 ft	4,001-6,000 ft	6,001-8,000 ft
Hot	Pints	75 min	11 lb	12 lb	13 lb	14 lb
	Quarts	90	11	12	13	14

Recommended process time for Ground or Chopped Meat in a weighted-gauge pressure canner				
			Canner Pressure (PSI) at Altitudes of	
Style of Pack	Jar Size	Process Time	0-1,000 ft	Above 1,000 ft
Hot	Pints	75 min	10 lb	15 lb
	Quarts	90	10	15

Strips, Cubes, or Chunks of Meat

Bear, beef, lamb, pork, veal, venison

Procedure: Choose quality chilled meat. Remove excess fat. Soak strong-flavored wild meats for 1 hour in brine water containing 1 tablespoon of salt per quart. Rinse. Remove large bones.

Hot pack — Precook meat until rare by roasting, stewing, or browning in a small amount of fat. Add 1 teaspoon of salt per quart to the jar, if desired. Fill hot jars with pieces and add boiling broth, meat drippings, water, or tomato juice (especially with wild game), leaving 1-inch headspace. Remove air bubbles and adjust headspace if needed.

Raw pack — Add 1 teaspoon of salt per quart to the jar, if desired. Fill hot jars with raw meat pieces, leaving 1-inch headspace. Do not add liquid.

Wipe rims of jars with a dampened clean paper towel. Adjust lids and process.

Recommended process time for Strips, Cubes, or Chunks of Meat in a dial-gauge pressure canner						
			Canner Pressure (PSI) at Altitudes of			
Style of Pack	Jar Size	Process Time	0-2,000 ft	2,001-4,000 ft	4,001-6,000 ft	6,001-8,000 ft
Hot and Raw	Pints	75 min	11 lb	12 lb	13 lb	14 lb
	Quarts	90	11	12	13	14

Recommended process time for Strips, Cubes, or Chunks of Meat in a weighted-gauge pressure canner				
			Canner Pressure (PSI) at Altitudes of	
Style of Pack	Jar Size	Process Time	0-1,000 ft	Above 1,000 ft
Hot and Raw	Pints	75 min	10 lb	15 lb
	Quarts	90	10	15

Meat Stock (Broth)

Beef: Saw or crack fresh trimmed beef bones to enhance extraction of flavor. Rinse bones and place in a large stockpot or kettle, cover bones with water, add pot cover, and simmer 3 to 4 hours. Remove bones, cool broth, and pick off meat. Skim off fat, add meat trimmings removed from bones to broth, and reheat to boiling. Fill hot jars, leaving 1-inch headspace. Wipe rims of jars with a dampened clean paper towel. Adjust lids and process.

Chicken or turkey: Place large carcass bones (with most of meat removed) in a large stock-pot, add enough water to cover bones, cover pot, and simmer 30 to 45 minutes or until remaining attached meat can be easily stripped from bones. Remove bones and pieces, cool broth, strip meat, discard excess fat, and return meat trimmings to broth. Reheat to boiling and fill jars, leaving 1-inch headspace. Wipe rims of jars with a dampened clean paper towel. Adjust lids and process.

Recommended process time for Meat Stock in a dial-gauge pressure canner						
			Canner Pressure (PSI) at Altitudes of			
Style of Pack	Jar Size	Process Time	0-2,000 ft	2,001-4,000 ft	4,001-6,000 ft	6,001-8,000 ft
Hot	Pints	20 min	11 lb	12 lb	13 lb	14 lb
	Quarts	25	11	12	13	14

Recommended process time for Meat Stock in a weighted-gauge pressure canner				
			Canner Pressure (PSI) at Altitudes of	
Style of Pack	Jar Size	Process Time	0-1,000 ft	Above 1,000 ft
Hot	Pints	20 min	10 lb	15 lb
	Quarts	25	10	15

Clams

Whole or minced

Procedure: Keep clams live on ice until ready to can. Scrub shells thoroughly and rinse, steam 5 minutes, and open. Remove clam meat. Collect and save clam juice. Wash clam meat in water containing 1 teaspoon of salt per quart. Rinse and cover clam meat with boiling water containing 2 tablespoons of lemon juice or 1/2 teaspoon of citric acid per gallon. Boil 2 minutes and drain. To make minced clams, grind clams with a meat grinder or food processor. Fill hot jars loosely with pieces and add hot clam juice and boiling water if needed, leaving 1-inch headspace. Remove air bubbles and adjust headspace if needed. Wipe rims of jars with a dampened clean paper towel. Adjust lids and process.

Recommended process time for Clams in a dial-gauge pressure canner						
			Canner Pressure (PSI) at Altitudes of			
Style of Pack	Jar Size	Process Time	0-2,000 ft	2,001-4,000 ft	4,001-6,000 ft	6,001-8,000 ft
Hot	Half-pints	60 min	11 lb	12 lb	13 lb	14 lb
	Pints	70	11	12	13	14

Recommended process time for Clams in a weighted-gauge pressure canner				
			Canner Pressure (PSI) at Altitudes of	
Style of Pack	Jar Size	Process Time	0-1,000 ft	Above 1,000 ft
Hot	Half-pints	60 min	10 lb	15 lb
	Pints	70	10	15

King and Dungeness Crab Meat

It is recommended that blue crab meat be frozen instead of canned for best quality.

Crab meat canned according to the following procedure may have a distinctly acidic flavor and freezing is the preferred method of preservation at this time.

Procedure: Keep live crabs on ice until ready to can. Wash crabs thoroughly, using several changes of cold water. Simmer crabs 20 minutes in water containing a cup of lemon juice and 2 tablespoons of salt (or up to 1 cup of salt, if desired) per gallon. Cool in cold water, drain, remove back shell, then remove meat from body and claws. Soak meat 2 minutes in cold water containing 2 cups of lemon juice or 4 cups of white vinegar, and 2 tablespoons of salt (or up to 1 cup of salt, if desired) per gallon. Drain and squeeze crab meat to remove excess moisture. Fill hot half-pint jars with 6 ounces of crab meat and pint jars with 12 ounces, leaving 1-inch headspace. Add 1/2 teaspoon of citric acid or 2 tablespoons of lemon juice to each half-pint jar, or 1 teaspoon of citric acid or 4 tablespoons of lemon juice per pint jar. Cover with fresh boiling water, leaving 1-inch headspace. Remove air bubbles and adjust headspace if needed. Wipe rims of jars with a dampened clean paper towel. Adjust lids and process.

Recommended process time for King and Dungeness Crab Meat in a dial-gauge pressure canner						
			Canner Pressure (PSI) at Altitudes of			
Style of Pack	Jar Size	Process Time	0- 2,000 ft	2,001- 4,000 ft	4,001- 6,000 ft	6,001- 8,000 ft
See above	Half-pints	70 min	11 lb	12 lb	13 lb	14 lb
	Pints	80	11	12	13	14

Recommended process time for King and Dungeness Crab Meat in a weighted-gauge pressure canner				
			Canner Pressure (PSI) at Altitudes of	
Style of Pack	**Jar Size**	**Process Time**	**0-1,000 ft**	**Above 1,000 ft**
See above	**Half-pints**	70 min	10 lb	15 lb
	Pints	80	10	15

Fish in Pint Jars

Blue, mackerel, salmon, steelhead, trout, and other fatty fish except tuna

Caution: Bleed and eviscerate fish immediately after catching, never more than 2 hours after they are caught. Keep cleaned fish on ice until ready to can.

Note: Glass-like crystals of struvite, or magnesium ammonium phosphate, sometime form in canned salmon. There is no way for the home canner to prevent these crystals from forming, but they usually dissolve when heated and are safe to eat.

Procedure: If the fish is frozen, thaw it in the refrigerator before canning. Rinse the fish in cold water. You can add vinegar to the water (2 table-spoons per quart) to help remove slime. Remove head, tail, fins, and scales; it is not necessary to remove the skin. You can leave the bones in most fish, because the bones become very soft and are a good source of calcium. For halibut, remove the head, tail, fins, skin, and the bones. Wash and remove all blood. Refrigerate all fish until you are ready to pack in jars.

Split fish lengthwise, if desired. Cut cleaned fish into 3-1/2-inch lengths. If the skin has been left on the fish, pack the fish skin out, for a nicer appearance or skin in, for easier jar cleaning. Fill hot pint jars, leaving 1-inch headspace. Add 1 teaspoon of salt per pint, if desired. Do not add liquids. Carefully clean the jar rims with a clean, damp paper towel; wipe with a dry paper towel to remove any fish oil. Adjust lids and process. Fish in half-pint or 12-ounce jars would be processed for the same amount of time as pint jars.

Recommended process time for Fish in Pint Jars in a dial-gauge pressure canner						
			Canner Pressure (PSI) at Altitudes of			
Style of Pack	Jar Size	Process Time	0-2,000 ft	2,001-4,000 ft	4,001-6,000 ft	6,001-8,000 ft
Raw	Pints	100 min	11 lb	12 lb	13 lb	14 lb

Recommended process time for Fish in Pint Jars in a weighted-gauge pressure canner				
			Canner Pressure (PSI) at Altitudes of	
Style of Pack	Jar Size	Process Time	0-1,000 ft	Above 1,000 ft
Raw	Pints	100 min	10 lb	15 lb

Fish in Quart Jars

Blue, mackerel, salmon, steelhead, trout, and other fatty fish except tuna

Note: Glass-like crystals of struvite, or magnesium ammonium phosphate, sometime form in canned salmon. There is no way for the home canner to prevent these crystals from forming, but they usually dissolve when heated and are safe to eat.

Caution: Bleed and eviscerate fish immediately after catching, never more than 2 hours after they are caught. Keep cleaned fish on ice until ready to can.

Procedure: If the fish is frozen, thaw it in the refrigerator before canning. Rinse the fish in cold water. You can add vinegar to the water (2 tablespoons per quart) to help remove slime. Remove head, tail, fins, and scales; it is not necessary to remove the skin. You can leave the bones in most fish, because the bones become very soft and are a good source of calcium. For halibut, remove the head, tail, fins, skin, and the bones. Wash and remove all blood. Refrigerate all fish until you are ready to pack in jars.

Cut the fish into jar-length filets or chunks of any size. The one-quart straight-sided mason-type jar is recommended. If the skin has been left on the fish, pack the fish skin out, for a nicer appearance or skin in, for easier jar cleaning. Pack solidly into hot quart jars, leaving 1-inch headspace. If desired, run a plastic knife around the inside of the jar to align the product; this allows firm packing of fish.

For most fish, no liquid, salt, or spices need to be added, although seasonings or salt may be added for flavor (1 to 2 teaspoons salt per quart, or amount desired).

For halibut, add up to 4 tablespoons of vegetable or olive oil per quart jar if you wish. The canned product will seem moister. However, the oil will increase the caloric value of the fish.

Carefully clean the jar rims with a clean, damp paper towel; wipe with a dry paper towel to remove any fish oil. Adjust lids and process.

Processing Change for Quart Jars: The directions for operating the pressure canner during processing of quart jars are different from those for processing pint jars, so please read the following carefully. It is critical to product safety that the processing directions are followed exactly. When you are ready to process your jars of fish, add 3 quarts of water to the pressure canner. Put the rack in the bottom of the canner and place closed jars on the rack. Fasten the canner cover securely, but do not close the lid vent. Heat the canner on high for 20 minutes. If steam comes through the open vent in a steady stream at the end of 20 minutes, allow it to escape for an additional 10 minutes. If steam does not come through the open vent in a steady stream at the end of 20 minutes, keep heating the canner until it does. Then allow the steam to escape for an additional 10 minutes to vent the canner. This step removes air from inside the canner so the temperature is the same throughout the canner. *The total time it takes to heat and vent the canner should never be less than 30 minutes. The total time may be more than 30 minutes if you have tightly packed jars, cold fish, or larger sized canners.* **For safety's sake, you must have a complete, uninterrupted 160 minutes (2 hours and 40 minutes) at a minimum pressure required for your altitude. Write down the time at the beginning of the process and the time when the process will be finished.**

Recommended process time for Fish in Quart Jars in a dial-gauge pressure canner						
			Canner Pressure (PSI) at Altitudes of			
Style of Pack	Jar Size	Process Time	0-2,000 ft	2,001-4,000 ft	4,001-6,000 ft	6,001-8,000 ft
Raw	Quarts	160 min	11 lb	12 lb	13 lb	14 lb

Recommended process time for Fish in Quart Jars in a weighted-gauge pressure canner				
			Canner Pressure (PSI) at Altitudes of	
Style of Pack	Jar Size	Process Time	0-1,000 ft	Above 1,000 ft
Raw	Quarts	160 min	10 lb	15 lb

Oysters

Procedure: Keep live oysters on ice until ready to can. Wash shells. Heat 5 to 7 minutes in preheated oven at 400 degrees F. Cool briefly in ice water. Drain, open shell, and remove meat. Wash meat in water containing 1/2 cup salt per gallon. Drain. Add 1/2 teaspoon salt to each pint, if desired. Fill hot half-pint or pint jars with drained oysters and cover with fresh boiling water, leaving 1-inch headspace. Remove air bubbles and adjust headspace if needed. Wipe rims of jars with a dampened clean paper towel. Adjust lids and process.

Recommended process time for Oysters in a dial-gauge pressure canner						
			Canner Pressure (PSI) at Altitudes of			
Style of Pack	Jar Size	Process Time	0- 2,000 ft	2,001- 4,000 ft	4,001- 6,000 ft	6,001- 8,000 ft
See above	Half- pints or Pints	75 min	11 lb	12 lb	13 lb	14 lb

Recommended process time for Oysters in a weighted-gauge pressure canner				
			Canner Pressure (PSI) at Altitudes of	
Style of Pack	Jar Size	Process Time	0-1,000 ft	Above 1,000 ft
See above	Half- pints or Pints	75 min	10 lb	15 lb

Smoked Fish

Salmon, rockfish and flatfish (sole, cod, flounder) and other fish

Caution: Safe processing times for other smoked seafoods have not been determined. Those products should be frozen. Smoking of fish should be done by tested methods. Lightly smoked fish is recommended for canning because the smoked flavor will become stronger and the flesh drier after processing. However, because it has not yet been cooked, do not taste lightly smoked fish before canning.

Follow these recommended canning instructions carefully. Use a 16 to 22 quart pressure canner for this procedure; do not use smaller pressure saucepans. Safe processing times have not been determined. Do not use jars larger than 1 pint. Half-pints could be safely processed for the same length of time as pints, but the quality of the product may be less acceptable.

Procedure: If smoked fish has been frozen, thaw in the refrigerator until no ice crystals remain before canning. If not done prior to smoking, cut fish into pieces that will fit vertically into pint canning jars, leaving 1-inch headspace. Pack smoked fish vertically into hot jars, leaving 1-inch head-space between the pieces and the top rim of the jar. The fish may be packed either loosely or tightly. Do not add liquid to the jars. Clean jar rims with a clean, damp paper towel. Adjust lids and process.

Processing Change for Smoked Fish: The directions for filling the pressure canner for processing smoked fish are different than those for other pressure canning, so please read the following carefully. It is critical to product safety that the processing directions are followed exactly. When you are ready to process your jars of smoked fish, measure 4 quarts (16 cups) of cool tap water and pour into the pressure canner. (**Note:** The water level probably will reach the screw bands of pint jars.) **Do not decrease the amount of water or heat the water before processing begins.** Place prepared, closed jars on the rack in the bottom of the canner, and proceed as with usual pressure canning instructions.

Recommended process time for Smoked Fish in a dial-gauge pressure canner						
			Canner Pressure (PSI) at Altitudes of			
Style of Pack	Jar Size	Process Time	0-2,000 ft	2,001-4,000 ft	4,001-6,000 ft	6,001-8,000 ft
See above	Pints	110 min	11 lb	12 lb	13 lb	14 lb

			Canner Pressure (PSI) at Altitudes of	
Style of Pack	Jar Size	Process Time	0-1,000 ft	Above 1,000 ft
See above	Pints	110 min	10 lb	15 lb

Table title: Recommended process time for Smoked Fish in a weighted-gauge pressure canner

Tuna

Tuna may be canned either precooked or raw. Precooking removes most of the strong-flavored oils. The strong flavor of dark tuna flesh affects the delicate flavor of white flesh. Many people prefer not to can dark flesh. It may be used as pet food.

Note: Glass-like crystals of struvite, or magnesium ammonium phosphate, sometime form in canned tuna. There is no way for the home canner to prevent these crystals from forming, but they usually dissolve when heated and are safe to eat.

Procedure: Keep tuna on ice until ready to can. Remove viscera and wash fish well in cold water. Allow blood to drain from stomach cavity. Place fish belly down on a rack or metal tray in the bottom of a large baking pan. Cut tuna in half crosswise, if necessary. Precook fish by baking at 250 degrees F for 2-1/2 to 4 hours (depending on size) or at 350 degrees F for 1 hour. The fish may also be cooked in a steamer for 2 to 4 hours. If a thermometer is used, cook to a 165 degrees to 175 degrees F internal temperature. Refrigerate cooked fish overnight to firm the meat. Peel off the skin with a knife, removing blood vessels and any discolored flesh. Cut meat away from bones; cut out and discard all bones, fin bases, and dark flesh. Quarter. Cut quarters crosswise into lengths suitable for half-pint or pint jars. Fill into hot jars, pressing down gently to make a solid pack. Tuna may be packed in water or oil, whichever is preferred. Add water or oil to jars, leaving 1-inch headspace. Remove air bubbles and adjust headspace if needed. Add 1/2 teaspoon of salt per half-pint or 1 teaspoon of salt per pint, if desired. Carefully clean the jar rims with a clean, damp paper towel; wipe with a dry paper towel to remove any fish oil. Adjust lids and process.

Recommended process time for Tuna in a dial-gauge pressure canner						
			Canner Pressure (PSI) at Altitudes of			
Style of Pack	**Jar Size**	**Process Time**	**0- 2,000 ft**	**2,001- 4,000 ft**	**4,001- 6,000 ft**	**6,001- 8,000 ft**
See above	**Half- pints or Pints**	100 min	11 lb	12 lb	13 lb	14 lb

Recommended process time for Tuna in a weighted-gauge pressure canner				
			Canner Pressure (PSI) at Altitudes of	
Style of Pack	**Jar Size**	**Process Time**	**0-1,000 ft**	**Above 1,000 ft**
See above	**Half- pints or Pints**	100 min	10 lb	15 lb

Appendix E

Canning Fermented Foods and Pickled Vegetables

— Courtesy of the USDA

Selection of Fresh Cucumbers

Quantity: An average of 14 pounds is needed per canner load of 7 quarts; an average of 9 pounds is needed per canner load of 9 pints. A bushel weighs 48 pounds and yields 16 to 24 quarts — an average of 2 pounds per quart.

Quality: Select firm cucumbers of the appropriate size: about 1-1/2 inches for gherkins and 4 inches for dills. Use odd-shaped and more mature cucumbers for relishes and bread-and-butter style pickles.

Low-Temperature Pasteurization Treatment

The following treatment results in a better product texture but must be carefully managed to avoid possible spoilage. Place jars in a canner filled half way with warm (120 degrees to 140 degrees F) water. Then, add hot water to a level 1 inch above jars. Heat the water enough to maintain 180 degrees to 185 degrees F water temperature for 30 minutes. Check with a candy or jelly thermometer to be certain that the water temperature is at least 180 degrees F during the entire 30 minutes. Temperatures higher than 185 degrees F may cause unnecessary softening of pickles. **Caution: Use only when recipe indicates.**

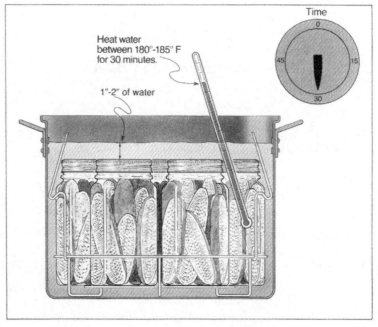

Illustration courtesy of the USDA

Suitable Containers, Covers, and Weights for Fermenting Food

A 1-gallon container is needed for each 5 pounds of fresh vegetables. Therefore, a 5-gallon stone crock is of ideal size for fermenting about 25 pounds of fresh cabbage or cucumbers. Food-grade plastic and glass containers are excellent substitutes for stone crocks. Other 1- to 3-gallon non-food-grade plastic containers may be used if lined inside with a clean food-grade plastic bag. **Caution: Be certain that foods contact only food-grade plastics. Do not use garbage bags or trash liners.** Fermenting sauerkraut in quart and half-gallon Mason jars is an acceptable practice, but may result in more spoilage losses.

Cabbage and cucumbers must be kept 1 to 2 inches under brine while fermenting. After adding prepared vegetables and brine, insert a suitably

308 The Complete Guide to Food Preservation

sized dinner plate or glass pie plate inside the fermentation container. The plate must be slightly smaller than the container opening, yet large enough to cover most of the shredded cabbage or cucumbers. To keep the plate under the brine, weigh it down with 2 to 3 sealed quart jars filled with water. Covering the container opening with a clean, heavy bath towel helps to prevent contamination from insects and molds while the vegetables are fermenting. Fine quality fermented vegetables are also obtained when the plate is weighted down with a very large, clean, plastic bag filled with 3 quarts of water containing 4-1/2 tablespoons of canning or pickling salt. Be sure to seal the plastic bag. Freezer bags sold for packaging turkeys are suitable for use with 5-gallon containers.

The fermentation container, plate, and jars must be washed in hot sudsy water, and rinsed well with very hot water before use.

Salts Used in Pickling

Use of canning or pickling salt is recommended. Fermented and nonfermented pickles may be safely made using either iodized or noniodized table salt. However, noncaking materials added to table salts may make the brine cloudy. Flake salt varies in density and is not recommended for use.

Reduced-sodium salts, for example mixtures of sodium and potassium chloride, may be used in quick pickle recipes, as indicated in this guide. The pickles may, however, have a slightly different taste than expected. **Caution: Use of reduced-sodium salt in fermented pickle recipes is not recommended.**

Fermented Foods

Dill Pickles

Use the following quantities for each gallon capacity of your container.

> *4 lbs of 4-inch pickling cucumbers*
> *2 tbsp dill seed or 4 to 5 heads fresh or dry dill weed*
> *1/2 cup salt*
> *1/4 cup vinegar (5%)*
> *8 cups water and one or more of the following ingredients:*
>> *2 cloves garlic (optional)*
>> *2 dried red peppers (optional)*
>> *2 tsp whole mixed pickling spices (optional)*

Procedure: Wash cucumbers. Cut 1/16-inch slice off blossom end and discard. Leave 1/4-inch of stem attached. Place half of dill and spices on bottom of a clean, suitable container (see page 307). Add cucumbers, remaining dill, and spices. Dissolve salt in vinegar and water and pour over cucumbers. Add suitable cover and weight. Store where temperature is between 70 degrees and 75 degrees F for about 3 to 4 weeks while fermenting. Temperatures of 55 degrees to 65 degrees F are acceptable, but the fermentation will take 5 to 6 weeks. Avoid temperatures above 80 degrees F, or pickles will become too soft during fermentation. Fermenting pickles cure slowly. Check the container several times a week and promptly remove surface scum or mold. **Caution: If the pickles become soft, slimy, or develop a disagreeable odor, discard them.** Fully fermented pickles may be stored in the original container for about 4 to 6 months, provided they are refrigerated and surface scum and molds are removed regularly. Canning fully fermented pickles is a better way to store them. To can them, pour the brine into a pan, heat slowly to a boil, and simmer 5 minutes. Filter brine through paper coffee filters to reduce cloudiness, if desired. Fill hot jar with pickles and hot brine, leaving 1/2-inch headspace. Remove air bubbles and adjust headspace if needed. Wipe rims of jars with a dampened clean paper towel. Adjust lids and process as below, or use the low temperature pasteurization treatment described below.

Recommended process time for Dill Pickles in a boiling-water canner				
		Process Time at Altitudes of		
Style of Pack	Jar Size	0-1,000 ft	1,001-6,000 ft	Above 6,000 ft
Raw	Pints	10 min	15	20
	Quarts	15	20	25

Sauerkraut

25 lbs cabbage

3/4 cup canning or pickling salt

Quality: For the best sauerkraut, use firm heads of fresh cabbage. Shred cabbage and start kraut between 24 and 48 hours after harvest.

Yield: About 9 quarts

Procedure: Work with about 5 pounds of cabbage at a time. Discard outer leaves. Rinse heads under cold running water and drain. Cut heads in quarters and remove cores. Shred or slice to a thickness of a quarter. Put cabbage in a suitable fermentation container and add 3 tablespoons of salt. Mix thoroughly, using clean hands. Pack firmly until salt draws juices from cabbage. Repeat shredding, salting, and packing until all cabbage is in the container. Be sure it is deep enough so that its rim is at least 4 or 5 inches above the cabbage. If juice does not cover cabbage, add boiled and cooled brine (1-1/2 tablespoons of salt per quart of water). Add plate and weights; cover container with a clean bath towel. Store at 70 degrees to 75 degrees F while fermenting. At temperatures between 70 degrees and 75 degrees F, kraut will be fully fermented in about 3 to 4 weeks; at 60 degrees to 65 degrees F, fermentation may take 5 to 6 weeks. At temperatures lower than 60 degrees F, kraut may not ferment. Above 75 degrees F, kraut may become soft.

If you weigh the cabbage down with a brine-filled bag, do not disturb the crock until normal fermentation is completed (when bubbling ceases). If you use jars as weight, you will have to check the kraut two to three times each week and remove scum if it forms. Fully fermented kraut may be kept tightly covered in the refrigerator for several months or it may be canned as follows:

Hot pack — Bring kraut and liquid slowly to a boil in a large kettle, stirring frequently. Remove from heat and fill hot jars rather firmly with kraut and juices, leaving 1/2-inch headspace.

Raw pack — Fill hot jars firmly with kraut and cover with juices, leaving 1/2-inch headspace.

Remove air bubbles and adjust headspace if needed. Wipe rims of jars with a dampened clean paper towel. Adjust lids and process.

Recommended process time for Sauerkraut in a boiling-water canner					
		Process Time at Altitudes of			
Style of Pack	Jar Size	0-1,000 ft	1,001-3,000 ft	3,001-6,000 ft	Above 6,000 ft
Hot	Pints	10 min	15	15	20
	Quarts	15	20	20	25
Raw	Pints	20	25	30	35
	Quarts	25	30	35	40

Bread-and-Butter Pickles

6 lbs of 4- to 5-inch pickling cucumbers
8 cups thinly sliced onions (about 3 pounds)

1/2 cup canning or pickling salt

4 cups vinegar (5%)

4-1/2 cups sugar

2 tbsp mustard seed

1 -1/2 tbsp celery seed

1 tbsp ground turmeric

1 cup pickling lime (optional) for use in variation below for making firmer pickles

Yield: About 8 pints

Procedure: Wash cucumbers. Cut 1/16-inch off blossom end and discard. Cut into 3/16-inch slices. Combine cucumbers and onions in a large bowl. Add salt. Cover with 2 inches crushed or cubed ice. Refrigerate 3 to 4 hours, adding more ice as needed.

Combine remaining ingredients in a large pot. Boil 10 minutes. Drain and add cucumbers and onions and slowly reheat to boiling. Fill hot pint jars with slices and cooking syrup, leaving 1/2-inch headspace. Remove air bubbles and adjust headspace if needed. Wipe rims of jars with a dampened clean paper towel. Adjust lids and process as below or use low-temperature pasteurization treatment.

Variation for firmer pickles: Wash cucumbers. Cut 1/16-inch off blossom end and discard. Cut into 3/16-inch slices. Mix 1 cup pickling lime and 1/2 cup salt to 1 gallon water in a 2- to 3-gallon crock or enamelware container. **Caution: Avoid inhaling lime dust while mixing the lime-water solution.** Soak cucumber slices in lime water for 12 to 24 hours, stirring occasionally. Remove from lime solution, rinse, and resoak for 1 hour in fresh cold water. Repeat the rinsing and soaking steps two more times. Handle carefully, because slices will be brittle. Drain well.

Storage: After processing and cooling, jars should be stored 4 to 5 weeks to develop ideal flavor.

Variation: Squash bread-and-butter pickles. Substitute slender (1 to 1-1/2 inches in diameter) zucchini or yellow summer squash for cucumbers.

		Process Time at Altitudes of		
Style of Pack	**Jar Size**	**0-1,000 ft**	**1,001- 6,000 ft**	**Above 6,000 ft**
Hot	Pints or Quarts	10 min	15	20

Recommended process time for Bread-and-Butter Pickles in a boiling-water canner

Quick Fresh-Pack Dill Pickles

8 lbs of 3- to 5-inch pickling cucumbers
2 gallons water
1-1/4 cups canning or pickling salt (divided)
1-1/2 qts vinegar (5%)
1/4 cup sugar
2 qts water
2 tbsp whole mixed pickling spice
    about 3 tbsp whole mustard seed (1 tsp per pint jar)
    about 14 heads of fresh dill (1 -1/2 heads per pint jar)
    or 4-1/2 tbsp dill seed (1-1/2 tsp per pint jar)

Yield: About 7 to 9 pints

Procedure: Wash cucumbers. Cut 1/16-inch slice off blossom end and discard, but leave 1/4-inch of stem attached. Dissolve 3/4 cup salt in 2 gallons water. Pour over cucumbers and let stand 12 hours. Drain. Combine vinegar, 1/2 cup salt, sugar, and 2 quarts water. Add mixed pickling spices tied in a clean white cloth. Heat to boiling. Fill hot jars with cucumbers. Add 1 tsp mustard seed and 1-1/2 heads fresh dill per pint. Cover with boiling pickling solution, leaving 1/2-inch headspace. Remove air bubbles and adjust headspace if needed. Wipe rims of jars with a dampened clean paper towel. Adjust lids and process as below or use the low-temperature pasteurization treatment described on page 306.

Recommended process time for Quick Fresh-Pack Dill Pickles in a boiling-water canner				
		Process Time at Altitudes of		
Style of Pack	**Jar Size**	**0-1,000 ft**	**1,001-6,000 ft**	**Above 6,000 ft**
Raw	Pints	10 min	15	20
	Quarts	15	20	25

Sweet Gherkin Pickles

7 lbs cucumbers (1-1/2 inch or less)

1/2 cup canning or pickling salt

8 cups sugar

6 cups vinegar (5%)

3/4 tsp turmeric

2 tsp celery seeds

2 tsp whole mixed pickling spice

2 cinnamon sticks

1/2 tsp fennel (optional)

2 tsp vanilla (optional)

Yield: About 6 to 7 pints

Procedure: Wash cucumbers. Cut 1/16-inch slice off blossom end and discard, but leave 1/4-inch of stem attached. Place cucumbers in large container and cover with boiling water. Six to 8 hours later, and again on the second day, drain and cover with 6 quarts of fresh boiling water containing 1/4-cup salt. On the third day, drain and prick cucumbers with a table fork. Combine and bring to a boil 3 cups vinegar, 3 cups sugar, turmeric, and spices. Pour over cucumbers. Six to 8 hours later, drain and save the pickling syrup. Add another 2 cups each of sugar and vinegar and reheat to boil. Pour over pickles. On the fourth day, drain and save syrup. Add another 2 cups sugar and 1 cup vinegar. Heat to boiling and pour over pickles. Drain and save pickling syrup 6 to 8 hours later. Add 1 cup sugar and 2 tsp vanilla and heat to boiling. Fill hot sterile pint jars with pickles and cover with hot syrup, leaving 1/2-inch headspace. Remove air bubbles and adjust headspace if needed. Wipe rims of jars with a dampened clean paper towel. Adjust lids and process as below, or use the low temperature pasteurization treatment described on page 306.

Recommended process time for Sweet Gherkin Pickles in a boiling-water canner				
		Process Time at Altitudes of		
Style of Pack	Jar Size	0-1,000 ft	1,001-6,000 ft	Above 6,000 ft
Raw	Pints	5 min	10	15

14-Day Sweet Pickles

Can be canned whole, in strips, or in slices

> *4 lbs of 2- to 5-inch pickling cucumbers*
> *(If packed whole, use cucumbers of uniform size)*
> *3/4 cup canning or pickling salt*
> *(Separated — 1/4 cup on each of the 1st, 3rd, and 5th days)*
> *2 tsp celery seed*
> *2 tbsp mixed pickling spices*
> *5-1/2 cups sugar*
> *4 cups vinegar (5%)*

Yield: About 5 to 9 pints

Procedure: Wash cucumbers. Cut 1/16-inch slice off blossom end and discard, but leave 1/4-inch of stem attached. Place whole cucumbers in suitable 1-gallon container. Add 1/4 cup canning or pickling salt to 2 quarts water and bring to a boil. Pour over cucumbers. Add suitable cover and weight. Place clean towel over container and keep the temperature at about 70 degrees F. **On the third and fifth days,** drain salt water and discard. Rinse cucumbers and re-scald cover and weight. Return cucumbers to container. Add 1/4 cup salt to 2 quarts fresh water and boil. Pour over cucumbers. Replace cover and weight, and re-cover with clean towel. **On the seventh day,** drain salt water and discard. Rinse cucumbers and re-scald containers, cover, and weight. Slice or strip cucumbers, if desired, and return to container. Place celery seed and pickling spices in small cheese-cloth bag. Combine 2 cups sugar and 4 cups vinegar in a saucepan. Add spice bag, bring to a boil, and pour pickling solution over cucumbers. Add cover and weight, and re-cover with clean towel. **On each of the next six days,** drain syrup and spice bag and save. Add 1/2 cup sugar each day and bring to a boil in a saucepan. Remove cucumbers and rinse. Scald container, cover, and weight daily. Return cucumbers to container, add boiled syrup, cover, weight, and re-cover with towel. **On the 14th day,** drain syrup into saucepan. Fill hot sterile pint jars or clean hot quart jars, leaving 1/2-inch headspace. Add 1/2 cup sugar to syrup and bring to boil. Remove spice bag. Pour hot syrup over cucumbers, leaving 1/2-inch headspace. Remove air bubbles and adjust headspace if needed. Wipe rims of jars with a dampened clean paper towel. Adjust lids and process as below or use low-temperature pasteurization treatment.

Recommended process time for 14-Day Sweet Pickles in a boiling-water canner				
		Process Time at Altitudes of		
Style of Pack	Jar Size	0-1,000 ft	1,001- 6,000 ft	Above 6,000 ft
Raw	Pints	5 min	10	15
	Quarts	10	15	20

Quick Sweet Pickles

May be canned as either strips or slices

8 lbs of 3- to 4-inch pickling cucumbers

1/3 cup canning or pickling salt

4-1/2 cups sugar

3-1/2 cups vinegar (5%)

2 tsp celery seed

1 tbsp whole allspice

2 tbsp mustard seed

1 cup pickling lime (optional) for use in variation below for making firmer pickles

Yield: About 7 to 9 pints

Procedure: Wash cucumbers. Cut 1/16-inch off blossom end and discard, but leave 1/4 inch of stem attached. Slice or cut in strips, if desired. Place in bowl and sprinkle with 1/3 cup salt. Cover with 2 inches of crushed or cubed ice. Refrigerate 3 to 4 hours. Add more ice as needed. Drain well.

Combine sugar, vinegar, celery seed, allspice, and mustard seed in 6-quart kettle. Heat to boiling.

Hot pack — Add cucumbers and heat slowly until vinegar solution returns to boil. Stir occasionally to make sure mixture heats evenly. Fill sterile jars, leaving 1/2-inch headspace.

Raw pack — Fill hot jars, leaving 1/2-inch headspace. Add hot pickling syrup, leaving 1/2-inch headspace.

Remove air bubbles and adjust headspace if needed. Wipe rims of jars with a dampened clean paper towel. Adjust lids and process as below or use the low temperature pasteurization treatment.

Variation for firmer pickles: Wash cucumbers. Cut 1/1 6-inch off blossom end and discard, but leave 1/4-inch of stem attached. Slice or strip cucumbers. Mix 1 cup pickling lime and 1/2 cup salt to 1 gallon water in a 2- to 3-gallon crock or enamelware container. **Caution: Avoid inhaling lime dust while mixing the lime-water solution.** Soak cucumber slices or strips in lime water solution for 12 to 24 hours, stirring occasionally. Remove from lime solution and rinse and resoak 1 hour in fresh cold water. Repeat the rinsing and resoaking two more times. Handle carefully because slices or strips will be brittle. Drain well.

Recommended process time for Quick Sweet Pickles in a boiling-water canner				
		Process Time at Altitudes of		
Style of Pack	Jar Size	0-1,000 ft	1,001-6,000 ft	Above 6,000 ft
Hot	Pints or Quarts	5 min	10	15
Raw	Pints	10	15	20
	Quarts	15	20	25

Storage: After processing and cooling, jars should be stored 4 to 5 weeks to develop ideal flavor.

Variation: Add 2 slices of raw whole onion to each jar before filling with cucumbers.

Other Vegetable Pickles

Pickled Asparagus

Yield: 6 wide-mouth pint jars

10 lbs asparagus
6 large garlic cloves

4-1/2 cups water

4-1/2 cups white distilled vinegar (5%)

6 small hot peppers (optional)

1/2 cup canning salt

3 tsp dill seed

Yield: 7 12-ounce jars

7 lbs asparagus

7 large garlic cloves

3 cups water

3 cups white distilled vinegar (5%)

7 small hot peppers (optional)

1/3 cup canning salt

2 tsp dill seed

Procedure: Wash asparagus well, but gently, under running water. Cut stems from the bottom to leave spears with tips that fit into the canning jar, leaving a little more than 1/2-inch headspace. Peel and wash garlic cloves. Place a garlic clove at the bottom of each jar, and tightly pack asparagus into hot jars with the blunt ends down. In an 8-quart saucepot, combine water, vinegar, hot peppers (optional), salt, and dill seed. Bring to a boil. Place one hot pepper (if used) in each jar over asparagus spears. Pour boiling hot pickling brine over spears, leaving 1/2-inch headspace. Remove air bubbles and adjust headspace if needed. Wipe rims of jars with a dampened clean paper towel. Adjust lids and process.

Recommended process time for Pickled Asparagus in a boiling-water canner				
		Process Time at Altitudes of		
Style of Pack	**Jar Size**	**0-1,000 ft**	**1,001- 6,000 ft**	**Above 6,000 ft**
Raw	12-ounce or Pints	10 min	15	20

Pickled Dilled Beans

4 lbs fresh tender green or yellow beans (5 to 6 inches long)
8 to 16 heads fresh dill
8 cloves garlic (optional)
1/2 cup canning or pickling salt
4 cups white vinegar (5%)
4 cups water
1 tsp hot red pepper flakes (optional)

Yield: About 8 pints

Procedure: Wash and trim ends from beans and cut to 4-inch lengths. In each hot, sterile pint jar, place 1 to 2 dill heads and, if desired, 1 clove of garlic. Place whole beans upright in jars, leaving 1/2-inch headspace. Trim beans to ensure proper fit, if necessary. Combine salt, vinegar, water, and pepper flakes (if desired). Bring to a boil. Add hot solution to beans, leaving 1/2-inch headspace. Remove air bubbles and adjust headspace if needed. Wipe rims of jars with a dampened clean paper towel. Adjust lids and process.

Recommended process time for Pickled Dilled Beans in a boiling-water canner				
		Process Time at Altitudes of		
Style of Pack	**Jar Size**	**0-1,000 ft**	**1,001-6,000 ft**	**Above 6,000 ft**
Raw	Pints	5 min	10	15

Pickled Three-Bean Salad

1-1/2 cups cut and blanched green or yellow beans (prepared as below)
1-1/2 cups canned, drained, red kidney beans
1 cup canned, drained garbanzo beans
1/2 cup peeled and thinly sliced onion (about 1 medium onion)

1/2 cup trimmed and thinly sliced celery (1-1/2 medium stalks)

1/2 cup sliced green peppers (1/2 medium pepper)

1/2 cup white vinegar (5%)

1/4 cup bottled lemon juice

3/4 cup sugar

1/4 cup oil

1/2 tsp canning or pickling salt

1-1/4 cups water

Yield: About 5 to 6 half-pints

Procedure: Wash and snap off ends of fresh beans. Cut or snap into 1- to 2-inch pieces. Blanch 3 minutes and cool immediately. Rinse kidney beans with tap water and drain again. Prepare and measure all other vegetables. Combine vinegar, lemon juice, sugar, and water and bring to a boil. Remove from heat. Add oil and salt and mix well. Add beans, onions, celery, and green pepper to solution and bring to a simmer. Marinate 12 to 14 hours in refrigerator, then heat entire mixture to a boil. Fill hot jars with solids. Add hot liquid, leaving 1/2-inch headspace. Remove air bubbles and adjust headspace if needed. Wipe rims of jars with a dampened clean paper towel. Adjust lids and process.

Recommended process time for Pickled Three-Bean Salad in a boiling-water canner				
		Process Time at Altitudes of		
Style of Pack	Jar Size	0-1,000 ft	1,001-6,000 ft	Above 6,000 ft
Hot	Half-pints or Pints	15 min	20	25

Pickled Beets

7 lbs of 2- to 2-1/2-inch diameter beets

4 cups vinegar (5%)

1-1/2 tsp canning or pickling salt

2 cups sugar

2 cups water

2 cinnamon sticks

12 whole cloves

4 to 6 onions (2- to 2-1/2-inch diameter), if desired

Yield: About 8 pints

Procedure: Trim off beet tops, leaving 1 inch of stem and roots to prevent bleeding of color. Wash thoroughly. Sort for size. Cover similar sizes together with boiling water and cook until tender (about 25 to 30 minutes). **Caution: Drain and discard liquid.** Cool beets. Trim off roots and stems and slip off skins. Slice into 1/4-inch slices. Peel and thinly slice onions. Combine vinegar, salt, sugar, and fresh water. Put spices in cheesecloth bag and add to vinegar mixture. Bring to a boil. Add beets and onions. Simmer 5 minutes. Remove spice bag. Fill hot jars with beets and onions, leaving 1/2-inch headspace. Add hot vinegar solution, allowing 1/2-inch headspace. Remove air bubbles and adjust headspace if needed. Wipe rims of jars with a dampened clean paper towel. Adjust lids and process.

Variation: For pickled whole baby beets, follow above directions but use beets that are 1 to 1-1/2 inches in diameter. Pack whole; do not slice. Onions may be omitted.

Recommended process time for Pickled Beets in a boiling-water canner					
		Process Time at Altitudes of			
Style of Pack	Jar Size	0-1,000 ft	1,001- 3,000 ft	3,001- 6,000 ft	Above 6,000 ft
Hot	Pints or Quarts	30 min	35	40	45

Pickled Carrots

2-3/4 lbs peeled carrots (about 3-1/2 lbs as purchased)

5-1/2 cups white vinegar (5%)

1 cup water

2 cups sugar

2 tsp canning salt

8 tsp mustard seed

4 tsp celery seed

Yield: About 4 pints

Procedure: Wash and peel carrots. Cut into rounds that are approximately 1/2 inch thick. Combine vinegar, water, sugar, and canning salt in an 8-quart Dutch oven or stockpot. Bring to a boil and boil 3 minutes. Add carrots and bring back to a boil. Then, reduce heat to a simmer and heat until half-cooked (about 10 minutes). Meanwhile, place 2 teaspoons mustard seed and 1 teaspoon celery seed into each empty hot pint jar. Fill jars with hot carrots, leaving 1-inch headspace. Fill with hot pickling liquid, leaving 1/2-inch headspace. Remove air bubbles and adjust headspace if needed. Wipe rims of jars with a dampened clean paper towel. Adjust lids and process.

Recommended process time for Pickled Carrots in a boiling-water canner				
		Process Time at Altitudes of		
Style of Pack	Jar Size	0-1,000 ft	1,001-6,000 ft	Above 6,000 ft
Hot	Pints	15 min	20	25

Pickled Cauliflower or Brussels Sprouts

12 cups of 1 to 2-inch cauliflower flowerets or small Brussels sprouts

4 cups white vinegar (5%)

2 cups sugar

2 cups thinly sliced onions

1 cup diced sweet red peppers

2 tbsp mustard seed

1 tbsp celery seed

1 tsp turmeric

1 tsp hot red pepper flakes

Yield: About 9 half-pints

Procedure: Wash cauliflower flowerets or Brussels sprouts (remove stems and blemished outer leaves) and boil in saltwater (4 tsp canning salt per gallon of water) for 3 minutes for cauliflower and 4 minutes for Brussels sprouts. Drain and cool. Combine vinegar, sugar, onion, diced red pepper, and spices in large saucepan. Bring to a boil and simmer 5 minutes. Distribute onion and diced pepper among jars. Fill hot jars with pieces and pickling solution, leaving 1/2-inch headspace. Remove air bubbles and adjust headspace if needed. Wipe rims of jars with a dampened clean paper towel. Adjust lids and process.

Recommended process time for Pickled Cauliflower or Brussels Sprouts in a boiling-water canner				
		Process Time at Altitudes of		
Style of Pack	Jar Size	0-1,000 ft	1,001-6,000 ft	Above 6,000 ft
Hot	Half-pints or Pints	10 min	15	20

Pickled Dilled Okra

7 lbs small okra pods

6 small hot peppers

4 tsp dill seed

8 to 9 garlic cloves

2/3 cup canning or pickling salt

6 cups water

6 cups vinegar (5%)

Yield: About 8 to 9 pints

Procedure: Wash and trim okra. Fill hot jars firmly with whole okra, leaving 1/2-inch head-space. Place 1 garlic clove in each jar. Combine salt, hot peppers, dill seed, water, and vinegar in large saucepan and bring to a boil. Pour hot pickling solution over okra, leaving 1/2-inch headspace. Remove air bubbles and adjust headspace if needed. Wipe rims of jars with a dampened clean paper towel. Adjust lids and process.

Recommended process time for Pickled Dilled Okra in a boiling-water canner				
		Process Time at Altitudes of		
Style of Pack	Jar Size	0-1,000 ft	1,001-6,000 ft	Above 6,000 ft
Hot	Pints	10 min	15	20

Pickled Pearl Onions

8 cups peeled white pearl onions

5-1/2 cups white vinegar (5%)

1 cup water

2 tsp canning salt

2 cups sugar

8 tsp mustard seed

4 tsp celery seed

Yield: About 3 to 4 pints

Procedure: To peel onions, place a few at a time in a wire-mesh basket or strainer, dip in boiling water for 30 seconds, then remove and place in cold water for 30 seconds. Cut a 1/1 6th-inch slice from the root end, and then remove the peel and cut 1/16-inch from the other end of the onion. Combine vinegar, water, salt, and sugar in an 8-quart Dutch oven or stockpot. Bring to a boil and boil 3 minutes. Add peeled onions and bring back to a boil. Reduce heat to a simmer and heat until half-cooked (about 5 minutes). Meanwhile, place 2 teaspoons mustard seed and 1 teaspoon celery seed into each empty hot pint jar. Fill with hot onions, leaving 1 inch headspace. Fill with hot pickling liquid, leaving 1/2-inch headspace. Remove air bubbles and adjust headspace if needed. Wipe rims of jars with a dampened clean paper towel. Adjust lids and process.

Recommended process time for Pickled Pearl Onions in a boiling-water canner				
		Process Time at Altitudes of		
Style of Pack	Jar Size	0-1,000 ft	1,001-6,000 ft	Above 6,000 ft
Hot	Pints	10 min	15	20

Marinated Peppers

Bell, Hungarian, banana, or jalapeno

*4 lbs firm peppers **

1 cup bottled lemon juice

2 cups white vinegar (5%)

1 tbsp oregano leaves

1 cup olive or salad oil

1/2 cup chopped onions

2 cloves garlic, quartered (optional)

2 tbsp prepared horseradish (optional)

*Note: It is possible to adjust the intensity of pickled jalapeno peppers by using all hot jalapeno peppers (hot style), or blending with sweet and mild peppers (medium or mild style).

For hot style: Use 4 lbs jalapeno peppers.

For medium style: Use 2 lbs jalapeno peppers and 2 lbs sweet and mild peppers.

For mild style: Use 1 lb jalapeno peppers and 3 lbs sweet and mild peppers.

Yield: About 9 half-pints

Procedure: Select your favorite pepper. **Caution: If you select hot peppers, wear plastic or rubber gloves and do not touch your face while handling or cutting hot peppers. If you do not wear gloves, wash hands thoroughly with soap and water before touching your face or eyes.** Peppers may be left whole. Large peppers may be quartered. Wash, slash two to four slits in each pepper, and blanch in boiling water or blister skins on tough-skinned hot peppers using one of these two methods:

Oven or broiler method to blister skins: Place peppers in a hot oven (400 degrees F) or under a broiler for 6 to 8 minutes until skins blister.

Range-top method to blister skins: Cover hot burner (either gas or electric) with heavy wire mesh. Place peppers on burner for several minutes until skins blister.

After blistering skins, place peppers in a pan and cover with a damp cloth. (This will make peeling the peppers easier.) Cool several minutes; peel off skins. Flatten whole peppers. Mix all remaining ingredients in a saucepan and heat to boiling. Place 1/4 garlic clove (optional) and 1/4 teaspoon salt in each hot half-pint jar or 1/2 teaspoon per pint. Fill hot jars with peppers. Add hot, well-mixed oil/pickling solution over peppers, leaving 1/2-inch headspace. Remove air bubbles and adjust headspace if needed. Wipe rims of jars with a dampened clean paper towel. Adjust lids and process.

Recommended process time for Marinated Peppers in a boiling-water canner				
		Process Time at Altitudes of		
Style of Pack	Jar Size	0-1,000 ft	1,001-6,000 ft	Above 6,000 ft
Raw	Half-pints or Pints	15 min	20	25

Pickled Bell Peppers

7 lbs firm bell peppers

3-1/2 cups sugar

3 cups vinegar (5%)

3 cups water

9 cloves garlic

4-1/2 tsp canning or pickling salt

Yield: About 9 pints

Procedure: Wash peppers, cut into quarters, remove cores and seeds, and cut away any blemishes. Slice peppers in strips. Boil sugar, vinegar, and water for 1 minute. Add peppers and bring to a boil. Place 1/2 clove of garlic and 1/4 teaspoon salt in each hot sterile half-pint jar; double the amounts for pint jars. Add pepper strips and cover with hot vinegar mixture, leaving 1/2-inch headspace. Remove air bubbles and adjust headspace if needed. Wipe rims of jars with a dampened clean paper towel. Adjust lids and process.

Recommended process time for Pickled Bell Peppers in a boiling-water canner				
		Process Time at Altitudes of		
Style of Pack	Jar Size	0-1,000 ft	1,001-6,000 ft	Above 6,000 ft
Hot	Half-pints or Pints	5 min	10	15

Pickled Hot Peppers

Hungarian, banana, chile, jalapeno

> *4 lbs hot long red, green, or yellow peppers*
> *3 lbs sweet red and green peppers, mixed*
> *5 cups vinegar (5%)*
> *1 cup water*
> *4 tsp canning or pickling salt*
> *2 tbsp sugar*
> *2 cloves garlic*

Yield: About 9 pints

Procedure: Caution: Wear plastic or rubber gloves and do not touch your face while handling or cutting hot peppers. If you do not wear gloves, wash hands thoroughly with soap and water before touching your face or eyes. Wash peppers. If small peppers are left whole, slash 2 to 4 slits in each. Quarter large peppers. Blanch in boiling water or blister skins on tough-skinned hot peppers using one of these two methods:

Oven or broiler method to blister skins: Place peppers in a hot oven (400 degrees F) or under a broiler for 6 to 8 minutes until skins blister.

Range-top method to blister skins: Cover hot burner (either gas or electric) with heavy wire mesh. Place peppers on burner for several minutes until skins blister.

After blistering skins, place peppers in a pan and cover with a damp cloth. (This will make peeling the peppers easier.) Cool several minutes; peel off skins. Flatten small peppers. Quarter large peppers. Fill hot jars with peppers, leaving 1/2-inch headspace. Combine and heat other ingredients to boiling and simmer 10 minutes. Remove garlic. Add hot pickling solution over peppers, leaving 1/2-inch headspace. Remove air bubbles and adjust headspace if needed. Wipe rims of jars with a dampened clean paper towel. Adjust lids and process.

		Process Time at Altitudes of		
Recommended process time for Pickled Hot Peppers in a boiling-water canner				
Style of Pack	**Jar Size**	**0-1,000 ft**	**1,001-6,000 ft**	**Above 6,000 ft**
Raw	**Half-pints or Pints**	10 min	15	20

Pickled Jalapeno Pepper Rings

3 lbs jalapeno peppers
1-1/2 cups pickling lime
1-1/2 gallons water
7-1/2 cups cider vinegar (5%)
1-3/4 cups water
2-1/2 tbsp canning salt
3 tbsp celery seed
6 tbsp mustard seed

Yield: About 6 pint jars

Procedure: Caution: Wear plastic or rubber gloves and do not touch your face while handling or cutting hot peppers. If you do not wear gloves, wash hands thoroughly with soap and water before touching your face or eyes. Wash peppers well and slice into 1/4-inch thick slices. Discard stem end. Mix 1-1/2 cups pickling lime with 1-1/2 gallons water in a stainless steel, glass, or food-grade plastic container. Avoid inhaling lime dust while mixing the lime-water solution. Soak pepper slices in the lime water, in refrigerator, for 18 hours, stirring occasionally (12 to 24 hours may be used). Drain lime solution from soaked pepper rings. Rinse peppers gently but thoroughly with water. Cover pepper rings with fresh, cold water and soak in refrigerator 1 hour. Drain water from peppers. Repeat the rinsing, soaking, and draining steps two more times. Drain thoroughly at the end. Place 1 tablespoon mustard seed and 1-1/2 teaspoons celery seed in the bottom of each hot pint jar. Pack drained pepper rings into the jars, leaving 1/2-inch headspace. Bring cider vinegar, 1-3/4 cups water, and canning salt to a boil over high heat. Ladle boiling hot brine solution over pepper rings in jars, leaving 1/2-inch headspace. Remove air bubbles and adjust headspace if needed. Wipe rims of jars with a dampened clean paper towel. Adjust lids and process.

Recommended process time for Pickled Jalapeno Rings in a boiling-water canner				
		Process Time at Altitudes of		
Style of Pack	**Jar Size**	**0-1,000 ft**	**1,001-6,000 ft**	**Above 6,000 ft**
Hot	**Pints**	10 min	15	20

Pickled Yellow Pepper Rings

2-1/2 to 3 lbs yellow (banana) peppers
2 tbsp celery seed
4 tbsp mustard seed
5 cups cider vinegar (5%)
1-1/4 cups water
5 tsp canning salt

Yield: About 4 pint jars

Procedure: Caution: Wear plastic or rubber gloves and do not touch your face while handling or cutting hot peppers. If you do not wear gloves, wash hands thoroughly with soap and water before touching your face or eyes. Wash peppers well and remove stem end; slice peppers into 1/4-inch thick rings. Place 1/2 tablespoon celery seed and 1 tablespoon mustard seed in the bottom of each empty hot pint jar. Fill pepper rings into jars, leaving 1/2-inch headspace. In a 4-quart Dutch oven or saucepan, combine the cider vinegar, water, and salt; heat to boiling. Cover pepper rings with boiling pickling liquid, leaving 1/2-inch headspace. Remove air bubbles and adjust headspace if needed. Wipe rims of jars with a dampened clean paper towel. Adjust lids and process.

Recommended process time for Pickled Yellow Pepper Rings in a boiling-water canner				
		Process Time at Altitudes of		
Style of Pack	Jar Size	0-1,000 ft	1,001-6,000 ft	Above 6,000 ft
Hot	Pints	10 min	15	20

Pickled Bread-and-Butter Zucchini

16 cups fresh zucchini, sliced

4 cups onions, thinly sliced

1/2 cup canning or pickling salt

4 cups white vinegar (5%)

2 cups sugar

4 tbsp mustard seed

2 tbsp celery seed

2 tsp ground turmeric

Yield: About 8 to 9 pints

Procedure: Cover zucchini and onion slices with 1 inch of water and salt. Let stand 2 hours and drain thoroughly. Combine vinegar, sugar, and spices. Bring to a boil and add zucchini and onions. Simmer 5 minutes and fill hot jars with mixture and pickling solution, leaving 1/2-inch headspace. Remove air bubbles and adjust headspace if needed. Wipe rims of jars with a dampened clean paper towel. Adjust lids and process or use low-temperature pasteurization treatment.

Recommended process time for Pickled Bread-and-Butter Zucchini in a boiling-water canner				
		Process Time at Altitudes of		
Style of Pack	Jar Size	0-1,000 ft	1,001- 6,000 ft	Above 6,000 ft
Hot	Pints or Quarts	10 min	15	20

Pickled Vegetable Relishes

Chayote and Pear Relish

   3-1/2 cups peeled, cubed chayote

   3-1/2 cups peeled, cubed Seckel pears

   2 cups chopped red bell pepper

   2 cups chopped yellow bell pepper

   3 cups finely chopped onion

   2 Serrano peppers, finely chopped

   2-1/2 cups cider vinegar (5%)

   1-1/2 cups water

   1 cup white sugar

   2 tsp canning salt

   1 tsp ground allspice

   1 tsp ground pumpkin pie spice

Yield: About 5 pint jars

Procedure: Caution: Wear plastic or rubber gloves and do not touch your face while handling or cutting hot peppers. If you do not wear gloves, wash hands thoroughly with soap and water before touching your face or eyes. Wash, peel, and cut chayote and pears into 1/2-inch cubes, discarding cores and seeds. Chop onions and peppers. Combine vinegar, water, sugar, salt, and spices in a Dutch oven or large saucepot.

Bring to a boil, stirring to dissolve sugar. Add chopped onions and peppers; return to a boil and boil for 2 minutes, stirring occasionally. Add cubed chayote and pears; return to the boiling point and turn off heat. Fill the hot solids into hot pint jars, leaving 1-inch headspace. Cover with boiling cooking liquid, leaving 1/2-inch headspace. Remove air bubbles and adjust headspace if needed. Wipe rims of jars with a dampened clean paper towel. Adjust lids and process.

Recommended process time for Chayote Pear Relish in a boiling-water canner				
		Process Time at Altitudes of		
Style of Pack	Jar Size	0-1,000 ft	1,001-6,000 ft	Above 6,000 ft
Hot	Pints	15 min	20	25

Piccalilli

6 cups chopped green tomatoes

1-1/2 cups chopped sweet red peppers

1-1/2 cups chopped green peppers

2-1/4 cups chopped onions

7-1/2 cups chopped cabbage

1/2 cup canning or pickling salt

3 tbsp whole mixed pickling spice

4-1/2 cups vinegar (5%)

3 cups brown sugar

Yield: About 9 half-pints

Procedure: Wash, chop, and combine vegetables with 1/2 cup salt. Cover with hot water and let stand 12 hours. Drain and press in a clean white cloth to remove all possible liquid. Tie spices loosely in a spice bag and add to combined vinegar and brown sugar and heat to a boil in a sauce pan. Add vegetables and boil gently 30 minutes or until the volume of the mixture is reduced by one-half. Remove spice bag. Fill hot sterile jars, with hot mixture, leaving 1/2-inch headspace. Remove air bubbles and adjust headspace if needed. Wipe rims of jars with a dampened clean paper towel. Adjust lids and process.

Recommended process time for Piccalilli in a boiling-water canner				
		Process Time at Altitudes of		
Style of Pack	Jar Size	0-1,000 ft	1,001- 6,000 ft	Above 6,000 ft
Hot	Half-pints or Pints	5 min	10	15

Pickle Relish

3 qts chopped cucumbers

3 cups each of chopped sweet green and red peppers

1 cup chopped onions

3/4 cup canning or pickling salt

4 cups ice

8 cups water

2 cups sugar

4 tsp each of mustard seed, turmeric, whole allspice, and whole cloves

6 cups white vinegar (5%)

Yield: About 9 pints

Procedure: Add cucumbers, peppers, onions, salt, and ice to water and let stand 4 hours. Drain and re-cover vegetables with fresh ice water for another hour. Drain again. Combine spices in a spice or cheesecloth bag. Add spices to sugar and vinegar. Heat to boiling and pour mixture over vegetables. Cover and refrigerate 24 hours. Heat mixture to boiling and fill hot into hot jars, leaving 1/2-inch headspace. Remove air bubbles and adjust headspace if needed. Wipe rims of jars with a dampened clean paper towel. Adjust lids and process.

Recommended process time for Pickle Relish in a boiling-water canner				
		Process Time at Altitudes of		
Style of Pack	Jar Size	0-1,000 ft	1,001-6,000 ft	Above 6,000 ft
Hot	Half-pints or Pints	10 min	15	20

Pickled Corn Relish

> 10 cups fresh whole kernel corn (16 to 20 medium-size ears), or
>   six 10-ounce packages of frozen corn
> 2-1/2 cups diced sweet red peppers
> 2-1/2 cups diced sweet green peppers
> 2-1/2 cups chopped celery
> 7-1/4 cups diced onions
> 1-3/4 cups sugar
> 5 cups vinegar (5%)
> 2-1/2 tbsp canning or pickling salt
> 2-1/2 tsp celery seed
> 2-1/2 tbsp dry mustard
> 1 1/4 tsp turmeric

Yield: About 9 pints

Procedure: Boil ears of corn 5 minutes. Dip in cold water. Cut whole kernels from cob or use six 10-ounce frozen packages of corn. Combine peppers, celery, onions, sugar, vinegar, salt, and celery seed in a saucepan. Bring to a boil and simmer 5 minutes, stirring occasionally. Mix mustard and turmeric in 1/2 cup of the simmered mixture. Add this mixture and corn to the hot mixture. Simmer another 5 minutes. If desired, thicken mixture with flour paste (1/4 cup flour blended in 1/4 cup water) and stir frequently. Fill hot jars with hot mixture, leaving 1/2-inch headspace. Remove air bubbles and adjust headspace if needed. Wipe rims of jars with a dampened clean paper towel. Adjust lids and process.

Recommended process time for Pickled Corn Relish in a boiling-water canner				
		Process Time at Altitudes of		
Style of Pack	**Jar Size**	**0-1,000 ft**	**1,001-6,000 ft**	**Above 6,000 ft**
Hot	Half-pints or Pints	15 min	20	25

Pickled Green Tomato Relish

10 lbs small, hard green tomatoes

1-1/2 lbs red bell peppers

1-1/2 lbs green bell peppers

2 lbs onions

1/2 cup canning or pickling salt

1 qt water

4 cups sugar

1 qt vinegar (5%)

1/3 cup prepared yellow mustard

2 tbsp cornstarch

Yield: About 7 to 9 pints

Procedure: Wash and coarsely grate or finely chop tomatoes, peppers, and onions. Dissolve salt in water and pour over vegetables in large kettle. Heat to boiling and simmer 5 minutes. Drain in colander. Return vegetables to kettle. Add sugar, vinegar, mustard, and cornstarch. Stir to mix. Heat to boiling and simmer 5 minutes. Fill hot sterile pint jars with hot relish, leaving 1/2-inch headspace. Remove air bubbles and adjust headspace if needed. Wipe rims of jars with a dampened clean paper towel. Adjust lids and process.

Recommended process time for Pickled Green Tomato Relish in a boiling-water canner				
		Process Time at Altitudes of		
Style of Pack	Jar Size	0-1,000 ft	1,001-6,000 ft	Above 6,000 ft
Hot	Pints	5 min	10	15

Pickled Horseradish Sauce

> 2 cups (3/4 lb) freshly grated horseradish
> 1 cup white vinegar (5%)
> 1/2 tsp canning or pickling salt
> 1/4 tsp powdered ascorbic acid

Yield: About 2 half-pints

Procedure: The pungency of fresh horseradish fades within 1 to 2 months, even when refrigerated. Therefore, make only small quantities at a time. Wash horseradish roots thoroughly and peel off brown outer skin. The peeled roots may be grated in a food processor or cut into small cubes and put through a food grinder. Combine ingredients and fill into sterile jars, leaving 1/4-inch headspace. Seal jars tightly and store in a refrigerator.

Pickled Pepper-Onion Relish

> 6 cups finely chopped onions
> 3 cups finely chopped sweet red peppers
> 3 cups finely chopped green peppers
> 1-1/2 cups sugar
> 6 cups vinegar (5%), preferably white distilled
> 2 tbsp canning or pickling salt

Yield: About 9 half-pints

Procedure: Wash and chop vegetables. Combine all ingredients and boil gently until mixture thickens and volume is reduced by one-half (about 30 minutes). Fill hot sterile jars with hot relish, leaving 1/2-inch headspace, and seal tightly. Store in refrigerator and use within 1 month. **Caution: If extended storage is desired, this product must be processed.**

Recommended process time for Pickled Pepper-Onion Relish in a boiling-water canner				
		Process Time at Altitudes of		
Style of Pack	**Jar Size**	**0-1,000 ft**	**1,001- 6,000 ft**	**Above 6,000 ft**
Hot	**Half-pints or Pints**	5 min	10	15

Tangy Tomatillo Relish

12 cups chopped tomatillos

3 cups finely chopped jicama

3 cups chopped onion

6 cups chopped plum-type tomatoes

1-1/2 cups chopped green bell pepper

1-1/2 cups chopped red bell pepper

1-1/2 cups chopped yellow bell pepper

1 cup canning salt

2 qts water

6 tbsp whole mixed pickling spice

1 tbsp crushed red pepper flakes (optional)

6 cups sugar

6-1/2 cups cider vinegar (5%)

Yield: About 6 or 7 pints

Procedure: Remove husks from tomatillos and wash well. Peel jicama and onion. Wash all vegetables well before trimming and chopping. Place chopped tomatillos, jicama, onion, tomatoes, and all bell peppers in a 4-quart Dutch oven or saucepot. Dissolve canning salt in water. Pour over prepared vegetables. Heat to boiling; simmer 5 minutes. Drain thoroughly through a cheesecloth-lined strainer (until no more water drips through, about 15 to 20 minutes). Place pickling spice and optional red pepper flakes on a clean, double-layer, 6 inch-square piece of 100 percent cotton cheesecloth. Bring corners together and tie with a clean string. (Or use a purchased muslin spice bag.) Mix sugar, vinegar, and spices (in cheesecloth bag) in a saucepan; bring to a boil. Add drained vegetables. Return to boil; reduce heat and simmer, uncovered, 30 minutes. Remove spice bag. Fill hot relish mixture into hot pint jars, leaving 1/2-inch headspace. Remove air bubbles and adjust headspace if needed. Wipe rims of jars with a dampened clean paper towel. Adjust lids and process.

Recommended process time for Tangy Tomatillo Relish in a boiling-water canner				
		Process Time at Altitudes of		
Style of Pack	Jar Size	0-1,000 ft	1,001-6,000 ft	Above 6,000 ft
Hot	Pints	15 min	20	25

Pickled Foods for Special Diets

No Sugar Added Pickled Beets

7 lbs of 2 to 2-1/2-inch diameter beets

4 to 6 onions (2 to 2-1/2-inch diameter), if desired

6 cups white vinegar (5 percent)

1-1/2 tsp canning or pickling salt

2 cups Splenda®

3 cups water

2 cinnamon sticks

12 whole cloves

Yield: About 8 pints

Procedure: Trim off beet tops, leaving 1 inch of stem and roots to prevent bleeding of color. Wash thoroughly. Sort for size. Cover similar sizes together with boiling water and cook until tender (about 25 to 30 minutes). **Caution: Drain and discard liquid.** Cool beets. Trim off roots and stems and slip off skins. Slice into 1/4-inch slices. Peel, wash, and thinly slice onions. Combine vinegar, salt, Splenda®, and 3 cups fresh water in large Dutch oven. Tie cinnamon sticks and cloves in cheesecloth bag and add to vinegar mixture. Bring to a boil. Add beets and onions. Simmer 5 minutes. Remove spice bag. Fill hot beets and onion slices into hot pint jars, leaving 1/2-inch headspace. Cover with boiling vinegar solution, leaving 1/2-inch headspace. Remove air bubbles and adjust headspace if needed. Wipe rims of jars with a dampened clean paper towel. Adjust lids and process.

Variation: *Pickled whole baby beets* — Follow the directions above but use beets that are no more than 1 to 1-1/2 inches in diameter. Pack whole after cooking, trimming, and peeling; do not slice.

Recommended process time for No Sugar Added Pickled Beets in a boiling-water canner					
		Process Time at Altitudes of			
Style of Pack	Jar Size	0-1,000 ft	1,001-3,000 ft	3,001-6,000 ft	Above 6,000 ft
Hot	Pints	30 min	35	40	45

No Sugar Added Sweet Pickle Cucumber Slices

3-1/2 lbs of pickling cucumbers
boiling water to cover sliced cucumbers
4 cups cider vinegar (5%)
1 cup water
3 cups Splenda®
1 tbsp canning salt

1 tbsp mustard seed

1 tbsp whole allspice

1 tbsp celery seed

4 one-inch cinnamon sticks

Yield: About 4 or 5 pint jars

Procedure: Wash cucumbers. Slice 1/16-inch off the blossom ends and discard. Slice cucumbers into 1/4-inch thick slices. Pour boiling water over the cucumber slices and let stand 5 to 10 minutes. Drain off the hot water and pour cold water over the cucumbers. Let cold water run continuously over the cucumber slices, or change water frequently until cucumbers are cooled. Drain slices well. Mix vinegar, 1 cup water, Splenda®, and all spices in a 10-quart Dutch oven or stockpot. Bring to a boil. Add drained cucumber slices carefully to the boiling liquid and return to a boil. Place one cinnamon stick in each empty hot jar, if desired. Fill hot pickle slices into hot pint jars, leaving 1/2-inch headspace. Cover with boiling pickling brine, leaving 1/2-inch headspace. Remove air bubbles and adjust headspace if needed. Wipe rims of jars with a dampened clean paper towel. Adjust lids and process.

Recommended process time for No Sugar Added Sweet Cucumber Pickle Slice in a boiling-water canner				
		Process Time at Altitudes of		
Style of Pack	Jar Size	0-1,000 ft	1,001-6,000 ft	Above 6,000 ft
Hot	Pints	10 min	15	20

Reduced-Sodium Sliced Dill Pickles

4 lbs (3- to 5-inch) pickling cucumbers

6 cups vinegar (5%)

6 cups sugar

2 tbsp canning or pickling salt

1-1/2 tsp celery seed
1-1/2 tsp mustard seed
2 large onions, thinly sliced
8 heads fresh dill

Yield: About 8 pints

Procedure: Wash cucumbers. Cut 1/16-inch slice off blossom end and discard. Cut cucumbers in 1/4-inch slices. Combine vinegar, sugar, salt, celery, and mustard seeds in large saucepan. Bring mixture to a boil. Place 2 slices of onion and 1/2 dill head on bottom of each hot pint jar. Fill hot jars with cucumber slices, leaving 1/2-inch headspace. Add 1 slice of onion and 1/2 dill head on top. Pour hot pickling solution over cucumbers, leaving 1/4-inch head-space. Remove air bubbles and adjust headspace if needed. Wipe rims of jars with a dampened clean paper towel. Adjust lids and process.

Recommended process time for Reduced-Sodium Sliced Dill Pickles in a boiling-water canner				
		Process Time at Altitudes of		
Style of Pack	**Jar Size**	**0-1,000 ft**	**1,001-6,000 ft**	**Above 6,000 ft**
Raw	Pints	15 min	20	25

Reduced-Sodium Sliced Sweet Pickles

4 lbs (3- to 4-inch) pickling cucumbers

Brining solution:
1 qt distilled white vinegar (5%)
1 tbsp canning or pickling salt
1 tbsp mustard seed
1/2 cup sugar

Canning syrup:

1-2/3 cups distilled white vinegar (5%)

3 cups sugar

1 tbsp whole allspice

2-1/4 tsp celery seed

Yield: About 4 to 5 pints

Procedure: Wash cucumbers and cut 1/16-inch off blossom end, and discard. Cut cucumbers into 1/4-inch slices. Combine all ingredients for canning syrup in a saucepan and bring to boiling. Keep syrup hot until used. In a large kettle, mix the ingredients for the brining solution. Add the cut cucumbers, cover, and simmer until the cucumbers change color from bright to dull green (about 5 to 7 minutes). Drain the cucumber slices. Fill hot jars, and cover with hot canning syrup leaving 1/2-inch headspace. Remove air bubbles and adjust headspace if needed. Wipe rims of jars with a dampened clean paper towel. Adjust lids and process.

Recommended process time for Reduced-Sodium Sliced Sweet Pickles in a boiling-water canner				
		Process Time at Altitudes of		
Style of Pack	Jar Size	0-1,000 ft	1,001-6,000 ft	Above 6,000 ft
Hot	Pints	10 min	15	20

Appendix F

Canning
Jams and Jellies

— Courtesy of the USDA

Making jelly without added pectin

Use only firm fruits naturally high in pectin. Select a mixture of about 3/4 ripe and 1/4 underripe fruit. Do not use commercially canned or frozen fruit juices; their pectin content is too low. Wash all fruits thoroughly before cooking. Crush soft fruits or berries; cut firmer fruits into small pieces. Using the peels and cores, adds pectin to the juice during cooking. Add water to fruits that require it, as listed in the table of ingredients below. Put fruit and water in large saucepan and bring to a boil. Then simmer according to the times below until fruit is soft, while stirring to prevent scorching. One pound of fruit should yield at least 1 cup of clear juice.

Extracting Juices and Making Jelly

To Extract Juice					
	Cups of Water to be Added per Pound of Fruit	Minutes to Simmer Fruit before Extracting Juice	Ingredients Added to Each Cup of Strained Juice		Yield from 4 Cups of Juice (Half-pints)
			Sugar (Cups)	Lemon Juice (Tsp)	
Apples	1	20 to 25	3/4	1-1/2 (optional)	4 to 5
Blackberries	None or 1/4	5 to 10	3/4 to 1	None	7 to 8
Crab apples	1	20 to 25	1	None	4 to 5
Grapes	None or 1/4	5 to 10	3/4 to 1	None	8 to 9
Plums	1/2	15 to 20	3/4	None	8 to 9

When fruit is tender, strain through a colander, then strain through a double layer of cheesecloth or a jelly bag. Allow juice to drip through, using a stand or colander to hold the bag. Pressing or squeezing the bag or cloth will cause cloudy jelly.

Using no more than 6 to 8 cups of extracted fruit juice at a time, measure fruit juice, sugar, and lemon juice according to the ingredients in the table above and heat to boiling. Stir until the sugar is dissolved. Boil over high heat to the jellying point. To test if jelly is done, use one of the following methods.

Temperature test — Use a jelly or candy thermometer and boil until mixture reaches the following temperatures at altitudes of:

Sea Level	1,000 ft	2,000 ft	3,000 ft	4,000 ft	5,000 ft	6,000 ft	7,000 ft	8,000 ft
220°F	218°F	216°F	214°F	212°F	211°F	209°F	207°F	205°F

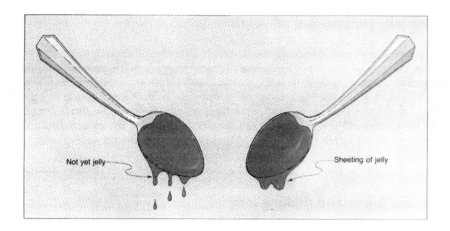

Sheet or spoon test — Dip a cool, metal spoon into the boiling jelly mixture. Raise the spoon about 12 inches above the pan (out of steam). Turn the spoon so the liquid runs off the side. The jelly is done when the syrup forms two drops that flow together and sheet or hang off the edge of the spoon.

Remove from heat and quickly skim off foam. Fill sterile jars with jelly. Use a measuring cup or ladle the jelly through a wide-mouthed funnel, leaving 1/4 inch headspace. Wipe rims of jars with a dampened clean paper towel. Adjust lids and process.

Recommended process time for Jelly without Added Pectin in a boiling-water canner				
		Process Time at Altitudes of		
Style of Pack	**Jar Size**	**0-1,000 ft**	**1,001-6,000 ft**	**Above 6,000 ft**
Hot	**Half-pints or Pints**	5 min	10	15

Making jam without added pectin

Wash and rinse all fruits thoroughly before cooking. Do not soak. For best flavor, use fully ripe fruit. Remove stems, skins, and pits from fruit; cut into pieces and crush. For berries, remove stems and blossoms and crush. Seedy berries may be put through a sieve or food mill. Measure crushed fruit into large saucepan using the ingredient quantities specified in the table below.

Ingredient Quantities				
Fruit	Cups Crushed Fruit	Cups Sugar	Tbsp Lemon Juice	Yield (Half-pints)
Apricots	4 to 4-1/2	4	2	5 to 6
Berries *	4	4	0	3 to 4
Peaches	5-1/2 to 6	4 to 5	2	6 to 7
*Includes blackberries, boysenberries, dewberries, gooseberries, loganberries, raspberries, and strawberries.				

Add sugar and bring to a boil while stirring rapidly and constantly. Continue to boil until mixture thickens. Use one of the following tests to determine when jams and jellies are ready to fill. Remember to allow for thickening during cooling.

Temperature test — Use a jelly or candy thermometer and boil until mixture reaches the temperature for your altitude.

Refrigerator test — Remove the jam mixture from the heat. Pour a small amount of boiling jam on a cold plate and put it in the freezing compartment of a refrigerator for a few minutes. If the mixture gels, it is ready to fill.

Remove from heat and skim off foam quickly. Fill sterile jars with jam. Use a measuring cup or ladle the jam through a wide-mouthed funnel, leaving 1/4 inch headspace. Wipe rims of jars with a dampened clean paper towel. Adjust lids and process.

Recommended process time for Jam without Added Pectin in a boiling-water canner				
		Process Time at Altitudes of		
Style of Pack	Jar Size	0-1,000 ft	1,001- 6,000 ft	Above 6,000 ft
Hot	Half-pints or Pints	5 min	10	15

Making jams and jellies with added pectin

Fresh fruits and juices as well as commercially canned or frozen fruit juice can be used with commercially prepared powdered or liquid pectins. The order of combining ingredients depends on the type of pectin used. Complete directions for a variety of fruits are provided with packaged pectin. Jelly or jam made with added pectin requires less cooking and generally gives a larger yield. These products have more natural fruit flavors, too. In addition, using added pectin eliminates the need to test hot jellies and jams for proper gelling. Adding 1/2 teaspoon of butter or margarine with the juice and pectin will reduce foaming. However, these may cause off-flavor in long-term storage of jellies and jams. Recipes available using packaged pectin include:

Jellies — Apple, crab apple, blackberry, boysenberry, dewberry, currant, elderberry, grape, mayhaw, mint, peach, plum, black or red raspberry, loganberry, rhubarb, and strawberry.

Jams — Apricot, blackberry, boysenberry, dewberry, loganberry, red raspberry, youngberry, blueberry, cherry, currant, fig, gooseberry, grape, orange marmalade, peach, pear, plum, rhubarb, strawberry, and spiced tomato.

Be sure to use pre-sterilized Mason canning jars, self-sealing two-piece lids, and a 5-minute process (corrected for altitude, as necessary) in boiling water. (See page 1-30 about spoilage of jams and jellies.)

Purchase fresh pectin each year. Old pectin may result in poor gels. Follow the instructions with each package and process as below:

Recommended process time for Jellies and Jam with Added Pectin in a boiling-water canner				
		Process Time at Altitudes of		
Style of Pack	Jar Size	0-1,000 ft	1,001-6,000 ft	Above 6,000 ft
Hot	Half-pints or Pints	5 min	10	15

Following are a few additional jelly and jam recipes for use with packaged pectin.

Pear-Apple Jam

2 cups peeled, cored, and finely chopped pears (about 2 lbs)
1 cup peeled, cored, and finely chopped apples
6-1/2 cups sugar
1/4 tsp ground cinnamon
1/3 cup bottled lemon juice
6 oz liquid pectin

Yield: About 7 to 8 half-pints

Procedure: Crush apples and pears in a large saucepan and stir in cinnamon. Thoroughly mix sugar and lemon juice with fruits and bring to a boil over high heat, stirring constantly. Immediately stir in pectin. Bring to a full rolling boil and boil hard 1 minute, stirring constantly. Remove from heat, quickly skim off foam, and fill sterile jars leaving 1/4-inch headspace. Wipe rims of jars with a dampened clean paper towel. Adjust lids and process.

Recommended process time for Pear-Apple Jam in a boiling-water canner				
		Process Time at Altitudes of		
Style of Pack	Jar Size	0-1,000 ft	1,001-6,000 ft	Above 6,000 ft
Hot	Half-pints or Pints	5 min	10	15

Strawberry-Rhubarb Jelly

1-1/2 lbs red stalks of rhubarb
1-1/2 qts ripe strawberries

1/2 tsp butter or margarine to reduce foaming (optional)

6 cups sugar

6 oz liquid pectin

Yield: About 7 half-pints

Procedure: Wash and cut rhubarb into 1-inch pieces and blend or grind. Wash, stem, and crush strawberries, one layer at a time, in a saucepan. Place both fruits in a jelly bag or double layer of cheesecloth and gently squeeze out juice. Measure 3-1/2 cups of juice into a large saucepan. Add butter and sugar, thoroughly mixing into juice. Bring to a boil over high heat, stirring constantly. Immediately stir in pectin. Bring to a full rolling boil and boil hard 1 minute, stirring constantly. Remove from heat, quickly skim off foam, and fill sterile jars, leaving 1/4-inch headspace. Wipe rims of jars with a dampened clean paper towel. Adjust lids and process.

Recommended process time for Strawberry-Rhubarb Jelly in a boiling-water canner				
		Process Time at Altitudes of		
Style of Pack	Jar Size	0-1,000 ft	1,001-6,000 ft	Above 6,000 ft
Hot	Half-pints or Pints	5 min	10	15

Blueberry-Spice Jam

2-1/2 pints ripe blueberries

1 tbsp lemon juice

1/2 tsp ground nutmeg or cinnamon

5-1/2 cups sugar

3/4 cup water

1 box (1-3/4 oz) powdered pectin

Yield: About 5 half-pints

Procedure: Wash and thoroughly crush blueberries, one layer at a time, in a saucepan. Add lemon juice, spice, and water. Stir in pectin and bring to a full rolling boil over high heat, stirring frequently. Add the sugar and return to a full rolling boil. Boil hard for 1 minute, stirring constantly. Remove from heat, quickly skim off foam, and fill sterile jars, leaving 1/4-inch headspace. Wipe rims of jars with a dampened clean paper towel. Adjust lids and process.

Recommended process time for Blueberry-Spice Jam in a boiling-water canner				
		Process Time at Altitudes of		
Style of Pack	Jar Size	0-1,000 ft	1,001-6,000 ft	Above 6,000 ft
Hot	Half-pints or Pints	5 min	10	15

Grape-Plum Jelly

3-1/2 lbs ripe plums

3 lbs ripe Concord grapes

1 cup water

1/2 tsp butter or margarine to reduce foaming (optional)

8-1/2 cups sugar

1 box (1-3/4 oz) powdered pectin

Yield: About 10 half-pints

Procedure: Wash and pit plums; do not peel. Thoroughly crush the plums and grapes, one layer at a time, in a saucepan with water. Bring to a boil, cover, and simmer 10 minutes. Strain juice through a jelly bag or double layer of cheesecloth. Measure sugar and set aside. Combine 6-1/2 cups of juice with butter and pectin in large saucepan. Bring to a hard boil over high heat, stirring constantly. Add the sugar and return to a full rolling boil. Boil hard for 1 minute, stirring constantly. Remove from heat, quickly skim off foam, and fill sterile jars, leaving 1/4-inch headspace. Wipe rims of jars with a dampened clean paper towel. Adjust lids and process.

		Process Time at Altitudes of		
Style of Pack	Jar Size	0-1,000 ft	1,001-6,000 ft	Above 6,000 ft
Hot	Half-pints or Pints	5 min	10	15

Recommended process time for Grape-Plum Jelly in a boiling-water canner

Golden Pepper Jelly

3 large fleshy yellow bell peppers

1 to 4 serrano chile peppers

1-1/2 cups white distilled vinegar (5%)

7 cups sugar

1 package (3 oz.) liquid pectin

Yield: About 7 half-pint jars

Procedure: Caution: Wear plastic or rubber gloves and do not touch your face while handling or cutting hot peppers. If you do not wear gloves, wash hands thoroughly with soap and water before touching your face or eyes. Wash all peppers thoroughly; remove stems and seeds from the peppers. Do not remove the membrane from the hot peppers, because the remaining capsaicin is located there. Place sweet and hot peppers in a blender or food processor. Add enough vinegar to puree the peppers, then puree. Combine the pepper-vinegar puree and remaining vinegar into a 6- or 8-quart saucepan. Heat to a boil; then, boil 20 minutes to extract flavors and color. Remove from heat and strain through a jelly bag into a bowl. (The jelly bag is preferred; several layers of cheesecloth may also be used.) Add the strained pepper-vinegar juice back to the saucepan. Stir in sugar until dissolved and return to a boil. Add the pectin, return to a full rolling boil and boil hard for 1 minute, stirring constantly. Remove from heat, quickly skim off any foam, and fill into sterile jars, leaving 1/4-inch headspace. Wipe rims of jars with a dampened clean paper towel. Adjust lids and process.

Notes: The use of yellow peppers gives this jelly a light golden color. Other colored sweet peppers can be substituted, but these will provide a different jelly color. Other hot peppers can also be substituted. It is best to start with a mild hot pepper flavor and increase it to suit personal tastes. If properly prepared, the jelly will have a mildly firm set; it is best to use half-pint jars.

Recommended process time for **Golden Pepper Jelly** in a boiling-water canner				
		Process Time at Altitudes of		
Style of Pack	**Jar Size**	**0-1,000 ft**	**1,001-6,000 ft**	**Above 6,000 ft**
Hot	**Half-pints**	5 min	10	15

Making reduced-sugar fruit spreads

A variety of fruit spreads may be made that are tasteful, yet lower in sugar and calories than regular jams and jellies. The following are recipes for reduced-sugar fruit spreads. Gelatin may be used as a thickening agent, as indicated in two of the following recipes. Sweet fruits, apple juice, spices, and/or a liquid, low-calorie sweetener are used to provide the sweet flavor of the fruit spreads. When gelatin is used in the recipe, the jars of spread should not be processed. They should be refrigerated and used within 4 weeks.

Peach-Pineapple Spread

4 cups drained peach pulp (procedure as below)
2 cups drained unsweetened crushed pineapple

1/4 cup bottled lemon juice
2 cups sugar (optional)

This recipe may be made with any combination of peaches, nectarines, apricots, and plums.

This recipe may be made without sugar or with up to 2 cups, according to taste or preference. Non-nutritive sweeteners may be added. If aspartame (a low-calorie nutritive sweetener) is used, the sweetening power of aspartame may be lost within 3 to 4 weeks.

Yield: 5 to 6 half-pints

Procedure: Thoroughly wash 4 to 6 pounds of firm, ripe peaches. Drain well. Peel and remove pits. Grind fruit flesh with a medium or coarse blade, or crush with a fork (do not use a blender). Place ground or crushed fruit in a 2-quart saucepan. Heat slowly to release juice, stirring constantly, until fruit is tender. Place cooked fruit in a jelly bag or strainer lined with four layers of cheesecloth. Allow juice to drip about 15 minutes. Save the juice for jelly or other uses. Measure 4 cups of drained fruit pulp for making spread. Combine the 4 cups of pulp, pineapple, and lemon juice in a 4-quart saucepan. Add up to 2 cups of sugar, if desired, and mix well. Heat and boil gently for 10 to 15 minutes, stirring enough to prevent sticking. Fill hot jars quickly, leaving 1/4-inch headspace. Wipe rims of jars with a dampened clean paper towel. Adjust lids and process.

Recommended process time for Peach-Pineapple Spread in a boiling-water canner					
		Process Time at Altitudes of			
Style of Pack	Jar Size	0-1,000 ft	1,001-3,000 ft	3,001-6,000 ft	Above 6,000 ft
Hot	Half-Pints	15 min	20	20	25
	Pints	20	25	30	35

Refrigerated Apple Spread (Made with Gelatin)

2 tbsp unflavored gelatin powder
1 qt bottle unsweetened apple juice
2 tbsp bottled lemon juice
2 tbsp liquid low-calorie sweetener
Food coloring, if desired

Yield: 4 half-pints

Procedure: In a saucepan, soften the gelatin in the apple and lemon juices. To dissolve gelatin, bring to a full rolling boil and boil 2 minutes. Remove from heat. Stir in sweetener and food coloring, if desired. Fill jars, leaving 1/4-inch headspace. Wipe rims of jars with a dampened clean paper towel. Adjust lids. Do not process or freeze. **Caution: Store in refrigerator and use within 4 weeks.**

Optional: For spiced apple jelly, add 2 sticks of cinnamon and 4 whole cloves to mixture before boiling. Remove both spices before adding the sweetener and food coloring.

Refrigerator Grape Spread (Made with Gelatin)

2 tbsp unflavored gelatin powder
1 bottle (24 oz) unsweetened grape juice
2 tbsp bottled lemon juice
2 tbsp liquid low-calorie sweetener

Yield: 3 half-pints

Procedure: In a saucepan, soften the gelatin in the grape and lemon juices. Bring to a full rolling boil to dissolve gelatin. Boil 1 minute and remove from heat. Stir in sweetener. Fill hot jars quickly, leaving 1/4-inch headspace. Wipe rims of jars with a dampened clean paper towel. Adjust lids. Do not process or freeze. **Caution: Store in refrigerator and use within 4 weeks.**

Remaking Soft Jellies

Measure jelly to be recooked. Work with no more than 4 to 6 cups at a time.

To remake with powdered pectin: For each quart of jelly, mix 1/4 cup sugar, 1/2 cup water, 2 tablespoons bottled lemon juice, and 4 teaspoons powdered pectin. Bring to a boil while stirring. Add jelly and bring to a rolling boil over high heat, stirring constantly. Boil hard 1/2 minute. Remove from heat, quickly skim foam off jelly, and fill sterile jars, leaving 1/4-inch headspace. Wipe rims of jars with a dampened clean paper towel. Adjust new lids and process.

To remake with liquid pectin: For each quart of jelly, measure 3/4 cup sugar, 2 tablespoons bottled lemon juice, and 2 tablespoons liquid pectin. Bring jelly only to boil over high heat, while stirring. Remove from heat and quickly add the sugar, lemon juice, and pectin. Bring to a full rolling boil, stirring constantly. Boil hard for 1 minute. Quickly skim off foam and fill sterile jars, leaving 1/4-inch headspace. Wipe rims of jars with a dampened clean paper towel. Adjust new lids and process.

To remake without added pectin: For each quart of jelly, add 2 tablespoons bottled lemon juice. Heat to boiling and boil for 3 to 4 minutes. Use one of the tests to determine if jelly is done. Remove from heat, quickly skim off foam, and fill sterile jars, leaving 1/4-inch headspace. Wipe rims of jars with a dampened clean paper towel. Adjust new lids and process.

Recommended process time for Remade Soft Jellies in a boiling-water canner				
		Process Time at Altitudes of		
Style of Pack	Jar Size	0-1,000 ft	1,001-6,000 ft	Above 6,000 ft
Hot	Half-pints or Pints	5 min	10	15

Appendix G

Recipes for Dried and Smoked Foods, Meats, and Cheese

Herbal Blends and Teas

Lemon Verbena Tea

1 cup lemon verbena leaves
3 tablespoons lavender flowers
1 teaspoon dried lemon peel

Pour the herbs into an airtight container, cover, and shake until thoroughly mixed. Place the lid tightly on the container. For a cup of tea, use 1 teaspoon in a cup of boiling water. Steep for 5 minutes and strain out the leaves and peel. Add sugar or honey, as desired.

Peppermint Tea

> 8 ounces peppermint leaves
>
> 1 teaspoon rosemary leaves
>
> 8 ounces lemon balm leaves
>
> 8 ounces fennel seeds

Pour the herbs into an airtight container, cover, and shake until thoroughly mixed. Place the lid tightly on the container. For a cup of tea, use 1 teaspoon in a cup of boiling water. Steep for 10 minutes and strain out the herbs. Note: this tea aids in digestion and stomach pains.

Soothing Chamomile Tea

> 3 teaspoon marjoram
>
> 3 teaspoon chamomile flowers
>
> 3 teaspoon bergamot leaves
>
> 2 teaspoon dried orange peel

Pour the herbs into an airtight container, cover, and shake until thoroughly mixed. Place the lid tightly on the container. Bring the water to a boil; then remove it from the heat. Add the herbs, and allow them to steep for 10 to 15 minutes. Remove herbs.

Italian Blend

> 3 tablespoons basil
>
> 1 tablespoon oregano
>
> 1 tablespoon thyme
>
> 3 tablespoons Italian flat-leaved parsley
>
> 3 tablespoons marjoram
>
> 1 tablespoon dried garlic, finely chopped

Pour the herbs into an airtight container, cover, and shake until thoroughly mixed. Place the lid tightly on the container. This seasoning is perfect as a rub for hearty meats or seasoning for sauces or stews.

Barbecue Rub

1 tablespoon paprika

2/3 cup brown sugar

1 tablespoon chili powder

1 tablespoon dry mustard

1 teaspoon ground coriander seeds

1 teaspoon ground black pepper

1 teaspoon dried rosemary, crushed

1 teaspoon dried thyme, crushed

1 teaspoon salt

1/2 teaspoon cayenne powder

1 teaspoon ground cumin

Mix together spices, herbs, and sugar and place in an airtight container. When ready to use, rub on meat cuts such as beef or pork ribs, steaks, or beef or pork loin. Let marinate for at least 30 minutes, and then brush the meat with vinegar. Grill or broil 3 to 4 inches from heat.

Recipe courtesy of Joe Williams Duea, Chicago, IL. Used with permission.

Cajun Spice Mix

2 1/2 tablespoons paprika

2 tablespoons chili powder

2 tablespoons salt

2 tablespoons dried garlic, finely chopped

1 tablespoon dried onion, finely chopped

1 tablespoon crushed cayenne pepper

1 tablespoon ground black pepper
1 teaspoon dried oregano, crushed
1 teaspoon dried thyme, crushed
1 teaspoon powdered cumin seeds

Mix together spices, herbs, and sugar and place in an airtight container. When ready to use, rub on fish or poultry, or use in stews, gumbo, or soup.

Meat and Fish

Basic Beef Jerky

Three to four pounds lean beef, such as sirloin or lean brisket, or any other meat or game (note: the original recipe uses buffalo meat).

1 cup soy sauce
½ teaspoon good curry powder
½ teaspoon garlic powder
½ teaspoon ground white pepper
½ teaspoon ground cumin
¼ teaspoon turmeric

Start with lean beef, trimming off as much fat as possible. Cut into strips about 1/8" to ¼" thick and 1" wide. Place meat in a dish and pour in soy sauce. Marinate the meat for at least 30 minutes.

Preheat oven to 150 degrees. Pull meat into strips ("jerk" it) and place on an ungreased baking sheet cookie sheet in a single layer. Do not allow pieces to touch each other. Coat the top side of the meat with the spice mix. Set oven or food dehydrator at the lowest temperature. If using an oven, be sure to keep it propped open during the drying time. It should not get above 140 to 150 degrees during the drying process. If you use a smoker to dry the meat, adjust the wood or coals to 140 to 150 degrees F and monitor during drying.

As soon as the meat stops dripping, turn it over so that the moister undersides of the meat are exposed to more heat. You can also rotate the upper and lower trays; the meat that is in the upper rack will have dripped moisture onto the lower rack. If the meat appears to be drying faster on the edges than in the center (or vice versa), move the pieces around on the racks.

Dry the meat until it is tough and chewy, approximately 4 to 6 hours in the oven. The drying time will depend on the oven temperature, house humidity, and size of the meat strips. Test a small piece every hour or so until it is dried to the right consistency. Note that the meat will become a little more brittle once it is cooled; do not over-dry the meat.

Place the cooled jerky in an airtight container, or freeze it in a plastic recloseable bag.

Other suggested marinades:

-   Hot sauce, molasses, seasoned salt, pepper, and garlic

-   Ground ginger, dry mustard, soy sauce, honey, and onion powder

-   Worcestershire sauce, garlic powder, molasses, pepper, and thyme

Yield: 2 to 3 pounds beef jerky strips

Biltong — a Variation of Jerky from South Africa

This South African beef jerky recipe is commonly known as biltong. There are many variations of this recipe, and South Africans experiment with different flavors by combining different spices, herbs, and peppers to the original recipe.

5 pounds fresh beef, such as lean brisket, sirloin, or eye of round

2 cups warm water

1/3 cup fine salt

4 tablespoons brown sugar

4 tablespoons ground coriander

1 teaspoon baking soda

1 teaspoon black pepper, ground

2 ounces red wine vinegar

Trim all fat from the meat to ensure the jerky will not grow rancid. Freeze the meat until ice crystals form. Slice the meat with the grain into very thin pieces (approximately 3/16" thick and 2" long).

Mix the salt, sugar, baking soda, pepper, and coriander together. Rub the seasoning mixture into the meat slices. Place the meat in a large mixing bowl or pan. Sprinkle some vinegar over the pieces as you add them to the container. Marinate in the refrigerator for at least 12 hours. The meat will become saltier the longer it marinates.

Remove the meat from the marinade and dip it in a mixture of vinegar and water; this will give the dried jerky the characteristic dark, shiny look of biltong. Preheat the over to 140 degrees F. If using an oven, be sure to keep it propped open during the drying time. It should not get above 140 to 150 degrees during the drying process. Completely cover the bottom rack of the oven with aluminum foil. To catch any meat dripping while positioning the meat, put a layer of rags or paper towels on the opened oven door — this will make cleanup easier. Place the oven racks on the highest positions and spray them with non-stick spray. Then put the prepared meat directly on the racks, without allowing any pieces to touch.

Alternatively, you can thread the meat on kitchen string and hang it in a cool, dry place. A fan placed in front of the meat will hasten the drying process. Drying will take much longer through this method than through oven-drying.

Dry the meat until it is tough and chewy, approximately 4 to 6 hours in the oven. The drying time will depend on the oven temperature, house humidity, and size of the meat strips. Test a small piece every hour or so until it is dried to the right consistency. Note that the meat will become a little more brittle once it is cooled; do not over-dry the meat.

Place the cooled jerky in an airtight container, or freeze it in a plastic recloseable bag.

Yield: Makes about 5 pounds

Bak Kua (Chinese Dried Meat Squares)

1½ to 2 pounds lean boneless pork shoulder or loin
½ teaspoon salt
2 tablespoons sugar
2 tablespoons honey
2 tablespoons rice wine
1 teaspoon Chinese five-spice powder
1 tablespoon soy sauce
½ teaspoon black pepper, ground

Partially freeze the loin or shoulder. Cut meat against the grain to a thickness of 1/8" and a length of 2." In a large bowl, stir together honey, rice wine, and seasonings. Place the slices in the marinade and turn several times to make sure each piece is coated evenly and completely. Cover and refrigerate for at least 24 hours, stirring the meat and turning it occasionally.

Preheat the oven to 140 degrees F. Place the marinated meat in a single layer on a baking sheet, being careful not to let the pieces touch. Dry the meat until it is about 70 percent dry and still a little flexible — approximately 3 hours in the oven. The drying time will depend on the oven temperature, house humidity, and size of the meat strips. Test a small piece every hour or so until it is dried to the right consistency. Note that the meat will become a little more brittle once it is cooled; do not over-dry the meat.

Grill each piece over a barbecue until brown, basting occasionally with oil until it is crisp.

Yield: 24 slices of dried meat

Dried Salmon Strips ("Salmon Jerky")

3 to 4 pounds skin-on salmon filet, Coho or sockeye preferred
1/2 cup soy sauce
1 teaspoon dried tarragon, crushed
1 teaspoon dried garlic

Slice the filets in ½" or thinner slices. Coat a baking sheet with non-stick spray. Place the slices onto the sheet without allowing the pieces to touch. Mix together all seasonings and brush onto the fish.

Preheat the oven to 140 degrees F, or put the dehydrator on the lowest setting. If the fish appears to be drying faster on the edges than in the center (or vice versa), move the pieces around on the racks. Make sure the oven is drying the food, not cooking it; adjust the temperature if needed. If you use a smoker to dry the fish, adjust the wood or coals to 140 to 150 degrees F and monitor during drying.

Dry the fish until it is tough but flexible. The drying time will depend on the oven temperature, house humidity, and size of the meat strips. Test a small piece every hour or so until it is dried to the right consistency.

Allow the salmon to cool. Using a blunt knife, separate the skin from the flesh, and discard the skin. Place the cooled jerky in an airtight container, or freeze it in a plastic recloseable bag.

Yield: 2 to 3 pounds of dried salmon

Wisconsin Cheddar Cheese

3 gallons fresh whole milk
¼ teaspoon Mesophilic-A starter culture
1½ teaspoons of 30% calcium chloride
½ rennet tablet dissolved in ¼ cup distilled water
1 teaspoon + 3 tablespoons coarse salt

Dissolve calcium chloride in 2 tablespoons of distilled water. Combine milk and calcium chloride mixture in the top pot of a large double boiler filled with water. Slowly heat the mixture to 86 degrees, stirring constantly. Turn off the heat and stir in the Mesophilic-A culture. Put the cover on the pot and allow it to process at 86 degrees for 90 minutes.

Turn on the heat and slowly increase the temperature of the milk to 90 degrees F. Dissolve rennet tablet in ¼ cup warm distilled water, then stir in 1 teaspoon of coarse salt. Pour this mixture into the milk and stir gently. Turn off the heat, cover the pot, and let the milk process for 90 minutes, or until the curd shows a clean break.

Cut the curds into ½ inch cubes and stir gently. Very slowly increase the heat of the double boiler until it reaches 100 degrees (about 30 minutes). Stir often to break up the curds. Once the mixture has reached the proper temperature, pour it into a colander lined with cheesecloth. Let the whey drain off in the sink until the curds are shiny and firm. Add three table-spoons of salt and mix well.

Line the bottom of a cheese press or other container with damp cheese-cloth, then press in the curds. Fold the cheesecloth over the top of the curds and place the follower (or a weight) on top of the curds. Press the cheese for 15 minutes. Open the cheesecloth, turn over the cheese, and re-wrap the curds. Place the weight or follower on top of the curds, and press for 12 hours longer.

Remove the cheese from the press and take it out of the cheesecloth, stir 1 tablespoon of salt into ½ cup of water, and brush this mixture onto each surface of the cheese. Place the cheese on a dish towel or cutting board, and allow to dry for 1 to 3 days. Turn the cheese over each day. When the cheese has formed the characteristic yellow color of cheddar cheese and the rind is dry, the cheese can be sliced or wrapped for storage.

Feta Cheese

2 gallons fresh pasteurized goat's milk (cow's milk can be substituted)
1/4 teaspoon Mesophilic-A starter culture
1/2 teaspoon calcium chloride
1/4 teaspoon liquid rennet
2 tablespoons coarse salt

Dissolve calcium chloride in 2 tablespoons of distilled water. Stir together milk and calcium chloride mixture in the top pot of a large double boiler filled with water. Slowly heat the mixture to 86 degrees, stirring constantly. Remove from heat and gently stir in the Mesophilic-A culture. Stir 1/4 teaspoon of liquid rennet into 4 ounces of cool distilled water, and gently mix with the milk. Put the cover on the pot and allow it to set at 86 degrees for 30 minutes, or until the curd shows a clean break, and the consistency has become hardened.

Cut the curds into ½ inch cubes and stir gently. Very slowly increase the heat of the double boiler until it reaches 95 degrees (about 30 minutes). Stir about every 10 minutes to break up the curds. After 1 hour, pour the curds into a colander lined with cheesecloth. Let the whey drain off in the sink for 1 hour. Cut up the curds and turn them over to drain for 30 minutes more.

Spoon the curds into a sterilized quart jar. Mix together 2 cups water and 2 tablespoons coarse salt to create a brine. Pour the brine into the jar, allowing ¼ inch headspace. Put the lid on the jar and refrigerate for at least 2 weeks.

Smoked Food

Dry-Cured Ham

15 to 20 pound fresh pork (hind quarter)
8 pounds of coarse salt
3 pounds sugar (white or brown)
4 ounces sodium nitrate

Trim fat and gristle from the meat. Mix together sugar, salt, and nitrate to create the dry cure mixture. Rub about ¼ of the of the dry cure mixture into the prepared ham, rubbing a little extra into the bone areas to protect against bone rot. Set the meat in a covered pan or container and let it cure in a dark, cool place. Every third day, rub more of the curing mixture into the ham until all the cure mix is used. A medium-size ham (about 15 pounds) will take about 30 days to cure; add 2 days of curing time for each pound more than 15 pounds. Note that you can keep curing longer than the recommended time, because the ham will not get any saltier.

Once the ham is cured, it can be thickly wrapped in netting or cheesecloth, and hung in a cool, dry place for up to 3 months. It will stay preserved in plastic wrap or a vacuum-sealed bag in the refrigerator for about 6 months, and up to 12 months in a freezer.

Basic Brine-Cured Ham

15 to 20 pound fresh pork (hind quarter)
3 gallons of water
1 cup of coarse salt

1 cup of brown sugar, packed (1 packed cup)
4 ounces sodium nitrate

Trim fat and gristle from the meat. Mix together sugar, salt, and nitrate with water to create the brine. Set the meat in a covered pan or container that is large enough to submerge the entire cut of meat. Pour the brine over the meat, and place a plate, lid, or other heavy object on the meat so that it remains submerged in the pan.

Place the pan in the refrigerator and check it every day or two. If enough water evaporates that the ham is not completely covered, add more brine. An average ham (about 15 pounds) will take about 7 to 10 days to brine-cure.

When the cure is completed, rinse the brine off the ham. The ham can be sliced and eaten fresh, smoked, boiled, or packaged for later use. It can be thickly wrapped in plastic wrap or a vacuum-sealed bag, and stored in a cool, dry place for up to three months. It will stay preserved in the refrigerator for about 6 months, and up to 2 years in a freezer.

Prosciutto

Prosciutto is a spicy Italian ham that can be difficult to find or very expensive in stores. Italians often eat this ham thinly sliced with fruit and cheese, as an appetizer.

12 to 15 cloves of garlic, peeled and chopped
2/3 cup coarse salt
1/4 cup sugar
2 tablespoons freshly ground black pepper
2 teaspoons ground nutmeg
2 teaspoons ground cinnamon
1 teaspoon ground cloves
1 teaspoon mace
1/3 cup sodium nitrate

20 to 25 pound fresh pork hind quarter

1 cup water

1 cup cider vinegar

Trim fat and gristle from the meat. Mix 1/3 of the salt and garlic with the rest of the ingredients in a bowl to create the dry cure mixture. Rub the dry cure mixture into the prepared ham, thickly covering all surfaces. Set the meat in a covered pan or container and let it rest in a dark, cool place for three days. Rub the next 1/3 of the garlic and salt mixture into the ham. Let rest for another 5 days, then rub with the remaining salt and garlic mixture.

Allow the ham to cure for about 30 days. Wipe up any seeping moisture from the pan during the curing time. After 30 days, rinse the ham with a mixture of 1 cup water and 1 cup vinegar. Once the ham is cured, it can be thickly wrapped in netting or cheesecloth, and hung in a cool, dry place for up to 3 months. It will stay preserved in plastic wrap or a vacuum-sealed bag in the refrigerator for about 6 months, and up to 2 years in a freezer.

Maple-Cured Bacon

10 pounds of fresh pork belly

2 cups of coarse salt

½ cup brown sugar, packed

½ cup maple syrup

1 tablespoon onion powder

1 tablespoon sodium nitrate

Cut the pork belly into 8 x 10" sections. Mix together all ingredients to create the maple cure. Rub about 1/3 of the mixture into the pork belly sections. Set the meat in a covered pan or container and let it cure in a dark, cool place. Every 3 days, rub more of the curing mixture into the meat until all the cure mix is used. The bacon will be cured in 2 to 3 weeks.

Once the meat is cured, hang it in the smoker. Using maple wood chips, smoke the bacon at 100 to 120 degrees for about 6 hours. Cut off the hard outside rind and wrap in cheesecloth or netting. Hang in a cool dry place for up to 1 month. It will stay preserved in plastic wrap or a vacuum-sealed bag in the refrigerator for about 4 months, and up to 2 years in a freezer.

Brine-Cured Bacon

10 pounds of fresh pork belly
1 gallon of water
1/2 cup coarse salt, divided
1/2 cup sugar
1 tablespoon sodium nitrate
¼ cup coarsely ground black pepper
¼ cup brown sugar

Cut the pork belly into 8 x 10" sections and rub the surface with half the salt. Mix together sugar, half of the salt, and nitrate with water to create the brine. Set the meat in a ceramic or plastic container that is large enough to submerge all the meat. Pour the brine over the meat, and place a plate, lid, or other heavy object on the meat so that it remains submerged in the pan.

Drain the liquid from the container 3 days later. Lay the meat on a cookie sheet or flat pan and allow the surface to dry completely. Turn over and dry the other side. Once the meat is dry, rub it with the mixture of pepper and brown sugar, and hang it in the smoker. Using apple, maple, or hickory wood chips, smoke the bacon at 100 to 120 degrees for about 6 hours. Cut off the hard outside rind, wrap in cheesecloth or netting, and hang in a cool, dry place for up to 1 month. It can be thickly wrapped in plastic wrap or a vacuum-sealed bag, for storage in a refrigerator or freezer. It will stay preserved in the refrigerator for about 6 months or up to 2 years in a freezer.

Polish Sausage

20 pounds finely ground meat, 80% lean

2 cups nonfat dry milk

1 cup fine salt

½ cup coarsely ground black pepper

½ cup sugar

1/3 cup onion powder

1/3 cup garlic powder

2 tablespoons celery seed

3 tablespoons coriander

2 tablespoons nitrite

1 tablespoon nitrate

2 quarts water

Thoroughly mix milk, spices, and nitrites into ground meat. Using a sausage stuffer, stuff into hog casings, twisting every 6 to 8 inches. Hang in a smoker or lay on smoking trays. Add hickory, cherry, or oak chips to the smoker. Heat the smoker to 185 degrees, and smoke until sausage has reddish-brown color and an internal temperature of 155 degrees.

Plunge the sausages into cold water and cool to 100 degrees. Hang the sausages in a cool, dark area to dry (approximately 1 hour). Refrigerate and use within 1 week, or individually wrap and freeze for up to 2 years.

Kippers

Kippers are split, smoked herrings that are popular in the United Kingdom. If they are "cold smoked," they must be cooked before eating; in the UK they can also be bought as packaged kipper snacks. They are often baked, fried, or poached and eaten with eggs and toast for breakfast, or served at tea.

> *15 to 20 fresh herrings*
> *1 gallon of water*
> *2/3 cup of coarse salt*
> *1 teaspoon freshly ground black pepper*
> *1 teaspoon sodium nitrate*

Cut the heads off herrings and split the fish lengthwise. Clean out the viscera and wash the fish. Mix together salt, pepper, and nitrate with water to create the brine. Set each fish, spread open, in a covered pan or container that is large enough to submerge all the fillets. Pour the brine over the fish, and place a plate, lid, or other heavy object on the meat so that it remains submerged in the pan.

Allow the fish to soak for several hours, and then drain the brine. Hang the fish on hooks in the smoker, or lay them flat on smoker trays. Add oak chips to smoker and allow to smoke for 4 to 6 hours at 120 degrees.

Kippers must be refrigerated, cooked, and eaten within 10 days of smoking. They can be wrapped and frozen for 12 to 18 months.

Appendix H

Resources

Canning

The following resources and canning experts can help you with canning supplies, questions, advice, and other guidelines.

National Presto Industries
(Presto canners, parts)
(800) 877-0441

National Center for Home Food Preservation (**www.uga.edu/nchfp**)
Guidelines posted to this site have been scientifically tested to make sure that foods that are preserved at home are safe to eat.

Wisconsin Aluminum Foundry Company
(Makers of All-American canners)
(920) 682-8627

Putting Food By By Ruth Hertzberg

Pressure Cooker Outlet
(Presto, Mirro, All American & Maitres Pressure Cookers & Parts; canning books and supplies)
(800) 251-8824

Canning supplies

Alltrista Corp.
(Manufactures Ball and Kerr canning lids, produces the Ball Blue Book of canning and other publications); Hotline: (800) 240-3340;
Order: (800) 392-2575

Kitchen Krafts
(Free catalog)
(800) 776-0575 or (563) 535-8000

Home Canning Supply
(Free catalog)
(800) 354-4070

Lip Smackin' Jams and Jellies, by Amy and Dave Butler
(**www.amybutlerdesign.com**)

Freezing

The National Center for Home Food Preservation
(**www.uga.edu/nchfp/how/freeze**)

USDA Food Storage and Inspection Service
(**www.fsis.usda.gov/home/index.asp**)

Juicing

Gary Null, radio and internet resource
"Natural Living with Gary Null"
(**www.PRNcomm.net**)
www.garynull.com

Mercola Natural Health website
(**www.mercola.com**)

Best Juicer Reviews — website offering feedback and ratings from actual users on some of the top home juicing equipment.
www.best-juicer-reviews.com

Smoking

Meat Smoking and Smokehouse Design, By Stanley Marianski, Adam Mariański, and Robert Marianski

The National Center for Home Food Preservation
Guide and Literature Review Series: Smoking and Curing
www.uga.edu/nchfp/publications/nchfp/lit_rev/cure_smoke_meats.html

Smoking Fish (Michigan State University Extension 1999a)
http://www.uga.edu/nchfp/publications/nchfp/lit_rev/cure_smoke_ref.html#msue99a

The Smoked-Foods Cookbook: How To Flavor, Cure, And Prepare Savory Meats, Game, Fish, Nuts, And Cheese, By Ed Park

Proper Processing of Wild Game and Fish (Cutter 2000)
http://www.uga.edu/nchfp/publications/nchfp/lit_rev/cure_smoke_ref.html#cutter

Smoking Meat website and Forum, hosted by Jeff Phillips, Tulsa, OK
www.smoking-meat.com

The Art and Practice of Sausage Making, by M. Marchello and J. Garden Robinson.

Harvest Essentials, Inc.
Provides injections, tools, preservatives, and equipment for curing meat and preserving other foods.
www.harvestessentials.com/meat-processing-meat-curing.html

Fermenting

Home Brew Talk Web Forum
www.homebrewtalk.com

Wild Fermentation, By Sandor Ellix Katz

The National Center for Home Food Preservation
www.uga.edu/nchfp/how/can6a_ferment.html

Wild Fermentation website, offering resources and information for all types of fermentation, including vegetables, cheese, beverages, bread, and condiments.
www.wildfermentation.com

Making Sauerkraut and Pickled Vegetables at Home: Creative Recipes for Lactic-Fermented Food to Improve Your Health By Klaus Kaufmann and Annelies Schoneck.

The Vinegar Book
www.vinegarbook.net

Root Cellaring

Root Cellaring: The Simple No-Processing Way to Store Fruits and Vegetables, By Mike Bubel.

Living Off the Grid website — resources for building and maintaining a root cellar.
www.livingoffgrid.org

About the Author

Angela Williams Duea

Angela Williams Duea is a freelance writer and photographer who is passionate about food and gardening. She is president of Pearl Writing Services, helping businesses communicate more effectively and helping individuals tell their stories. Angela lives in Chicago with her superhero husband; she has two daughters in college.

Index